I0141189

THE STRANGER I CAME TO LOVE

Also by Steve Jaffe

Fiction

The Haven House Chronicles-The Conspiracy
Children With Invisible Faces
God's Looking Glass

The Mind Diet Series Books

Count Your Life With Smiles, Not Tears
Healing From Within, Emotionally Surviving Cancer
A Recipe for Healing, Coming Together as a Team
Beyond Valentine's Day, Making Love All Year Long
Re-Defining Stress to Prevent Disease

THE STRANGER I CAME TO LOVE
A Psychological Thriller

STEVE JAFFE
Steve Jaffe Books
www.stevejaffebooks.com

This first international edition published 2011 in the USA and the
UK by Lightning Source Inc, 1246 Heil Quaker Blvd, LaVergne,
TN. 37086 and Steve Jaffe Books, Palm Desert, Ca. 92211

Copyright © 2011 by Steve Jaffe
ISBN 978-0-9819410-3-5
Cover Design by To The Point Solutions

ACKNOWLEDGEMENTS

I have to once again thank my wife Nancy for her commitment, dedication, suggestions, editorial advice and her good memory, as well as her love, all of which helped me complete my fourth novel. Without her support, this book would still be hiding somewhere inside my computer.

I want to thank my daughter Stephanie who at the beginning stages of this book shared her thoughts and suggestions.

And, I want to thank all of the relationships I have known most of my life for the fodder they provided in bringing this story to life.

AUTHOR'S NOTE

This book is dedicated to relationships and all the challenges they pose for anyone looking for love, passion and security. No matter how challenging or how difficult an emotional commitment can be or how crazy being in love will make you, there is always hope that the perfect relationship, the one that has that storybook ending, is waiting to capture you. Unfortunately, for some people, a committed relationship, the one that you dedicate your entire being for, can drain your life force and make you totally crazy.

And, this is why *A Stranger I Came to Love* is not a love story.

ONE

Marc thought again about Nora, in fact, he incessantly thought about his wife. He pondered about things he had no control over. This kept his obsession in overdrive.

His thoughts constantly ricochet against each other wondering, if he were just a little bit kinder to her, more respectful, or even more tolerant, his marriage would be better. Well, that's what Nora kept telling him anyway. Sadly, his wife never felt that he ever got it right.

He believed her. Why wouldn't he? She was his wife and wives should be trusted. So, thinking that he was the problem, he tried harder to anticipate her every whim. Accomplishing this feat would bring him nirvana, wouldn't it? It was the carrot Nora dangled each day in front of him, keeping him on edge, like a dog chasing his tail. Marc wanted to figure out how to correct his flaws—so that Nora would feel passionate toward him and give him the loving he so wanted. He was certain of it.

The more Marc thought about it, it actually made such good sense…—*tit-for-tat, you scratch my back, I scratch yours* and the marriage would be perfect. When he pictured getting Nora's passion and her sexual intimacy, it made his heart race wildly. When that image filled his mind, he became quite excited. He imagined how her supple breasts would feel in his hands, how warm and soft they were and how her lips would taste…he was getting very aroused at the thought of that dream with Nora.

He wanted to wake her up right now and make love to her. But then, the excitement evaporated as quickly as it came. His sad reality struck and he remembered how hateful her eyes were when they met his. It was his downfall, those eyes. He could see a person's soul in their eyes and Nora's showed she had the soul of Satan.

Marc's mind was on fire now as he gazed at Nora. A strange rage exploded within. He did not blink. His breathing became rapid, making him a little lightheaded. He prayed he was not going to blackout. Bad things always happened when he blacked out. He forced himself to slow down and stay calm.

He had to get back to his ritual. The one he did each and every morning. He had a need to sit on his communal bed and stare at Nora while she slept, allowing his thoughts to run wild.

He envied her in a perverted sort of way. Not because she was a warm caring human being, but because she could just sleep so peacefully as soon as her head hit the pillow. Experiencing Nora every day made him realize that people who were self-centered, egotistical, and downright nasty could sleep peacefully. Nora, his wife of twenty-five years, had become the poster child for: *Be a bitch to get a good night sleep—no drugs needed.*

He believed that people like her were blessed with good sound sleep because they had their soul removed at an early age due to a mutated gene. They were manipulators. They had political smarts. They knew how to create scenarios that got others to worry about them. Thus, the other humans lost sleep each and every night because they incessantly thought about people like his Nora and how they could make those people's lives better.

Peaceful sleep each night had become difficult for Marc. His cynicism for Nora occupied his mind. Her provocations were escalating toward him, and his disgust and contempt for her had begun to grow to new levels—and for the first time that scared him. He needed Nora. She helped fill in a lost past that he did not remember.

Empty flashbacks of another life took up much of his days and evenings. It was the vague memories of a past that scared him.

For the briefest of moments, each day, something familiar, that déjà vu sense, that disagreeable familiarity, tempted him with a glimpse of a distant memory. Any morsel of hope he experienced would quickly vanish before he could grab onto it and fill-in the many missing pieces to his confusing past life. From Nora's point of view, he was just a little too crazy and should stop trying to remember things that did not exist and to instead focus his attention on her and how to make her life better.

Nora was the trigger to his flashbacks—he was sure of it. Her piercing shrill voice or her special way of pressing his emotional buttons would send his mind into overdrive. Once she started her attack, Marc would get a nanosecond of a memory and then, whoosh, it would be gone, leaving him empty and confused. He reasoned that he was blocking out a traumatic event…before he married Nora. Oh, how Marc envied people who remembered their past, their history in such detail, but he was not so lucky. P.N., pre-Nora was a blank slate, as if he never existed.

Each morning Marc would awake, assume his position on their bed with the confidence that this day would be the one that would trigger the floodgates of locked away memories, and all of his questions would be answered. That's why he stared so much. When Nora did not talk or scream, he could have the peaceful freedom to put his brain on recall and attempt to see his past.

He would come so close at times, like when he'd enter a room only to forget what he was looking for, or going to do, and he'd have to walk backwards to the beginning of his thought to recapture it. So like every morning, Marc just stared at Nora, hoping he would be able to trigger a memory. To just remember something or evoke what his brain was trying to get him to recall. Today, his morning had begun once more.

As Marc's brain spiraled out of control, another aggravation came to light. One that was magnified with their friends…Nora's friends. She'd brag to them or sometime complain, about how Marc watched her each morning. Her bragging happened with the few friends they saw socially. She would tell them how cute and romantic he was, but, to her best girlfriends, she told them how weird it made her feel.

However, only Marc knew his real reason for his morning routine. He knew that she was the keeper of the key that could unlock his Pandora's Box of memories, but kept it hidden from him for her own selfish reasons. He started drifting again back in time, his eyes closing tightly.

* * * * *

The flashbacks had started when they first began dating and have continued throughout their marriage. At the beginning they didn't bother Marc. He had the strange recollections of a life that seemed distant and lost. He reasoned that it was his guilt from losing his aunt and uncle during high school or losing his parents at an earlier age. Marc had always tormented himself with self-doubt, flailing his mind constantly with so many "what ifs". When Nora complained and battered him emotionally, he looked within his soul and hurried to make changes that would please her. Each time she'd demand more and each time Marc would grow unhappier, as he conformed to the image Nora demanded.

Even though his wish was for a better life, his thoughts never stopped hoping that he'd one day have a life with a woman who had passion, one who really loved him for who he was. They had no children to bond their marriage, but Marc was a man of principle and his word. He took his marriage vows seriously.

After twenty five years of this wretched life, Marc's emotional well-being had began to unravel. He was now waiting for his pardon from his prison sentence to a woman, more a warden than a loving wife.   As he stared at Nora, he was overwhelmed, to say the least.

His penetrating eyes were not the only ones focusing on Nora. Marc could feel it. It had been happening for quite some time. It gave him the shivers. He abruptly turned his head to the sliding glass window that faced the backyard, looking to see if someone was there, looking in. However, like all the previous times that he had felt the presence of someone else, it once again proved to be false. Marc closed his eyes, squeezing the pillow that was resting on his lap, his grip getting tighter, and as the pressure became more intense, so did the feeling that someone else was now in the bedroom with him.

* * * * *

Brad's cold eyes stared at Nora, keeping his distance. It was not his time. He was always waiting, always watching, and always hoping that the woman he loved would give him a sign to end Marc's existence. He was impatient, but trusted that Nora knew best.

Brad loved Nora, in a perverted sense. They had a long violent history together before Marc. Her marriage to Marc was a necessary alternative for all of them. It was part of their perfect plan so that Brad could disappear and become invisible from the police.

The plan was that they would remain apart until they both felt he could return after Nora had completed her part that involved Marc. However, patience was not one of Brad's positive attributes and it was running out quickly. He knew Nora could not be trusted. She was a self-centered bitch and he knew she'd have to be out of the picture one day. But, he needed her for now so he could return and assume his life once more.

He had prayed that Marc would step up to the plate and do the deed, but Marc was a weak, wimp of a man, too sensitive and too good natured. He glanced at the letter he wrote—the letter that would jog Marc's memory and help put him back on his journey to recovery. Brad knew that once Marc had his memory back, Nora would be history.

* * * * *

Marc looked up, catching a glimpse of his bare chest in the wardrobe mirror. He was an athletic man who prided himself on staying fit. He was also a man of few words and many controlled emotions. He hid his melancholy through denial. He kept his temper under check, even though he understood he was masking a hidden personality that he sensed was about to explode against Nora.

This violent rebellion had crossed his mind on many occasions, even while watching her blissfully sleeping. However, the days crept on with no action, as the real Marc continued to fight to exist inside his tormented mind. He still believed he needed Nora in his life, at least until he could figure out how to bring to the surface a past he knew nothing about.

Their marriage had become superficial since he had said his "I Do's". How unusual he thought, as he gazed over at Nora that a husband and wife could put across their shell of a marriage in such a warm, loving, and positive manner, yet hide their true feelings so elegantly, as their abrasive emotional conflict lurked inside the walls of their home.

For Nora it was easy. She had a way of creating emotional debt for Marc after each argument she'd create. They happened mostly at the times when Marc wanted sex.

There were infrequent times, when Nora would show her loving side toward Marc. These bursts of affection happened only at social gatherings witnessed by their many acquaintances, making

them the "perfect couple".   She'd do this as a game. She knew
how Marc melted from her outwardly loving gestures. They would
give him hope that for at least one night he'd receive the passion
he so desperately craved.   However, when they would return to the
sanctuary of their home, away from prying eyes and Marc prepared
for his starved love making—Nora would explode into a rage and
get upset about trivial things. Car keys not in the right place, not
screwing on the toothpaste cap tight enough, even looking at her
while she removed her clothing would create a screaming frenzy
that would evaporate any passion that was left inside Marc's heart.
Sex had now become mercy fucking, love making when Nora
sensed Marc was going to bolt.

One-on-one, Marc and Nora had no life together. He was a
married-single man. Deep within his subconscious there was
something that kept him drawn to her, but it just wasn't making
sense to him anymore.

Their marriage was filled with a suburban social life that kept
Nora in the limelight and Marc in the shadows. He would have
loved to have had children, but Nora on the other hand had no
energy except for herself and her vanity.

He always believed that Nora had wanted to marry someone
else. She always complained about how her high school
sweetheart Brad Stevens had been the love of her life. But, over
the long years of their marriage Marc had come to believe that it
was his ability to make a comfortable living that kept Nora married
to him.

Marc, with his clean-cut features and powerful build, combined
with his innate calmness, projected an air of strength, controlled
energy and confidence, but this was totally the opposite of how he
really felt inside. He was a pedantic man, always fussing over
minute details. He knew it drove Nora up-the-wall. However, it
was the only button he knew how to press so he could have some
power over his life.

He had recently begun to fantasize about being a widower,
being in the limelight, watching Nora's casket lowered into a deep
grave. The daily nightmares of this mean spirited bitch kept
building day after day, and like a time bomb were ready to
explode.

On many occasions he would count to ten, hold his breath, and
walk away from Nora and their fighting. He was unable to
confront the important issues that spun out of control inside his

head. He had hopes that he could turn the corner one day. That day, he prayed, could not come soon enough.

His eyes remained riveted on Nora in her blissful state. Today, his emotions had sunk to an all-time low. A distant voice was calling him to take action once and for all.

As he continued to gaze at Nora, his pathetic life flashed in front of him. He glanced at the clock on his nightstand. It was 6:28 A.M. and within minutes his serenity would come to an abrupt end and once again, there would be no answers to his past.

He held his breath—his eyes closed tight—the pillow gripped firmly in his hands, praying that Nora would sleep forever and grant him the greatest gift, one of solitude and peace.

He made his left hand into an imaginary gun, *bang, bang* he mouthed the words, blowing gently on the fantasy plume of gunpowder escaping his finger. *"Maybe one day, if they ever put into law a battered husband syndrome defense,"* he thought. *"Not likely. Men continue to be the bastards women make us out to be. Who'd believe me anyway? Our façade of a marriage is perfect,"* he thought, his frustration building. *Nora is smarter.*

Marc knew he was a lost soul in search of some excitement, some passion, and most of all, someone to share a happy life with. He wished he could remember his teenage years. The memory of that major part of his life was missing. It was as if he had popped out of an egg and became Marc, the older teenager.

He was not the type of man who blamed others for his troubles, but his memories traversed only as far back to when his aunt and uncle died when he had begun dating Nora. She had become his historian, constantly telling him about how his aunt and uncle were extremely demanding. He tried to believe they had good intentions, but without his own memories he was at Nora's mercy. Nevertheless, she explained how they robbed him of his teenage years, sheltering him from the few friends he had.

He heard stories from Nora how his aunt, a certified home care nurse, imparted her worldly wisdom on him, which, from Nora's point of view, was the foundation that made him the weak man he was today.

However, somewhere deep within his heart he believed he had loved his aunt and uncle. He tried to ignore Nora's take on it, but she was persistent and very convincing, telling him how he always gave in to their desires to protect him from drugs, peer pressure, and the imaginary violence that loomed outside their home. How could he not believe her?

"They made you a weak person, something less than the man I thought I'd married," she'd tell him over and over again. *"Grow a pair, it might turn me on."*

Emotionally battered, he had given up on his dreams. His todays were not building for any happy tomorrows. It was the safe thing, the only thing he had control of and the easy way out. He relegated himself to becoming everyone's doormat.

Marc sucked in a trembling breath feeling his hopelessness once again over take him. He knew, like every morning, that as long as he was married to Nora, he had no future and no happiness.

He sighed, looking at the inanimate object that was his wife, the large pillow clutched tightly in his hands.

Marc's mind seemed to drift to a far away place, a familiar place, the illusion of having previously experienced what he was thinking. He felt a sense of happiness, but like in a dream, it was sketchy and indistinct.

He raised the pillow up against his face; the tension in his arms caused his heart to pound.

"Do it," he heard a voice say. He nodded. "I can do it," he whispered.

What seemed like slow motion, the pillow drifted toward Nora's face, eclipsing her from view. His heart was racing, his eyes were squeezed tight, a single tear rolled down his cheek. Soon it would be over.

Without warning, a squealing car alarm startled him from his aggressive thoughts, causing his body to become limp and the supportive voice in his head to vanish.

Nora popped straight up in bed.

Within an instant she began demanding of Marc with her high-pitched voice to put a stop to that incessant noise.

Like every morning, Nora awoke without a smile or even a *"good morning"*, just a harsh scowl and a machine-gun barrage of demands for him to jump up and accomplish.

Massaging her scalp with her perfectly manicured fingernails, she turned her eyes away from Marc and in rapid succession, spoke.

"Is my coffee ready?"

"Where's the paper?"

"Were the cats fed?"

She swung around and placed her bare feet on the soft shag carpet and pounded the mattress. "Where the hell are my fucking slippers?" she yelled.

His shoulders instantly hunched, his face turned beet red, as he dropped the pillow and jumped off the bed in search of Nora's pink bunny slippers. The devil had awoken.

Another day had begun for Marc.

* * * * *

Brad tried to contain his laughter. He had seen this same scene for the last three weeks. "You're one miserable coward," he mumbled. "This is not going to be easy," he said, disappearing into thin air.

TWO

Marc was barely out the door when Nora pressed the phone on her nightstand hard against her ear. She tapped her sharp nails anxiously on the receiver impatient for her best girlfriend, Gail, to answer. "Come on…come on," she muttered. The ringing stopped and Gail's voice replaced the bothersome beep, beep noise Nora hated.

"What took you so long?" Nora barked arrogantly.

"I was in the bathroom," Gail barked back. "You should install a little red light that flashes on your phone so you'd know when I'm indisposed and can't grab the damn phone. I should be allowed some personal time alone, don't you think?" she hesitated, wanting to rip into Nora, but realized she was talking to a wall.   She paused and waited for one of Nora's ridiculous self-absorbed remarks.

"If you'd put a phone by your toilet, I wouldn't have this problem," Nora said curtly.

Gail let out a long breath. "I guess Marc's done something again? What didn't he do for you this morning, my little princess?" Sarcasm was bleeding out of her mouth.   Gail had been talking to Nora for less than a minute and was ready to climb the walls.

Like most jabs, Nora missed the irony of Gail's remarks. "Well…the moron did not have my slippers by my side of the bed. My coffee was not hot, just lukewarm. The paper was out of order," her voice quivered as she tried to get out the last complaint. "He…he forgot to feed the cats." She almost sounded like she was about to faint. "Why I ever married him…I miss Brad so much, he knew how to satisfy me."

An uncontrolled explosion of mucus shot out of both of Gail's nostrils, her cupped hand unable to contain her laughter. "Doesn't Marc have to go to work so you can live in the style you've created for yourself? That was the plan all along, wasn't it? Brad had no potential in that area." Gail said, her tone more acerbic than usual. "It was your decision, not his, to get married. You should have waited for Brad to return. I just don't know why you're keeping up this charade? He's never going to be Brad no matter how hard you try."

Nora gasped, finally understanding the severe harshness from her friend. As if she never heard a word Gail had said, she verbally ripped into her. "How can you talk to me that way? You know how the cats get when they're not fed. You know what I mean? They jump on the bed; they force me to get up before my time. Marc is so inconsiderate…I just don't know why I put up with this anymore!" she whined.

Gail couldn't contain her frustration. "Boy, you're one nutty bitch. Marc still doesn't know who he really is and if you open up a can of worms, get him to remember before its time, we're both going to be in deep shit. Stop being a spoiled princess. You've not changed since high school."

"I've got everything under control. I just know if I keep pushing Marc, the stress will make him snap and my life will be better again."

"I think you're nuts. Don't go messing up a good thing for both of us. I have as much to lose as you do. What's so wrong about keeping Marc around? Brad got us all into too much trouble."

There was a long pause at Nora's end of the phone line. Then, in a low serious voice Nora spoke. "Once I have control over Marc's money and if he should die mysteriously after the divorce, I would have our assets and his life insurance. Then it won't matter anymore. Ten million dollars can keep us all very happy, even without Brad."

"Right. How are you going to pull that off? You keep pushing Marc and it's not working anymore. That might have worked for you in the past, but I've seen the look in Marc's eyes…well, you might want to learn to be sweet and caring if you want to keep Marc around long enough to get his money. You lose him and you lose any chance of getting Brad back. There's no guarantee that Brad's ever going to return and carry you away on his white horse." Gail had become exhausted from the meaningless conversation and stopped talking. She was worn out.

Nora started shouting at Gail. "I think Marc's going to hurt me. I can sense it every morning before I wake."

Gail moaned exasperated. "You're being paranoid."

"He has that look. The same one Brad had before he did something bad." She was rambling, making no sense. "Plus, he's been forgetting to do too many things and making my life a living hell."

Gail let out a long loud breath. "Marc would never hurt a fly. That's why he's Marc. His personality is the opposite of Brad in every way. If only you could enjoy a nice caring man for once, you might find true happiness like Peter and me."

"That's the stupidest thing you've ever said to me. Marc's just not exciting enough, not like Brad. I won't believe that Brad's not coming back and ridding me of Marc. If that won't happen then Marc's gotta go away permanently." Nora let out an exasperated breath. There was a long silence before she continued her twisted rationalizing. "His new five million dollar life policy has upped the total for me to ten million, but the new policy has not been approved yet. Once it's approved, then I'll have some real options. I won't need Brad or Marc. I'll just start over again. I've done it…we've done it before, and we can do it again."

"You're one crazy bitch," Gail said in a serene calming voice. "Don't make any impulsive decisions. Just think about what you're saying before you make the biggest mistake of your life," Gail said patronizingly curt.

Nora was silent for a moment. "If Marc's gone, I'll be richer. I'll have the life insurance and our assets."

Gail knew that when Nora had a wild idea she'd act before thinking everything through. She's seen it since high school and each time it backfired. "Give Marc a call and apologize. Don't do anything rash. I'm tired of running. Maybe a romantic dinner, a little cuddling in front of your wonderful fireplace, then…well you know what I mean? Spread those gorgeous legs of yours, close your eyes and dream of Brad, and Marc will be under your spell again," she said containing her frustration. "I'm just getting nervous that you're going to do something stupid. I have a great life and want to keep it."

Nora looked at the clock on her nightstand. "Shit, I've got to go. Rita's coming for my Yoga lesson and she'll be here any minute. We'll talk later. Thanks for your help. I think I've got it all figured out now," Nora said, abruptly hanging up.

Gail looked at her phone, shaking her head. "Yeah, I'm afraid of what you've figured out."

* * * * *

This was Nora's time. She jumped out of bed, letting her silk nightgown fall to the floor. She slipped into her silk kimono totally naked underneath. She fussed with her hair, a touch up of make-up, with her bright red lipstick. She was ready for her yoga lesson and Rita.

THREE

Marc arrived at Lou's, a small coffee shop, vintage 1950's. It was a block from his financial planning office that overlooked Carlsbad beach. The owner, cook, and waitress, Louise was wiping her hands on her soiled white apron when she saw Marc enter.

"Hey sweetie," she called out in her sultry southern drawl. She always had a big loving smile on her face when she saw him. "The usual?" she said throwing him a big kiss with her hand.

Marc stared at her, his eyes sad, as he nodded. He sat down in the same booth he took every day for the last five years. He looked up and saw Lou prancing over with his glass of OJ and coffee. She was the only person in his life that even knew he existed, always making time to ask how he was doing.

Lou, a divorcee three times over, constantly teased Marc every chance she had, hinting that he could be the right man that could win over her heart—unfortunately, her message, directed at Marc, skidded past him each time.

Lou's personality made Marc uncomfortable. He did not believe he deserved so much loving attention from such a beautiful woman. In a bubbly voice, the back of her hand to her forehead, she with as much drama as she could muster said, "I love being in love. 'Mister Right' could be staring me right in the eye." She said fluttering her eyelashes at him, as she grabbed his chin lifting it up so their eyes met.

She still had a youthful look about her and Marc's heart raced every time he spoke to her, but he was oblivious to her suggestiveness. He sensed she was flirting with him, but he was a married man and couldn't venture down that path. It just wasn't who he was. Trying not to be rude, he just ignored her aggressive comments.

"You look so sad this morning," she said, squeezing his hand lovingly.

Marc blushed, feeling an excitement rush over him. Her cool hand made him feel lightheaded. "Same old thing. Nora's pissed at me. I forgot to do some stuff before she got up. It's nothing. I don't want to bother you with my problems." His tone and body language said something else.

"Are we friends, honey? You can tell me anything you like. That's what friends are for…right?"

Marc slowly shook his head. "It's nothing really. I don't want to bring Nora here. I like our time together.   I'll have to go home soon enough and attend to my spousal chores." His chin had fallen to his chest again.

Lou's smile faded as she slipped into the bench across from Marc. "I like our time together too," she said cupping his hands with hers. "If you weren't married…well…I just don't know what I'd do," putting her finger to her cheek, pretending to be helpless. "You're a great man, a wonderful person that has so much to offer any woman. One day you'll see it."

Marc's face turned red, as he stared into Lou's eyes. _You don't really know what kind of fucked up person you're talking about!_ His eyes had become glassy. "But, thank you anyway."

Lou squeezed Marc's hand, a big smile appeared on her face. "You're one of the good guys." She was just about to tell him about a friend of hers that helped men in Marc's same situation when his cell phone rang. She closed her eyes and shook her head. She knew it had to be Nora, by the frustrated look on his face.

Marc raised his finger, gesturing Lou to hold that thought. He flipped open his phone. He mouthed it was Nora. Lou stood up, pursing her lips sadly and walked back toward the kitchen. He noticed her shaking her head, as he listened to Nora rant.

"Are you able to come home early today?" she begged seductively. I'm making your favorite meal. I was terrible to you this morning. I can be such a bitch. You're the best," she said in a flat monotone. "We could cuddle by the fireplace—" Nora stopped in mid-sentence. "Thanks Rita, I totally enjoyed it. I can't wait for our next lesson. Oh, where was I? Oh, yes, we could cuddle by a fire and then, well maybe, you could apologize, make up for this morning's screw ups and I could feel so much better," she said with as much excitement as paint drying.

Marc wanted to say no. But, he couldn't, this could be the turning point for their marriage. It was another opportunity for him to make Nora love him or at least show some passion toward him. He let out a soft breath. "I'll see what I can do. How's four o'clock sound?" he said tentatively, glancing at his Blackberry. He had three appointments in the early afternoon.

Nora sighed impatiently. "Let's try for three o'clock. You're trying to get me to forgive you…aren't you?"

"Sure," he replied unable to hide his sadness. "Three it is." He flipped his phone shut. He looked up to see that Lou had placed his two sunny-side eggs with hash-browns and toasted sourdough bread on the table. She was back behind the counter before he could thank her. He could tell she was sad and buried his fork in the yellow yoke, letting it ooze off the eggs and into his hash browns. This was his ritual, the blending of food, the one of many things that drove Nora crazy. One of the small insignificant things he had control of and he loved it. He knew full well that he should have stood up to Nora's demands and said no, but, she had a way about her that always gave him hope that his marriage would finally work out.

He called out, "Did you finish what you wanted to tell me?" he said, his voice cracking. He sensed Lou was disappointed with him and when he saw that she just waved him off, it confirmed his suspicions. Sadness swept over him. *Marc…you're such a fuck up at relationships,"* a familiar voice inside his head said. *I can help you if you'd like?* The familiar voice whispered. "Leave me alone. I can ruin my own life," he muttered.

Marc was feeling the weight of his guarded emotions that had twenty-five years of abuse etched onto his soul. Now the scars of his calculated avoidance, as well as his defensive seclusion, surfaced. He wanted to learn to walk again. He wanted to unhook the chain that was held fast to his ankle, leaving him powerless. While he struggled to survive with Nora and the inner voice that was telling him to do things he did not want to even consider, he remained a coward and trapped.

For most of his life, the period he could remember, his emotions had been rationally restrained. He had denied most of them. It was that plain and simple. He had allowed himself to feel only what seemed safe to feel, which in reality, was nothing. He had at times shown anger, but only in moderation, holding inside a demon that wanted to escape and pillage his world. He feared that if one drop of hatred, one ounce of anger surfaced it would unleash a raging river that he couldn't control. It had happened before, but it was met with a blackout and no memory of what transpired during his lost hours. He believed there was a stranger lurking inside his body, one he did not want to meet.

He stood at the cash register staring blankly at Lou counting out his change. He wanted to tell her that he was sorry about the phone call. He wanted to apologize for interrupting their conversation, but, like everything in his life, he knew it really didn't matter.

Lou handed him his change, intentionally lingering her cool hand to caress his. "I just hate seeing you being taken advantage of sweetie. You're a wonderful man and deserve better."

All he could do was shrug his shoulders, unable to mutter a word. Lou lifted his hand to her lips and kissed the back of it. No words had to be said. Marc understood she was just being a friend.

"When you're ready to discover a world outside of your marriage, I'll be here for you." Without giving him a choice to back away, she leaned forward and gave him a kiss on the cheek, this time it did not feel like any kiss a friend would have given him.

Outside in the cool morning air, a marine layer had blanketed the area, making visibility tenuous. He waited to cross over State Street. Through the fog he could feel the piercing eyes, he had sensed early that morning, burning the back of his neck. He turned abruptly. He couldn't see anything within ten feet. He was sure someone was there, as he crossed the street.

He arrived at his office wondering if he was going crazy, if his paranoia had worsened. On his desk was a bouquet of carnations, a mixture of yellows, pinks, and whites and a letter resting against the vase. Something about the arrangement seemed familiar, but yet again, like most of his flashing memories, the answer escaped him.

He immediately opened the envelope and was shocked at what was written. Who would send him the flowers…definitely not Nora? It was the powerful words in the letter that had gotten his heart to race, the pounding against his ribcage made his entire body shudder. The confusing message inside the letter was making his head spin. Once again distant memories had begun to surface, but this time they stayed longer, they were becoming real. The excitement made him lightheaded. Marc had no control over it as his eyes closed tightly, as darkness blanketed his body.

FOUR

Brad thought it was time to call Nora and begin the process so he could return. He knew he needed Marc out of the way, permanently out of the way, for the next steps to all work.

Nora had never been the brightest egg he had ever known, but she was the most ruthless.   The phone only rang three times when she picked up.

At first, Brad was silent, it had been too many years since he'd spoken to Nora and it seemed awkward.

Nora had become impatient with the silence and was about to hang up when she heard the familiar voice. She cupped her hand to her mouth, gasping.

"Yeah, it's me. It's been a long time," Brad said his tone raspy with a cold edge to it. "I don't have much time to talk."

Nora couldn't stop herself from breathing hard—her excitement had put her in an uncontrollable state. "Did you do it? Is…is Marc finally gone?" was all that could come out of her mouth.

"Not yet.   You need to get control of his money. Without it, coming back won't work. I've given him a letter that should begin to trigger his memories. I pray it'll be fast. I miss you so much and can't keep waiting like this. I'm going mad."

Nora tried to control her giggles, but couldn't. "You're already mad sweetheart, that's what I like so much about you. I've missed you so much. Marc's nothing like you. But, what if his memories come back and he realizes what we've done? I could go to jail."

"Once he comes to grips with everything, I'll be able to control him once again and he'll fall back into place. He'll realize that what we've done, had to be. It's who we all are."

"I hope you're right. I'll call Gail and Rita and tell them to be ready."

"I don't know when I'll be able to call you again, but don't do anything stupid until I speak to you with the final plan."

Nora sounded excited. "I'm a lot better now. I have Marc wrapped around my finger, but don't wait too long. He's starting to change. He's getting some surprising confidence and it's beginning to worry me."

Curtly Brad said. "Just don't do anything stupid until you hear from me, understand?" and hung up.

FIVE

Like most of Marc's days they were spent in and out of his crazy daydreams and fantasies about his marriage and the passive ineffective actions he'd take when Nora treated him badly. Lately his customers were suffering. His financial advice had become questionable and they were becoming angry as their portfolios lost money in the stock market. Even though it wasn't Marc's fault, his confidence in his abilities had begun to erode, placing him in a spiraling black-hole of despair.

However, Marc was a master at finding sleeper stocks, companies that would have a short-term upturn, placating his complaining clients with more profits than losses. He just had to keep himself focused while he was away from Nora, which was becoming a difficult struggle.

Alone in his office that overlooked the whitewater of the Pacific Ocean, he stared off into the distance, dreaming of better times. He loved closing his eyes and seeing himself pulling the trigger on a gun pointed at Nora, or using a sniper rifle and popping her right between the eyes. He understood it was just a pathetic act of imaginary courage that he could only dream about within the serenity of his office. But now, with the mysterious letter looming over him, he could sense that everything was about to change. His alarm on his Blackberry went off, bringing him back to his reality and have to get home for Nora.

* * * * *

As he pulled into his driveway, he was not looking forward to an evening with his crazy wife. He sucked in a deep breath, turned off the engine, pressed his eye lids tight and listened to the garage door vibrate close.

His mind flashed back to breakfast at Lou's and the warm caring words she had said to him. His eyes remained closed, his head pressed hard against the car's headrest. His emotions were tumbling out of control, a convergence of anger and sadness, culminating inside his pounding heart. He had begun to feel a change coming over him. A terrifying change he had never felt before, yet it felt familiar. A cold chill had started him shivering.

Get out now! Run! A distant voice cried out. Marc tried to scream, his mouth had opened wide, and his lips had become twisted, ready to explode with anger, ready to curse profanities at his Nora. He then opened his eyes, fully aware of what was happening to him. He accepted it without complaint.

His thoughts raced to Lou and then back to Nora. Would another woman be any different toward him after getting to know him? Would he just screw up another new relationship? He felt like he was the floating dot on a game of Pong. Back and forth, back and forth, his emotions bounced, going faster and faster until the dot (Marc) had become a faint blur.

That was his life and Nora was at the controls.

Nora had always been the chameleon. She was able to change her personality to suit her situation. One moment she'd be smiling, appearing happy, the next moment she'd be in a crazed fury with eyes like pools of lava. She never allowed Marc to escape her seductive ways.

Everything that happened around Nora had come with flashing yellow lights warning him to be cautious, and then when he entered her lair the flashing red lights would go off, but by then it was too late, Marc had been captured, a helpless toy for her desires. Nora knew where every button was on his body and had mastered how to press them to destroy his resolve. He knew she wanted him to be more like Brad, her previous boyfriend who disappeared suddenly.

Marc constantly tried to accomplish what Nora wanted on so many occasions, but unfortunately for Marc, he continued to fail miserably.

"One day…one day really," he sighed. "I'll be stronger. I'll leave that bitch," he whispered softly inside his car. "Maybe she'll disappear and make it easier," he said without conviction.

A loud piercing noise broke his serenity.   He jerked his knees, startled, hitting the steering column hard.   Nora was standing by the door to the garage, her air horn outstretched in her hand, her finger creating an alarming intermittent blast inside the garage.

He straightened up, his heart pounding wildly. His resolve was again evaporating when he saw Nora standing by the door to the kitchen, dressed in a green see-through nightie, tapping her foot on the floor and with her long sharp fingernail in unison tapping her watch-face.

"What are you doing?" she screamed like a drill Sergeant. "I've been waiting for ten minutes since you got home. "Get your butt inside, eat the snack I've prepared with your favorite tea, and get me to forgive you." Her voice, like fingernails on a chalkboard, made his body shiver.

Even though Nora was demanding and self-centered, her attempt at thoughtfulness preparing his peanut butter, cream cheese and jelly sandwich, with a cup of hot tea, would usually help him feel a little more cared for. Comfort food always made him happy. However, today, it was not working. This button was not going to be pressed. He would stand his ground for one small victory.

The color drained from Marc's face, as he opened the car door. His legs had become rubbery and his hands would not stop shaking. He waved his arm at her, controlling himself from flipping her "The Bird" and said, "Just go to the bedroom. I'll be there shortly," he said without any emotion.

Nora let out a grunt, giving the air horn one long final blast before slamming the door shut. "I hope "Mister Shortie" is not coming to our bedroom today," she shrieked.

In his hand was the mysterious letter he had received with the flowers. Usually a note came attached to a floral arrangement, not a letter, and not a letter that was stirring up so many frightening emotions.   The letter was vague, its message convoluted, but not so much, as it placed Marc into a heart pounding flashback at his office. The one thing he did know is that he had to distance himself from Nora immediately. It was a matter of life or death. He folded the letter and stuffed into his shirt pocket.

For the first time Marc's inner voice echoed outside his head. It was loud and clear calling out to him. He looked around believing someone was in the garage with him. He realized it was inside his head. *If you don't leave now, you will never get out until she's dead or you're dead."*

He stared blankly at the closed garage door, visualizing Nora, seeing clearly the meaningless merry-go-round they rode together. A strong man could step off if he wished. Even though he knew the logic of that reasoning, he had tried before to jump, but something had kept him tethered on this sick perpetual ride.

As light bulb went off inside his head, it brought him face-to-face with his imprisoned self. He looked at his reflection in the car window. His face seemed to have changed. He did not recognize the image that was staring back at him. "Maybe you're right." he responded to the reflection nodding. "Maybe you're right."

Right then he knew he had to escape or he would never be free. He knew that it was Nora who stood in his way for happiness and that needed to change.

Just the thought of Nora being out of his life permanently brought a warm happy rush over his body. He smiled, then walked into the kitchen and took a cold beer out of the refrigerator. He looked at his sandwich and smiled. "A nice romantic dinner?" he muttered sarcastically.

He stared at the carving knives in their wooden block holder. He pulled out the one with the longest and widest blade. He ran his finger gently over the sharp edge pretending it was Nora's neck. *Now you're talking,* the voice said.

He turned, the knife by his side grasped tightly in his hand. He had made his decision. There would be no compromise, no turning back on what he had to do. He bounded up the steps to their bedroom two at a time, happy, for the first time in a long time, and feeling in control.

SIX

Marc kicked opened the door. Nora did not seem startled, but her eyes went wide with surprise seeing the carving knife that was raised above Marc's head. She slid up, propping her back stiffly against the headboard, her large remanufactured breasts at attention.

"What's going on here?" she screamed, anger pouring out of her mouth. Within an instant, her expression went from anger to fear. She folded her arms across her chest and continued talking.

"Are you crazy? Put that goddamned knife down this minute. You've totally ruined this romantic moment. Didn't you like the snack?" she asked innocently.

"You're not going to control me this time! I'm fed up with you and this marriage." An unfamiliar scream shot out of his mouth. Marc seemed startled. He did not feel like himself.

Nora had a vacant expression. "You just seem to screw things up lately. I just don't know what I'm to do with you?" she said allowing her manipulative tears to flow. "Is it something I've done? Said? I can try to be the woman you want. Just tell me what you need from me and I can try to do it," she cried turning on a faucet of tears.

"It's over Nora. I've been down this road many times. Each time you say you're going to try, it only lasts until you know you have me back within your clutches. I'm not going to live this way anymore." His voice was now trembling. The knife had started shaking wildly in his hand. "I can't even remember a day in our twenty-five year marriage when I was happy. In fact, I can't even think of a time you were happy with me. I've wasted too many years. I can't do this any longer," he yelled, his voice more angry than it had ever been.

Nora jumped out of bed moving toward Marc, her arms opened wide, her nightie falling seductively to the carpet. She looked sexy and beautiful; her pubic hair perfectly shaved. She looked like a little girl in puberty. At that moment Marc was not buying her manipulation. She stopped abruptly, her new breasts barely jiggling, when he shook the knife at her.

Marc's voice rose, his rage culminating into an explosion. "Don't come near me. It's over. This time I mean it," He said with conviction.

Nora appeared impervious to his words and the pending danger. He felt an eerie sensation flow through his veins. As his intensity grew, Nora's mocking laughter kept pace.

Nora's chuckle had become hysterical. In an eerie tone she answered him. "It's over when I say it's over. Now put that fucking knife down and see if you can get me back into the mood."

Without hesitation Marc drew the knife back and flung it toward Nora. Before she could react, the knife blew past her and lodged in the padded headboard. She fell back onto the bed, the color drained from her face. "You're not even worth the effort," he said in a hushed tone. "I've wished you dead for many years and now…well…I don't care what happens to you."

Marc turned away from Nora and opened his closet door grabbing from the upper shelf a small suitcase. With his back to her he said, "I'll be back to get the rest of my things in a few days. Until then, you should find an attorney and think of returning to work."

Nora's face went from ashen to bright red. She wiggled the knife from the headboard and lunged toward Marc's back. Within seconds, the knife was plunging downward, penetrating his left shoulder blade. He screamed at the searing pain radiating over his entire body.

She pulled the knife out quickly and was ready to stab him again when he turned and grabbed her arm twisting the knife from her hand. She was looking in his eyes, a happy smile stretching on her face. It was as if she was seeing someone else.

He kicked the knife under the bed and with his fist clenched tight, slammed it into her nose. The sound of cartilage breaking filled the bedroom. "You're one fucking crazy bitch. I don't know who the hell I've been with all these years, but what you're seeing now is the new Marc who won't take it anymore."

A river of blood gushed from Nora's nose as she went down hard, her head impacting the carpet with a bounce. She was now screaming, holding her nose with her hands. "Look what you've done...bastard. You're going to have to pay for a new nose again. You're nothing but a wife beater," she ranted.

Ignoring the pain in his shoulder and the warm moist fluid that was soaking his shirt he continued to pack his suitcase. Five minutes later he was out the door and heading as far away from Nora as he could. He started to cry. It was a crying that was different than any emotion he had ever felt. It was orgasmic in a sense, feeling what it was like to release pent up emotions.

He was painfully happy for the first time in his life. He had closed a door, which he hoped would remain closed forever. A rush of insecurity flowed through his veins. This would be his first time on his own. His guilt was consuming his every thought. He was now wondering if he had overreacted. He began to recall the violence that exploded only moments earlier. The rage had felt familiar, but he knew he had never done anything close to that in his life. He prided himself on being gentle, respectful of others and very polite. He knew that about himself, but something had just happened in his bedroom and it scared him.

Heading west toward Carlsbad beach, the late afternoon sun glistened off the blue ocean. With it was hope and promise that life could be perfect. For Marc, he couldn't absorb the warmth and bounty of the moment. He felt compelled to self-analysis, his normal rationalizing that he had done for so many years. However, at the moment, it was the burning anger that consumed him, trying to transfer what was once a gentle soul into something that had him terrified.

As the shock of the moment wore off, the throbbing from his wound had become too excruciating to drive anymore. He decided to head to the emergency room.

SEVEN

Nora called Gail, crying hysterically. She told her everything Marc said and how he left with a suitcase. "My beautiful nose is broken. My eyes are black and blue," she wept. "I heard from Brad this morning. Marc can't leave me like this. Brad's close now. How will I control Marc? I won't allow it," she was ranting and screaming. "Plus the fucking life insurance hasn't been issued yet. What if Marc cancels it?"

"Did you call the police? He can't hit you. Have him arrested. Let him get a taste of jail. It might knock some sense into him," Gail said, her tone angry. "Now call 911. You need this officially recorded. And get your ass to the emergency room, pronto. I'll meet you there." Gail could hear Nora's hesitation in her voice.

"Are you sure we want the police involved? Other shit might surface if they start investigating Marc and me. Shouldn't we call Rita and discuss it first? He had a different look about him. If I didn't know better I'd say he is beginning to remember. What if he's questioned by the police and says something? I don't like this idea to call the police idea," Nora whimpered.

"There's nothing to be worried about. The police will never suspect anything. All they're going to be thinking about is that Marc attacked you and beat you. Now call 911 and get to the hospital. After he's spent a night in jail you can drop the charges. Everything's going to be just fine."

Nora was in one of her stubborn moods. "Just get over here. I need you at the house when the police and EMT arrive."

* * * * *

Gail had been consoling Nora as the cute fireman was checking her blood pressure. A moment later the police knocked on the door. Standing in front of Gail were two police officers, both looking like they didn't want to be bothered with another domestic violence complaint. Gail invited them in, directing them toward the living room where Nora sat with a bloodied towel pressed firmly against her face.

Both officers introduced themselves, flashing their badges, indifferent as they stood in front of another sobbing battered wife. They knew that after all their investigation and throwing the bastard in jail, the wife nine out of ten times would recant and want the husband back.

Officer Monroe was first to ask questions. "When did this happen?" he asked in a serious monotone.

"I don't know. I wasn't looking at the clock when the knife flew past me," Nora said sarcastically.

Officer Monroe ignored her remarks. "I need a time of day, Mrs. Richards. I need to establish a timeline."

"He came home…I mean, Marc came home at three this afternoon. He threw it at me sometime right after that. That's the best I can remember." Her tears were flowing in gushes as she patted her face with her bloodstained towel. "I don't know what got into him. I fixed his favorite snack and was ready for him…I mean ready to submit to his demands…for sex," she said her voice cracking. "He's a sex maniac, you know."

Still ignoring her theatrics, Officer Monroe continued with his questions. He knew that there were always two sides to every domestic abuse complaint. He had been there a few minutes and already wanted to slap Nora across her face. "What prompted him to punch you in the nose?" he asked coldly.

Nora seemed confused at his question. "He hit me. Isn't that all you need to know so you can arrest him?"

"Possibly, but in most domestic disputes there are two sides to every situation. Did you do something to provoke him?"

"Look at me. Do I look like I could do anything to a man, other than being a woman?" She allowed her silk blood stained robe to fall off her shoulder, as well as the towel to drop in her lap. A real Victoria Secret moment, except for the swollen nose and black and blue rings round her eyes. She looked like a sexy raccoon.

The line of questioning and answering went on for forty-five minutes. Before the two officers left, they took photos of Nora's face and the gash in the headboard where the knife landed, then put the knife, with Marc's blood in an evidence bag.

Officer Monroe had two more questions for Nora. "What type of car was your husband driving?" Monroe was already using his two-way to call in a BOLO on Marc Richards. "If you have the car's license plate it would speed things up a bit?" he asked

Nora pulled out her Blackberry and read the number to the officer. "I want him arrested," she whined. "Then, throw away the key…throw the damn thing away. He's a bastard for doing this to me." Then, with an emotionless calm, she asked a question. "If he's in jail would I get control of our assets? He wants to leave me," Nora said her eyes fluttering as if she was about to faint.

Gail let out an exasperated sigh.

Both officers rolled their eyes, frustration written on their faces. They turned and left without a good-bye.

"What was that all about?" Gail barked. "Are you nuts asking them that question? Now they're probably thinking you started this," Nora looked at Gail and resumed her hysterics, oblivious to what her friend was saying.

* * * * *

Officer Monroe looked at his partner, his eyebrows raised and said, "She's a real looker that one, but I bet you she deserved what she got. She's probably trying to steal him blind. She acts like she's high maintenance," he said sarcastically. "What was with that stupid question at the end? Do we look like 411?"

Officer Anita Perez scowled at her partner. "So you think women need a little battering to keep them in line? Most women have no control over their finances and when a bastard like this Marc Richards leaves, they have no means to support themselves. I thought it was a valid question," Perez said. "Let's get this Marc character's side of it.   I'll bet he's a real winner too."

Ten minutes later, Officer Perez got a confirmation that Marc Richards' car had been spotted at the Tri-Cities emergency room in Oceanside.

EIGHT

Marc was talking to a police officer while a doctor stitched up his knife wound. It was poetic justice. It took twenty-five stitches, one for each year of his dysfunctional marriage. He just wanted to scream. *"What else could go wrong now?"* he said to himself.

It was hard to talk to a stranger about what Nora had done and how he had reacted to her stabbing him. He tried to down play it as an unfortunate accident between two angry people. After he finished answering the officer's questions, Officer Monroe and Perez barged their way into the ER. They took over the interview.

"Mister Richards, I'm Officer Monroe and this is my partner Officer Perez. We have a report—" he was interrupted by his partner.

Officer Perez took out her handcuffs and snapped one on Marc's left wrist. He winced at her rough tug of his arm. "Hey, you're hurting me. I just had twenty-five stitches in my shoulder. What's this all about?"

Perez stared unemotionally at him while he complained. "Your wife made out a domestic abuse complaint. It seems that you like to beat women," she said coldly. "Do I detect you'd like to do something to me? I'd love you to try," she said coldly.

Marc's eyes widened with fear. "Abuse? Are you crazy?" he screamed. "I just got sliced and diced from the knife my wife stabbed me with because I wanted to leave her. She's the one that should be arrested."

Officer Perez said sternly, "Didn't you throw a knife at her? Don't you think Mrs. Richards thought her life was in danger?" Perez argued.

"I aimed at the bed and hit the bed. I did not aim the knife at her. I was angry and just threw the knife at the headboard. That was it…a fitting ending to a horrible marriage. She came at me with the knife almost immediately after I threw it. She stabbed me in the back!" He said his voice cracking. "Her life was not in danger. She only stabbed me because I told her I wanted a divorce. She can't tolerate anyone telling her what to do," Marc's voice showed his frustration. "If she's filing this domestic abuse report…then…shit, I want to file a report about what she did to me. Or are you going to believe her story only?"

Officer Perez glanced at her partner. He was nodding his head, a little smile forming on his face. She reluctantly said yes. "We can if you want. She did in fact commit a violent crime." Officer Perez was unhooking the cuffs she had put on Marc and grumbling. "I hate these things. I guess it's her word against yours, as to what happened inside your home."

Marc shook his head pursing his lips, disgust exploding on his face. "I just want this behind me. If she drops her complaint, I won't pursue mine. The less I have to deal with her the better. I just want a divorce," he said, his eyes staring down at the cold linoleum hospital floor.

Officer Perez apologized to Marc and handed him her business card. "We'll talk to your wife and get back to you."

Marc smiled. "Thank you."

* * * * *

On the way to his motel Marc called Lou. His head was spinning out of control. His shoulder hurt, but his emotions were hanging on a thread. He got her answering machine. He tried to tell her what happened, but before he could finish her machine beeped and ended this call. He pressed re-dial on his cell and told her to just call him.

He needed someone to talk to and Lou was the only person he could think of who would even understand what he was going through.

* * * * * *

Brad had followed Marc to the ER. He overheard everything and loved what was happening. He was beginning to see some daylight. Marc was slowly changing, which for him was a good thing. He had to find a way to speak to Nora to tell her what to do now, but the police were too close right now. He couldn't risk being exposed.

NINE

The phone at the motel had a ring like a fire alarm. Marc sprang up in bed. Disoriented, he felt the searing pain in his shoulder and he instantly remembered the events of yesterday.

"Hello?" he said his voice gravelly.

"Marc? It's Lou." She said anxiously. "I got your message this morning…I know you called last night, but I didn't check my messages until now. I'm so sorry I couldn't be with you at the hospital. It must have been frightening." She couldn't contain the trepidation in her voice.

"It was more painful than frightening. Well, maybe when the officer put the handcuffs on me—"

"Officer? Handcuffs? What haven't you told me?" she said alarmed.

"Let's meet for breakfast in a few hours. I'll bring you up-to-date. Right now I need someone to talk to. You're the only one I could think of calling," he said shyly.

Lou was speechless. "See you at Morgan's Café on State Street at ten-thirty."

"See you then." Thanks Lou.

* * * * *

Marc and Lou arrived at Morgan's at the same time. Lou hugged him a little too hard, causing the stitches to stretch.

"Ouch," he said causing Lou to jump back a foot.

Her hand was over her mouth. "I'm so sorry," she said.

"No, no, no. Don't stop hugging it feels good, just be gentle." Marc reached for her, pulling her closer. "I don't want you to stop. It feels good. I love that perfume you're wearing. It's a lot better than that fried, greasy stuff you wear everyday," he said mischievously.

Lou drew herself even closer, melding her head against his chest. "It does feel good," she purred.

After a few minutes hugging, oblivious to all the people walking past them, they untwined and walked inside the cafe. Marc walked to a booth toward the back. He wanted privacy. He needed to talk freely.

At first, Marc just gazed at Lou, his mind drifting. He seemed lost inside her eyes. He wanted to show her the letter before telling her about what happened with Nora, but thought better of it, at least for now. Not until he understood its meaning.

Lou looked at him with a soft smile. Her eyes were glassy. It was obvious how much she cared for him, but it was going unnoticed. Lou sensed that Marc was somewhere else, staring blankly past her. He was deep in thought, almost trance-like.

His thoughts traveled back to the letter and another time, when Ashley Wayburn had come into his life. She was similar to Lou, but much more reserved. She was ten years younger than him, a natural blonde, with gorgeous ocean blue eyes that sparkled in a photogenic way. It had not taken him long after they met to become captivated by her innocent charm.

The affair with Ashley, Marc's first, was hypnotic and he found himself deeply lost within her coquettish ways. The passion came on fast and furious, as his emotions for Nora waned, opening his thoughts up to a divorce. He knew leaving his wife would be difficult, but he was madly in love and liked how it felt.

His recollection of Ashley would pop into his mind now and then, but his memory of their time together had too many holes in it, especially the timeline of her disappearance that still remained unsolved. Now, the mysterious letter was triggering a flashback that scared him.

Marc's emotional loss back then had spiraled into a deep depression. Nora, with her cold-hearted emotions, had sensed his weakness and dug her sharp talons deep into his heart, bringing him back into their marriage. Nora always seemed to know more about him than he even did. Like a bloodhound, she used the guilt of his affair to control him once again. It was impossible that Nora even knew about Ashley, he had kept his secret world hidden, he had thought. He had wished that those last few days of memories with her had not vanished, that they had not abandoned him like so many of his memories. It was as if someone had surgically removed Ashley from his brain.

Marc slipped back to the first time he had decided to leave Nora. Her rage back then had stunned him. The night when Ashley had gone missing, he had suspected Nora had a hand in it, but she was with him that night. He knew Nora was crazy, but didn't want to believe she was capable of scaring off or even harming his lover.

The mysterious letter was triggering so many memories of a violent Nora. Seeing the fury in her eyes as she wielded the knife at him in their bedroom, he knew that Ashley's disappearance could be more than her just going away.

Marc shook off these frightful thoughts and refocused on Lou.

Marc forced a smile and finally spoke. "After leaving your coffee shop yesterday, all I could think about was our conversation. It wasn't really that thought provoking, but it did get me to think about my life and who I've become." He paused, taking a nervous breath. "The sad thing is that I don't know me. I knew I was the husband of Nora and that was it. When you said I was a wonderful man…well I really didn't know who you were talking about." He saw that she wanted to say something, but he held up his finger. "Hold that thought. I have more I need to say and I'm afraid that if you interrupt me I'll forget what's inside my befuddled mind." He gently patted her hand.

Marc continued. "I heard what you said, but it sounded like you were talking about someone else. How can you see me like that when my wife of twenty-five years sees me as a total fuck-up and horrible person? Fighting with Nora is not easy to do. She becomes so melodramatic that all you can do is just watch and tune it out. Then, as she ranted on about me and my lack of trying, a light bulb went off in my head. I knew then that I had to get off the merry-go-round Nora and I were on. When I am around you, everything seems easy and simple."

Lou nodded her head, showing Marc she understood. "That's what you'll feel like everyday once you surround yourself with adults and people who care about you," she said.

Marc forced a smile. "The crazy thing about all of this is that once I told Nora that I wasn't going to do this crazy dance with her anymore, she went ballistic and that's when she stabbed me. The scar I'm going to have will be my reminder of a life that no longer exists." He was squeezing Lou's hand a little too tightly, making her wince.

"I really can feel what you're saying," she said, shaking her hand.

"I'm so sorry. I guess I'm a little emotional about this subject. I've never told anyone what I'm about to tell you. Eighteen years ago, I tried to leave Nora. I had met a wonderful young woman. Her name was Ashley Wayburn." Marc paused taking a big breath. "She made me feel, alive, like you're making me feel right now."

Lou had a puzzled look on her face. "You're speaking of her in the past tense. Did something happen to her?"

Marc let out a deep emotional breath. "She disappeared off the face of the earth. One day she was there and without a word she was gone. My affair was not public knowledge, so I couldn't file a missing person's report."

"She must have had some family. Someone who might look for her? Maybe there's a police report. Have you ever checked it out?" Lou asked.

Marc shook his head. "I was so devastated, even angry that she'd leave so abruptly that I ended up back with Nora, trapped inside my prison."

Lou gave him a dubious look. "Losing Ashley should not have changed your plans to leave Nora. Why would you go back after taking such a positive step?"

Marc swallowed hard, nervous about his reasons. "At the time Nora did not know I was leaving. I was just having an affair during my private time away from her. You know, testing the waters before I made a wrong decision. You can't imagine the guilt I felt, lying to Nora, each day."

"How could escaping from that woman be a bad decision? You were doing something positive for yourself. While I don't think having an affair is the mature thing to do, it was a good first step any way."

"I guess I was too weak to see it that way. She was the only person in my life after my aunt and uncle's accident. I had no friends, no other family. I must have been afraid of being alone. While Nora was a horrible choice, she was a choice nonetheless."

Lou's eyes grew wide with disbelief. "I don't think you're weak, sweetie. What I think is your self-image sucks and you believe you deserve the prison you remain in."

At first Marc felt compelled to argue, but he constrained himself to self-analysis, seeing the truth in her words.

Over the last five years he felt comfortable talking to Lou; however, the subject matter had been about other things in his life that did not include Nora. Now, faced with exposing the sad truth about his marriage, his ill attempt at an affair seemed filled with evidence of his recondite life. Everything at this moment appeared very obscure and difficult to explain. He did not like exposing his weakness to a woman he wanted to be close to.

Today, Lou looked more beautiful than he had remembered. Seeing her outside of her everyday environment put her in a different light. Her green eyes had a deeper more vibrate color to them. Her auburn hair, flawlessly down from the bun she normally wore, surprised him with its length, falling seductively over her shoulders. Each strand on her wavy mane was a rainbow of colors as the sun's rays came through the diner's windows.

How opposite she was to Nora's beauty, which now seemed vociferous in nature—Nora's disposition was loud and clamorous.

Marc wanted to be careful about how he would explain to Lou about his marriage. His mind drifted to the precise moment he raised the knife and saw Nora as the monster she was. He was wishing the knife had not missed last night and how by sheer chance he didn't kill Nora. The confusing part about his emotional outburst is that he did not remember actually throwing the knife. As his emotions soared, as his anger became intense, he felt like he blacked out. It was only for a second, but nevertheless, those seconds were gone from his memory, like Ashley was gone from his life.

Lou asked sweetly, "Are you going to fill me in on what has you smiling so brightly?"

Marc blushed. "Just thinking of a few things I should have done before I left my house yesterday. I really was thinking how Nora spends so much time taking care of herself, eating right, exercising and fussing over how bad she thinks she looks. The crazy thing is that she has always looked fantastic. But, she has never really been happy with herself, even after her boob job and nose job. I just might have to fix her nose again," he said embarrassed.

"You broke her nose?" Lou asked gently rubbing Marc's hand.

"Only after she stabbed me. It was self-defense," he said sadly. "A knee-jerk reaction. Just another thing for her to complain about."

"You know that good health is merely the slowest possible rate at which one can die and in your case it appears that Nora is the type that uses her obsession with her health as a 'Chinese Water Torture'. She will feel very stupid someday lying in a hospital bed dying of nothing."

Marc, for the first time that morning, laughed. "That's a nice visual. It just seems so ridiculous that I stayed married to her for so long. I'm so angry with myself that I could allow her to consume me and deny me my identity. I look in the mirror and see a misfit, someone who should become a hermit and avoid contact with people. I'm so tired of walking on eggshells and trying to second guess what the 'right thing" is to do or say."

Marc's smile had shifted and painful sadness came over his face. He wanted to tell Lou about the letter, the flashbacks, but again, thought better of it.

Lou slowly shook her head, a disapproving look on her face. "You'll need a lot of work, but there is hope and a light at the end of your tunnel. I know it's hard to see it now, but trust me that life is beautiful and is better when you surround yourself with people who care about you."

Marc shrugged his shoulders. "Right now, you're my only friend. I can't allow you to take me on as a charity case. I'm so uncomfortable opening myself up to you, let alone strangers. I've been very private for so long."

Lou rolled her eyes. "My father used to say 'All of us could take a lesson from the weather. It pays no attention to criticism,' and he's right." Lou could see that her words had returned Marc's smile. "My mother took acid in the 60's to make the world look weird, and now that the world is really weird, people, like your wife, are taking Prozac to try to make it normal. The thing for me is that I like the weirdness of the world. It's like a rainbow of challenges that makes every day more interesting. As you get to know me, you'll see that I'm extremely weird and sometimes impetuously crazy about how I go about my daily chores. I do have a habit of taking in strays," she said effervescently, "and I do talk about my life openly."

Marc seemed confused. "You believe I'm a stray that needs your care? Well, this stray might like your company, but it will be like pulling teeth to get me to open up about my sordid and unremarkable life."

"You'll let me know when you want me in your world." Lou smiled. "Now about you being a stray, I only meant it in a loving and caring way. I believe that we are all mentors to the people in our lives and should offer help and advice when needed. I know it sounds strange and a little bizarre, especially from where you're coming from, but once you open yourself up to embracing change, everything I want to offer will feel just right."

"Your version of bizarre sounds good right now. Nora is creepy in her own way. She seems to sense when other people want something from her, especially me. As much as I've grown to despise her, I never could bring myself around to cheating on her after losing Ashley. I'm embarrassed to tell you how frustrating it is to not having a loving physical relationship."

Lou nodded, seeming to understand. "I do know. But, as you learn to be on your own, discovering yourself, you'll find that loving, caring friendships can be more satisfying than sex. I'm not saying that I don't enjoy a good romp in the hay, but it is the emotional connection with the person that makes the sex so much better."

Marc had a goofy grin on his face. "I was just remembering Nora's perfect radar when she knew I was horny. It was like she believed that men, especially me, had two emotions: hunger and horny. When she saw me with an erection, she made me a sandwich and some tea. I'd eventually fall asleep after my snack. That was the extent of our foreplay."

Lou tried to contain her giggles, but it was difficult. "That's very funny and a little sad. I believe that life is sexually transmitted and should not be practiced safely. It should be turned on and experienced every moment of a person's day. We only have a short time on this planet and if we miss a day, even a minute of pleasure and joy, it's an unfathomable crime."

Marc and Lou kept talking for the next four hours—most of the conversation about Marc and what he really wanted in his life. Nora, for the first time had disappeared from the conversation and for the moment, from his thoughts.

Lou had begun to transform right before Marcs eyes. He had never in his life met a woman he could talk to for so long and who would truly listen to him. Life, as Lou put it, was being sexually transmitted to him. She understood his look and did not offer him a sandwich and tea. They spent the rest of the afternoon at her place exploring a new world for Marc: intimacy.

TEN

Nora was livid that Marc had not been arrested. Officer's Monroe and Perez stood at her door telling her that the evidence reflected that she attacked her husband first and her broken nose was the result of Marc's self-defense.

"What do you mean self-defense?" she screamed. "He hit me. I'm a woman. I have to have rights here, don't I?" she said instantly turning on her sniffling.

Officer Monroe shrugged his shoulders. "Your husband said he wouldn't press charges if you dropped yours. We'd like to close this case and get on with more serious crimes."

 Nora's face turned beet red, contempt on her face. She looked at Officer Perez who yesterday seemed on her side, but now appeared aloof and uninterested. "So what happens if I don't dismiss my complaint? Will you still arrest my husband?"

Officer Perez spoke before her partner. She looked straight at Nora, her expression serious. "Look, the evidence reflects that you attacked your husband with a lethal weapon. He thought he was in mortal danger. I've seen this before and someone turns up dead. You're lucky you've only got a broken nose."

Nora almost passed out. "What the fuck are you talking about?" she said seemingly puzzled.

"Look, we're here to see if you want to be reasonable, like your husband, and just leave this as a private matter. If not, we're here to arrest YOU on charges of attempted murder," she said unsympathetically. "It's really your choice. You can do this the easy way or the hard way, we really don't care."

The color had already drained from Nora's face, making her colorful bruises around her eyes and her swollen nose more grotesque. "What do I have to do?" she asked despondently.

"Just initial this report that you're dropping your complaint so we can be on our way," Officer Monroe said.

* * * * *

Nora was such a capricious woman it was hard to know how she'd react to Marc's bold move. Her moods were unpredictable, her anger petty, and her actions vicious. If she couldn't have Marc arrested, she was determined to ruin him financially if he didn't come back to her.

She reached Gail and begged her to come over immediately. She needed help to plan her strategy. "If that bastard wants a divorce, he's going to get one that will destroy him."

Gail had just woken up when Nora started ranting and raving. "Hold on a second. What about him being arrested?" she asked groggily.

Nora told her about her meeting with the two officers and what they told her. Gail was shocked, but knew that she really did not have all the facts about what really happened to Nora yesterday. She knew all too well how prone Nora was to exaggerate to get her way.

Gail sighed and told Nora she'd be there as soon as she could.

Nora sat on the living room couch pouting. What Marc had done brought back memories of eighteen years ago when he thought of leaving her for that bimbo slut Ashley. She was surprised then that the affair had been going on before Marc had said he wanted to leave her. *Did Marc re-grow some balls*, she thought. *Has he been having another affair?* Her blood was now boiling.

Marc's infidelity was never the problem. As far as she was concerned, he could do as he pleased as long as he stayed married to her. If seeing other women diminished his sexual desires toward her that was a win-win. But, now that he wanted a divorce, to reduce her standard of living, to see her money go to another woman, well, that wouldn't be tolerated. Marc was hers and only hers until Brad came back. They both needed Marc.

* * * * *

Marc prepared to leave Lou's late in the afternoon. He had a few appointments with rental agents to preview some apartments. He also had to get to his office and sign payroll before the weekend started. He was about to kiss Lou good-bye and thank her for a wonderful day, but their intimacy, the type of closeness he experienced made his mind wander.

He reflected on their conversation. She was truly different, but comfortable. He realized he had spent most of the afternoon talking about his problems. Talking so much had surprised him. He had always been a private person and now he had opened up to someone else. Somewhere deep in his subconscious he knew opening up would become a problem and was regretting having said so much. Nevertheless, he trusted Lou and hoped she would respect his privacy.

He then realized he did not know much about her, even though they saw each other every day for the last five years. All he knew at that moment was that she was a woman he wanted to get to know better. Then a bad memory flashed before his eyes. A cold sweat had made his body clammy remembering he had once had those same feelings for Ashley. *Could Lou disappear if Nora found out about her?* He thought. *Not this time.*

"Can I call you later? Maybe some dinner?" Marc asked tentatively.

"I'm not sure if I can do dinner tonight, but maybe a late drink. I have a friend I'd like you to meet. I was trying to tell you about him yesterday, but you were preoccupied with that call you got from your wife."

Marc's heart sunk at the mention of another man in Lou's life. "You're not that weird that you're introducing me to your understanding boyfriend? This isn't some kind of open relationship thing you're into, is it?"

Lou patted his cheek and smiled. "You're jealous. That's very flattering. It's nothing like that. Call me later and we'll see what time we can get together with my friend. Today was wonderful. You know…I was right about you all along."

"What was that?" he asked a curious expression on his face.

"You're a great guy. The way you made love to me, tells me you have a gentle heart. We're going to be great friends."

Marc was whistling as he walked to his car. The embers of the lovemaking he and Lou experienced still warmed his heart. *I've been a fool*, he told himself. *Why have I waited so long?*

He never whistled in his life. It felt very good, something he wanted to do more often.

ELEVEN

Nora sat across from Albert Rankin, one of the best attorneys in San Diego County. His reputation was legendary: destroy the spouse at all costs and to the victor goes the spoils. His clients, mostly women, had become some of the wealthiest divorcees in California. It also meant that Rankin was one of the richest divorce attorneys in the United States, or, as he would call himself, a family lawyer. In practical terms he was more like the local butcher who would throw his scraps out in the alley for any stray dogs, which in this case was going to be Marc.

Rankin was a brutal man who even if both parties wanted a conciliatory divorce, stirred up enough animosity and distrust that it would be a battle between the attorneys, as the husband and wife just watched and fed the retainer coffers.

Nora, with Gail's recommendation, chose Rankin. "Girl, you better pray Marc doesn't get him first," she said seriously. "You really won't have any problems. He only likes female clients. It's the wealthy husbands he enjoys destroying. Most wives don't have a pot to piss in. So he doesn't represent men very often."

Rankin tapped his knuckles on his desk, bringing Nora back to the present. "Did you bring copies of your bank checking and savings statements for the last year?"

She opened a red manila folder and pulled out her copies. "Here. I believe I have the last two years."

"That's my girl. Now, were you able to find any of his corporation tax returns?" Rankin kept his temperament serious and business like. "In addition, did you bring me a list of all the assets the two of you have accumulated during the marriage?"

Nora nodded. "I found the last five years but, the list of assets is incomplete. I only have so much time in my day. I couldn't miss my yoga lesson and I had to have my hair and nails done before seeing you. Even though my face is a mess I must keep up the rest of my appearance. Don't you think?" she said impishly.

Rankin glared at her, a puzzled look on his face. "Let's get one thing straight. I'm not interested in how you look. In fact, the worse you look the better. If I get Judge Edith Johnson, we're in. She hates it when women come to her courtroom all beat up. So let yourself go. You'll have plenty of time to get back to your beautiful self when we have all of Marc's money."

Nora looked aghast. Her pout did not seem to win over her attorney. "I can't let myself go like that. Won't the judge see the photos of the brutal beating Marc gave me?"

"Look Mrs. Richards. When I tell you to do something, you do it. I won't have you wasting my time. If you won't listen to me, then find yourself another lawyer. Is that clear?" He was closing his file when Nora spoke.

"You can be a little sweeter," she said biting her quivering lip. "I just thought I'd ask."

"Sweet is not who I am. Are you going to cooperate or should I put your file in the trash bin?" he said curtly holding it above his wastebasket.

"I'll do whatever you want. Don't be in such a pissy mood,' she said fretfully.

"Good. I'll look over everything you've given me. I'll have a preliminary balance sheet for you to approve. What I want you to start thinking about is how much money you'll need to live on. Not what you've been accustomed to, but what you'd like for your pain and suffering."

Nora had a puzzled look on her face. "Pain and suffering? You mean for my broken nose?"

Rankin rolled his eyes in frustration. "He's leaving you to fend for yourself. You won't have the companionship you're used to. You'll have to start dating again. You're no spring chicken and the bars are full of women like you. That's pain and suffering in my book and your husband will have to pay. With enough money, any man, especially the young ones, will be clamoring for your attention. Just one thing I need to know: are there any skeletons in your closet that you don't want coming out during the trial?"

Her face turned bed-sheet white as Rankin's words felt like Marc's fist felt against her nose. "No," she said way too fast. She was thinking about Rita and Gail, especially Rita, holding back a worried look. "I'll have your stuff as soon as I can."

* * * * *

"Rita, we have a problem," Nora cried. "What if our relationship comes out during my divorce proceedings? What if they learn about all of us?" She was now frantic.

Rita let out a frustrated gasp. "How's anyone going to find out? Marc's not smart enough to get a PI and we all live in California, which is a no-fault state. California judges do not care about your personal life. It's simple accounting and alimony calculations. Let's not worry about it right now."

"Can you follow Marc and check on what he's up to? Maybe we can find some dirt on him that will help?"

"Sure. Maybe Marc can have a nice accident and we can get on with our plans. You've been with him longer than you've wanted to be," Rita complained. "You don't need Brad either once you get control of Marc's finances."

"We need Brad and Marc around a little bit longer. If my plan works…and we kill two birds with one stone…then we will be set for life." Nora had one of her evil looks popping up on her face.

TWELVE

Murphy's Irish tavern in downtown Carlsbad, built in the early fifties, kept a quaint atmosphere by proudly never remodeling. The lounge was always packed around the long wooden bar and the old-timers were fixed to a bar stool they've occupied since the tavern's grand opening forty years ago. Like always, the place was noisy.

This evening Marc wanted to be seated some place away from the noise and prying eyes. He sometimes hung out at the bar drinking flavored beers with his lunch. Some of the bar-flies recognized him and waved.

Marc needed privacy tonight, not the borderless atmosphere the bar created. He did not want the normal chit-chat from strangers who had a light buzz and who were looking for someone to talk to.

Murphy's restaurant was larger than the lounge and was dimly lit, hiding the old worm-wood paneling that was in dire need of repair. Tonight, he liked being in the big dark room. He wanted to be away from the happy drunken chatter that seemed to not have a care in the world.

Marc ordered a Microbrew Honey Blond beer and walked to his table. As usual, he was early. Being early allowed him enough time to adjust to a new environment. Unlike Nora, he who was never on time and loved making a grand entrance.

Marc had learned to tell Nora a time, at least two hours earlier than needed, just so he could have his ten minutes to adjust to his new environment.

Marc's heart ached. He had long understood he was invisible to everyone that knew him. Even his employees didn't seem to acknowledge that he even existed. Except for Lou. She seemed to listen to him and understand where his feelings were coming from. He was starting to trust. However, these new feelings were new for Marc. It made him nervous and uncomfortable now that he was on his own. His worries had triggered him to think about his past with Nora.

She had been a beautiful woman when they first married. But, as the years crept on, her inner beauty faded, masked by a shell that needed constant cosmetic attention. She had become a pain-in-ass victim, not only within their marriage, but also around the scattered few who still saw them socially.

While Marc waited for Lou and her friend to arrive, he used that time to savor his new found freedom. He started thinking about what he could do with all of it. No more waiting on Nora, listening to Nora, fighting with Nora…Nora, Nora, Nora. "Shit, she took up a lot of my time and energy," he sighed quietly.

He thought about his recent hook-up with Lou, earlier that day. Just the thought of it made him excited, as well as anxious. Most of the time Marc was so wrapped up in his pain that he did not realize how obsessed he was about his marriage and Nora.

During the last twenty-five years, he had never been able to be out on his own, especially after dark, in an environment that would allow him to make new friends. He even allowed Nora the final vote on anyone new he wanted to bring into their lives. His heart ached at the thought of all the friends he had lost over the years…all because of Nora. Staring across the restaurant looking at the bar, he was enjoying the people-watching and wondered if someday people might watch him and want his life.

What he did not see was Rita at the far end of the bar sipping a cosmopolitan. She had an oversized hooded sweatshirt covering her fit petite body and a black baseball cap covering her long black hair.

But, what he did notice were two attractive young women talking at the far left end of the bar, deep in a happily animated conversation. Since turning forty, he had lost all perspective of estimating someone's age, especially someone much younger than himself. He thought they were in their late twenties or early thirties.

Two barstools down from the young women were two older men dressed in business attire. They were loud and drunk, staggering on and off their barstools and bunking into other people standing around the bar. Then they started leering and leaning toward the two attractive ladies—who did not even know that the men existed. The most inebriated guy staggered off of his barstool, stumbling a bit as he weaved his way toward the women. He put his face rudely between the two chatty women.

Whatever the he had said caused the two ladies to shake their heads in disgust— however that didn't discourage him from wedging himself further between the two of them. He must have said something really crude, because the first gal slapped him and the other pushed him stiffly away. A few words were exchanged by the women and the man, but he still did not get the message. His friend came to his rescue, and now the two women seemed frightened.

Marc remained riveted, his eyes focused on what was happening at the bar. A strange feeling washed over him. He was not a brave assertive man, but something was happening and he felt more powerful than he had felt before. He briskly walked toward the bar and grabbed both men by the back of their collars, pulling them backwards and causing one of them to stumble and fall to the sawdust floor. The other man took a reactionary swing at him, which he blocked and with cat-like reflexes landed a hard punch to the man's midsection. The power from Marc's fist caused the man to bend over and lose his last meal, which amused everyone at the bar, as it spewed on his fallen friends face.

By that time Eddie the bartender had come around to help, a small baseball bat in his hand. Marc joked, "I think a mop might be what you need instead."

Eddie was a short burly man, but appeared very strong as he lifted both men up and dragged them outside, warning them to never return to his bar again.

Marc gingerly stepped over the puke and went over to the two young women. "Are both of you all right?" he said, his heart pounding inside his chest.

The first woman gave him a big hug and a warm wet kiss on the lips. Then it was the other woman's turn, and her kiss was even more sensuous.

"That was such a brave thing you did. Those two men were much bigger than you," the first woman said. "Oh, please excuse my bad manners, I'm Lisa and this is my friend Samantha. Can we buy you a drink? It's the least we can do."

He surprised himself when he said 'yes'. "I'm Marc Richards. I've never done anything like that before in my life. I can't get my heart to stop pounding," he said drawing in a deep breath.

Lisa, with a very gentle touch, slipped her hand through the opened button on his shirt and put her cool hand on his chest. "Oh my, it is pounding hard! Sam, take a feel," she said playfully.

Samantha smoothly slipped her hand inside his shirt, which almost made Marc pass out. Her hand was cooler than Lisa's. He had to sit down so the two women couldn't see the excitement bulging inside his pants.

Lisa must have noticed as she sat down on his lap and purred. "Is that your cell phone, or are you just happy to have me sitting on your lap?" she giggled, further embarrassing him.

Samantha said. "You must be new at the bar scene. Newly divorced? Separated?"

Marc gently lifted Lisa off of his lap. "A little over twenty-four hours…getting a divorce…I was meeting a friend here tonight," he said shyly.

Samantha already had her business card out and handed it to Marc. "You seem like a nice guy. Maybe we could do drinks or dinner sometime when the dust settles on your divorce?"

Marc was speechless. They were so young and he felt so old at the moment. Lisa repeated what Samantha had said, handing him her business card too.

Unbeknownst to Marc, Lou and her friend were standing behind him, observing the interactions between the three of them. In a soft seductive voice she said, "Are you going to introduce us to your new friends?"

Marc spun around. He was shocked, but mostly embarrassed. Lou was all dressed up, looking more beautiful than he had ever seen her before. He was blushing. "How long have you been standing there?" he asked clumsily.

"Long enough to witness you defending the honor of these two damsels in distress." Lou couldn't contain her smile. "I never pictured you with this tough sort of swagger."

"Neither did I," Marc said a little red-faced. "Let's move to the back. I have a table in the corner," he pointed. "I'll be right there."

Marc gave Lisa and Samantha a warm strong hug. "Nice meeting you two. I hope this isn't how I'm going to meet women at bars," he said, a broad smile exploding on his face.

Lisa replied first. "I wouldn't suggest using that technique too often. You have a great smile, just be yourself. We girls like men who are honest and sincere."

"I kind of like having my honor defended," said Samantha coyly. "I hope you'll give us a call. We'd like to get to know you better, Mr. Marc Richards," said Samantha rolling her "R's".

"Maybe I'll do that. I could use some nice friends."

Lisa and Samantha stared at Marc as he strode back to his friends. "Nice butt," Sam said.

"I'd like to see that cock of his. It almost penetrated my panties. We do owe him at least one free romp."

"I might do him for a year for free," Samantha said dreamily.

"What did you think of those two ass-holes? Are we dressed like we're hookers tonight?" Lisa asked.

"Not on your life. These are our *"lady"* outfits. It's our night off and we deserve a little respect," Samantha said, waving at Marc who had glanced back at them.

* * * * *

Rita had already emailed the video from her cell phone of Marc's barroom brawl to Nora. The magic of cell phones, she thought.

"Did you get the fight?" Rita asked.

"Perfect. I'll see if Rankin wants them. Might help prove how violent Marc really is. Anything else to report?"

He was meeting an attractive woman and another guy. Marc seemed pretty friendly with the woman. He didn't know the guy," Rita told her.

Nora was silent for a moment and then an empty chuckle. "Do you think he's seeing that woman?"

"How should I know?"

"Why don't you hang around longer and find out," Nora said.

Rita heard the phone disconnect. She waved to Eddie to give her another Cosmo.

THIRTEEN

Marc's gait had an air of confidence, blending with his smile that stretched from ear to ear when he turned and walked toward Lou and her friend. As he got closer to their table and his eyes met Lou's friend, he stumbled, a nervous clumsiness, catching his foot on a table leg. He was no longer "Mister Cool". He flopped helplessly into his chair. "Well that was exciting," he said, his confidence gone.

For some reason a distant memory had exploded inside his brain, stirring up a cold chill of fear. The words in the mysterious letter had just become more clear and vivid. Was it from his adrenaline that had come to the surface at the bar or was it something else. He wasn't sure. He was seeing a car accident that was fading in and out of his head. He felt someone touch his hand and the memory evaporated.

Lou took his hand unable to contain her giggles, not noticing that Marc was in a far-away place. "From knife throwing to barroom fights, you're really beginning to blossom."

Marc's blank stare looked past Lou. He was oblivious to his surroundings.

"Are you okay?" Lou asked, a worried expression had formed on her face. She put her hand gently on his cheek. Her touch startled him, bringing him back to the present with a big smile on his face. He was unaware that he had come back from another place.

"For the life of me, I don't really know what got into me. Do men really do those obnoxious things to women?"

Lou, with concern, watched Marc's transformation.   Then she remembered that she had not introduced her friend to Marc. She forgot that he was not comfortable meeting people for the first time.

"Marc, excuse my rudeness. I'd like you to meet Doctor Edward Kaplan. He's a psychologist.   I thought it would be nice for the two of you to get to know each other."

Doctor Kaplan stood and extended his hand. "Nice to meet you," he said in a deep baritone voice. "If I may answer your question?" he said in a clinically professional tone, ignoring Marc's puzzled expression.   "There are way too many men who think women like being treated as tramps. The interpretive part of a man's brain truly believes that women, especially in barroom settings, are there looking for a stud and that every woman sitting alone at a bar has sex on their minds. What you did was quite amazing. Lou has told me about your marriage situation and what it's been like for you. What I just witnessed, though, did not match the picture Lou painted of you."

Marc did not know if he should feel flattered or upset that a stranger had been given personal information about him. Either way, he was feeling his rage start to boil. It was one thing that someone had just sent him a letter with information about a past he couldn't remember, but now to have Lou violate the trust he had given her, that was just not right. He had thought he had made it clear that he was uncomfortable sharing his life with strangers and assumed she would keep his confidence.   He was pissed. Something unexpected started boiling inside him. He scowled at Lou.

"I thought you were MY FRIEND! I thought—" he hesitated, pointing his finger at her, "that you understood how uncomfortable I was about exposing my personal life to strangers…" he glared at her, his disappointment showing,   "What I told you during our intimacy was private."

Lou gasped. "Marc, I'm so sorry. I didn't mean anything by it. I just thought Doctor Kaplan could help you move on with your divorce. He's helped so many other men who have been with women like your Nora," her eyes had welled up as she bit her lower lip. "I'm so sorry. I've made a grave error…please forgive me."

Marc couldn't explain what was churning inside of him. His emotions felt like they were inside a blender being chopped and diced. Anger was consuming him at the moment, a kind of anger that was very comfortable, and it was taking everything he had to control it.

"You have asked me first if you could talk on my behalf. What I need are friends right now, not gossip mongers. If I'm going to expose my problems to the world, it'll be done on my terms, not yours," he said loudly.

Doctor Kaplan, in a calm voice, interrupted the two of them. "It sounds like you're afraid of being open to your problems?"

Marc's face had turned red, his veins ready to explode on his forehead. "Don't give me your psycho-babble. Because I'm upset having my trust violated doesn't mean I'm afraid of anything," he said, his fists clenching.

Kaplan and Lou noticed the rage building on Marc's face. "Please give me a chance to explain myself," the doctor said cautiously. "Lou did not delve into any of your personal affairs. All I know is that you have been married over twenty-five years and have not had much of a life for yourself. That's about the extent of what Lou had told me. I just assumed that you fit the standard profile of my other patients. "

Lou tried to hold Marc's hand, but he yanked it away harshly. "I just feel that I'm being controlled and that's exactly what I don't need right now. I've lived that way most of my life and I'm done with it. Lou doesn't know what's best for me." Marc stood abruptly knocking over his chair. "I'm out of here," he shouted. "I'm too upset right now and don't want to say something that I'll regret later."

Lou gasped, her hands cupping her mouth. She had never seen Marc with such rage before.

Doctor Kaplan stood and handed Marc his card. "When you're ready to talk, I'll be there. No charge until you feel you can trust me," he said his lips pursed with concern.

Lou tried to say something, but Marc put his finger on her lips. "Not now. I'll call you when I'm ready to see you again," he said despondently. He spun around and marched out of the tavern.

FOURTEEN

Marc felt overwhelmed, as he sped out of the parking lot. He smiled at himself with an approving wink, adjusting the rearview mirror. He didn't know when the epiphany had struck him, but it did, and it came on like a bolt of lightning. Driving down State Street toward his motel he was thinking about what he had just done, especially the rage he had felt back at the tavern. He had never before spoken up for himself, especially in public. He was puzzled why he had been able to tell Lou how he felt, when he never could have done it toward Nora. But what seemed nonsensical to him was that he had put himself at risk for two beautiful strangers, acting as if he were Steven Segal. The courage that had come over him felt wonderful and vaguely familiar.

Also, how he was able to throw the knife at Nora with the accuracy of a knife thrower from the circus, surprised him. But, there was a certain déjà vu to it all. Maybe it was the intimate connection with Lou just a day ago that gave him confidence? He didn't comprehend it fully—he was just feeling something powerful flowing though his veins and he did not want it to stop. The violence that had sprung out of him in the bar was an orgasmic jolt of sheer pleasure he wanted to keep nurturing.

He did know one thing was for sure—a transformation had started the instant he had read the mysteriously confusing letter. Alarms had instantly exploded inside his head, igniting a strange past he had once been a part of, whatever it was, still seemed unclear.

The strange sensations, the paranoia, the eyes he felt were watching him, left him bewildered. They had begun to reveal an assortment of trepid beginnings, uncomfortable middles, and the frightening new endings that seemed to be in perpetual motion inside his confused mind. He did not understand why these feelings felt like a comfortable sweatshirt and at other times felt like a scratchy pair woolen of slacks. He knew he had to put the memories in some type of order and connect the dots. He was becoming scared of what he might have awakened that had been lying hauntingly dormant for so many years.

The letter, while brief and incomplete, yanked him up, as if he was on a bungee cord, and had taken him back to his senior year in High School. Before the mysterious letter, Marc had remembered only tidbits of that period of time. What he did remember never seemed to be meaningful or complete.

Now he had started to have visions of violent behavior, a pretty high school cheerleader, and two other girls. The brutality had a familiar feeling to it, but the faces of the victims that crept inside his mind where engulfed in a fog. He was witnessing everything, as if he were a man peeking through binoculars, unable to know what his involvement, if any, might have been. He just sensed he had been there, an eye witness to things. Unfortunately, they were blocked inside his head.

These new sparks of memory seemed very real, and included his guardians, his aunt and uncle, who lovingly took him in after his parents died. One thing the letter made clear was that he had to return to his old home and go back to where his aunt and uncle had died in a car accident during his senior year.

His clouded visions seemed to involve the three young girls and a young man around his age. It didn't make any sense to him. His aunt and uncle's death had been ruled an accident by the police. They had died on a rain slicked road two miles from their house.

Marc had always made excuses for his memory loss. Per Nora, it stemmed from his unconscious need to block out the horrible accident after his parents died that left him an orphan. Even today, he had no recollection of how his parents died. His past evaporated further from the trauma of his aunt and uncle's death, and from their death the only link to his past evaporated.

Nora, back then, had taken on the responsibility of telling Marc about himself and the snippets of past he could not see clearly. After months of therapy that failed to unlock his past, he gave up and began his new life with Nora.

Reading the letter, he was confused. It was directing him to go read the police report. *Why the police report?* It had been over twenty years since he had gone anywhere close to his aunt and uncle's home. A cold chill climbed up his spine. Just thinking of taking this action was stirring up some unpleasant memories he knew were not going to be enjoyable.

He was remembering how Nora had filled in all of his blank memories. She had told him that he had grown up in a dysfunctional family before his mother and father died. He never questioned as to how she knew so much about his past. He believed her when she said that his aunt and uncle had told her how he had been the whipping post for his father's physical abuse and verbal put-downs. What he could not truly believe was Nora's account of the loveless care he had received from his mother.

Nora painted Marc's aunt in a selfish way also. She told him how self-centered his aunt had been, just like his mother, which was the reason he felt empty and un-nurtured.

Nora in her infinite wisdom would drill into Marc that he was a product of his environment and it had turned him into an introverted, spineless man.

It had been hard for Marc to believe the stories Nora would tell him about his past and all the abuse dished out to him from everyone who was supposed to have loved and cared for him. Since he couldn't remember anything after any of his blackouts, he allowed Nora to control him in such a manner that he had shut himself off from the world, afraid to be himself.

He had made the conscious decision to use silence to survive the meanness being inflicted on him by Nora. She controlled him by embarrassing him in front of their social acquaintances, interrupting him whenever he tried to talk to anyone who'd listen, and battered him with her abusive and painful words that he actually believed and which kept him from fighting back. All he had was his silence and the voice, which had become his best friend. Deep inside his tormented mind lurked a memory of a past, something he continued to struggle to find..

His memory returned to his relationship with Ashley, who had seen Marc as a wonderful man who had something to say and to offer. Soon after they became lovers and Marc took a big step and approached Nora with the offer of a divorce. She became livid, and a very dark side of her emerged. Less than a week later he had received a short typewritten note from Ashley saying that she needed to end the relationship. No reason. No forwarding address. She was gone…forever.

Marc searched for her. Her belongings were still at her apartment. It appeared that she had left in a hurry. He wanted her to tell him to his face that it was over. He wanted to see it in her eyes. He really wanted to beg her to stay with him, but she was nowhere to be found.

He was tossed out of his daydream when a loud erratic car horn and blinking headlights signaled him that he was veering into oncoming traffic on Leucadia Boulevard. Then the flashback of Ashley vanished.

He kept driving above the speed limit, his head whirling. He did not like how he felt about his outburst toward Lou. He knew deep down in his heart that Lou was not like anyone from his past or like Nora. He knew she had the best intentions for him. He felt ashamed for getting angry when all she was trying to do was help.

Most of Marc's life had been a kaleidoscope in black and white, at times boring gray, but nevertheless, always bleakly changing. Once he had decided to leave Nora, it was like walking through a portal that took him into a world filled with colors and fireworks. He did not know what to do about all of it just yet. Doubt started festering inside his brain telling him that he should be wary, that no one should be trusted. He was fighting the urge to run back to Nora, starting to think that being with her was better than being alone and on his own. As irrational as it seemed, Nora was familiar.

While Marc kept struggling with his demons, a loud voice inside his head began shouting at him. He turned thinking someone was in the car. But he was all alone. The voice was now screaming, *"Grow some balls for once in your life!"*

"It's not that easy," Marc answered timidly. "I'm tired. I'm worn out."

"Let me cry you a river," the voice replied sarcastically. *"You've got the letter, figure it out and take a chance. It can't be any worse than going back to that dumb bitch of a wife you have."*

While driving he was wondering if he was going crazy. He had never before really had this many conversations with himself. Nevertheless, the words kept flowing out his lips. "I just don't know what I'm looking for."

"You won't know until you try." Then everything went silent and all he could hear was the faint buzzing of the car's engine. He

was back at his motel's parking lot, the car idling, his foot pressed hard on the brake, while he shifted into park.

Marc was struggling at the moment. He wasn't sure if he was confused about his existing life or the exciting changes that were happening to create his new identity. What kept popping into his brain was the previous time he had come this close, and how it failed horribly. He lost Ashley then, and now with Lou in his life was afraid of losing her, too.

For Marc who had been emotionally abused for the last twenty-five years by Nora, change was a scary thing. He knew his first major hurdle was going to be the divorce.

He thought that he'd be able to convince Nora with his new found bravery that a divorce was the best thing for both of them. He believed he could make her see that they never really had a mutually agreeable marriage. What he wanted to say to Nora sounded great inside his head: *Let's act like adults. We should move on with our lives and learn from our mistakes.* The only problem he had was that Nora never listened to anything he had to say. Being sensible was not one of Nora's strengths, especially if it inconvenienced her.

He slapped himself across his forehead with the palm of his hand. "Stupid Marc," he chastised himself. "Nora and you never saw eye-to-eye on anything. It's Nora's way or no way."

Marc started shivering—a cold nervous shaking that comes when hope seems lost. Lou had advised him a while ago to call Albert Rankin, the number one divorce attorney in San Diego County. She had said that some of her female customers told her that he was the best out there.

"Pray Nora doesn't get him first," she had warned. "You'll be living at the YMCA for a while if she's retained him."

He really didn't think much about it then, since it had been only two days since he walked out on Nora. "Maybe it's not too late," he mumbled.

* * * * *

Marc couldn't stop his hand from shaking as he tried to punch in Rankin's number into his cell phone. After three unsuccessful attempts, the call went through.

A young perky voice answered. "The law firm of Albert Rankin, how may I direct your call?"

Marc liked the sound of her voice. He was having a good feeling about this already. "I'd like to speak to Mr. Rankin please."

"On whose behalf are you calling for?" the woman asked matter-of-factly.

Marc got a lump in his throat the size of a grapefruit. It was trying to hold back the bile that was trying to explode up from his stomach. "I..huh..need a divorce lawyer. It's…it's for me," he said nervously. "Can I please speak to Mr. Rankin?

"Please hold," she said coldly. His opinion of the woman was changing rapidly.

Horrible thoughts had begun to form inside his head while he waited on-hold listening to the Dixie Chicks sing *"Good bye Earl"*. He actually wanted to hang up and cut his own throat, but he believed that good things were about to happen for him and Albert Rankin was going to be his divorce lawyer.

As he continued to wait and the Dixie Chicks song did another loop, his mind started imagining the worst. *Did Nora already retain him? Should I book a room at the YMCA? Will I have a pot to piss in?* Marc's thoughts were interrupted when a man's voice came on the line.

"Albert Rankin here. How can I help you?" he asked in a relaxed cordial tone.

The lump evaporated and the bile returned to its home in his stomach. *"Maybe I beat Nora to this lawyer?"* He thought, his confidence growing.

"Thank you for talking to me. My name's Marc Richards and I'd like to set—" He was cut off abruptly.

"Mr. Richards, Nora must have told you that I represent her in your divorce. I'm sorry, but I can't speak to you. I suggest you retain another attorney and have him or her give me a jingle so we can set up a time for all of us to meet and begin the division of your *ASSETS*," Rankin said, emphasizing the word assets.

The lump came back. This time it felt like a watermelon coated with the bitterest bile he had ever tasted. "You're her attorney?" he stuttered. "I don't have an attorney just yet," he said feebly.

Rankin's voice had become harsh. "Then I suggest you get one immediately. You'll soon be receiving a court document that will compel you to turn over every financial record you have in your possession, including everything about your very successful business. If you don't contest what Nora rightly deserves from you,

I might go easy and leave you something. Please have your attorney call me," he said, then abruptly hung up the phone.

Marc stared at the receiver that was soaked from his sweaty palm. His hand could not stop shaking. The Dixie Chicks song had been replaced by what he now believed would be his new theme song: "Y.M.C.A". He started signing the letters with his arms, as if he were on the dance floor. A single tear rolled down his cheek. He didn't know what to do next except to call Lou.

FIFTEEN

Nora was overjoyed by the phone call from her attorney. She had already begun, with some help from Gail, making a list of some prospective replacements for Marc. Sensing the enthusiasm from Rankin, it made her afternoon even better.

Gail couldn't contain her enthusiasm. "Peter has two co-workers that would fit the bill perfectly. I know one man, who might just be a clone of Marc. He's been divorced four years and hasn't adjusted well to the dating scene. He'd be perfect to put your hooks into. He's a little desperate, which will work well for you. What makes him perfect is that he works long hours and makes a ton of money."

Nora began to giggle. "And Rankin said I'd have a problem. Ha. He doesn't know how well my charms work on men," she boasted. "I'll just keep up my poor little me appearance for a while, and then I'll be back in the saddle again."

"Are you so sure Marc's going to roll-over and not fight you for what you're asking?" Gail asked.

"Marc? I cannot see him fighting for anything. He'll probably curl up in a fetal position and cry for his mommy. Oh, I forgot. That bitch is dead. The fool has been so beat up all of his life, especially from me, that he'll probably let Rankin gut him from his balls to his throat. The buzzards are probably circling his carcass right now," Nora said, unable to control her laughter.

"Don't be so confident," said Gail. "He did leave *you*, right? He even threw a knife at you and broke your nose," she said pointing at Nora's swollen face. "That doesn't sound like the Marc I know. It's more like Brad. In fact, what about Brad? He's not going to like that you are planning on taking Marc's money before he returns."

Nora laughed. "When I get everything I want, I won't need Marc or Brad. Now, as for handling Marc right now...what he did was just a little temper tantrum. The old Marc will reappear soon enough, especially when Rankin begins to cut him down to size. When I start pressing some of his buttons, he'll explode and it will all be over."

Gail tried to change the subject, holding back her frustration. "Do you think he's seeing someone?" she asked cautiously.

Nora grunted. "No way. He's a one woman guy who can't multi-task. Anyway, who would want such a spineless loser?" she said confidently. "I know Rita said she saw him the other night with a woman, but she did say it ended badly. Marc's personality and confidence could never attract another woman. But, if that happened before I get what I deserve, then she'd be history, just like Ashley."

Gail nervously laughed. "Yeah, we did get rid of that bimbo."

Nora high-fived Gail. "The three of us are still a good team." Nora said. "The divorce will be over soon enough and Marc will be road kill." Without taking a breath, Nora kept talking. "Have you thought of leaving Peter? Maybe we could find two guys that will give us what we want?"

Gail felt her blood begin to boil. "Peter and I are doing just fine. He's great in bed and really loves me. Doesn't ask questions when I'm with you and Rita. You just worry about your own life," she said her tone biting.

"Bitch," Nora barked, turning her back on Gail and walked away.

SIXTEEN

"I won't stoop to her level," Marc barked, his face beet red. "I won't let her or her damn attorney control me. I've been manipulated way too long by her. I'm not going to take it anymore."

Lou had never seen Marc so livid talking about Nora. "First, see my lawyer. You need to know your alternatives. A good one will help you not give away the store. You have a good heart. It's sad that Nora knows how to exploit it."

Marc expelled a long breath. "Are you sure your attorney friend is any good? You told me that Rankin was the best," he said anxiously waving his finger at her.

Lou sighed before responding. She reached across the table and took Marc's hand in hers. "Look, just because Nora has Rankin doesn't mean you're going to lose your shirt. What I said then was just figuratively speaking. Lindsey Warren is the "female" Rankin of divorce attorneys. She'll keep Nora's lawyer in check, while watching over you and your assets."

Marc threw his hands in the air. "Where the hell is a rule book on divorce when you need it? Is it me or do all guys feel like they are being gang raped when they decide to leave their wives?"

Marc tried not acting too frustrated in front of Lou, but Nora had her talons dug deep into his ass and wouldn't let go. His entire world revolved around Nora and her whims. Every thought he had was about Nora. Every emotion revolved around Nora. Every memory he had was born with Nora.

Marc let loose a low groan. He pictured Nora's attorney dragging out his hourly fee and then draining every penny from him. He was deep within his normal worry-state.

"Welcome to the world of wanting your own life," Lou said. "It's not easy taking that first step and breathing fresh air. It causes severe brain freezes, as well as Eleutherophobia," Lou said, seeing a puzzled look on Marc's face. "Marc, it means the fear of freedom. So many men want to be on their own, but can't handle all that responsibility after decades of being with one woman. Most first time attempts to divorce end up with a temporary reconciliation, a sort of partial castration affect."

"Oh brother," he said slapping his forehead. "She's always gotten her way. Maybe I should just buy myself a ball and chain and rollover and play dead."

Lou shrugged her shoulders. "I'm just the messenger. You're going to be ready for this. You did airmail a dangerous weapon at her, warning her to not mess with you. Not to mention the new nose job you gave her. I think you're well on your way to having your freedom. It might just cost a few dollars, but it will be well worth it."

Marc rolled his eyes at Lou's philosophical wisdom. He knew she was trying to ease his fears, but it was not working. He was so conditioned to worry about everything, that it drained the confidence right out of him.

Lou had a broad smile on her face as she consoled Marc. "You'll have to stand up to Nora and her attorney. Maybe some of those cute martial art moves you did the other night? Don't take anything too lightly and don't fall for any of those seductive wiles Nora puts on you."

"Can we be serious right now? It's hard seeing any levity in fighting with Nora. She has no soul."

Lou wrinkled her nose. "I'm not trying to joke with you, well not too much. You know I've been in your shoes on three occasions? There are things that you will need to be ready for and on your game. If you lack confidence, Rankin will smell it and rip you apart. You just have to be strong." Lou raised her finger wanting to make another point. "One other thing will definitely happen..." she said tentatively, her eyes wide with delight begging to tell him more.

Marc put his hand on his forehead feigning exasperation. "Go ahead…tell me. I can't stop you anyway," He tried to force a smile, but his upper lip had begun to quiver.

"Anuptaphobia, the fear of staying single," she said, her face more serious than when she had said Eleutherophobia. If you're anything like me, and I think you are, I believe you love being in love. That trait led me into three failed marriages. It's still a trait I have and respect. I'll keep it in my arsenal until mister right comes along. It might take you a few tries to find the right gal…or maybe not…who's to say. If, when the time comes, you feel comfortable and happy, just go with it until it doesn't feel good anymore. Just don't become anal about a relationship. Too many people second guess what the other person might want and never give of themselves a hundred and ten percent."

Marc couldn't contain his laughter anymore. "You're so weird. The crazy thing is that you're making sense, and that scares me." He saw Lou glance at her watch. "Time to go?"

"I've got so much to do at the coffee shop. I'll be free around six this evening. Want to do dinner and then some dessert at my place?" she said coyly.

"After meeting with my attorney I might need the dessert first. You have a phobia for that craving?" He said rolling his eyes.

Lou grinned. "That's easy. Galeophobia, the fear of sharks. You will probably feel it from Rankin. Then, Decidophobia will overwhelm you. But, if you haven't figured that one out, I'll tell you over dessert."

Lou bounced up from her chair, kissed him on the lips, spun around, and was out the door of the motel room.

Marc felt a warm rush blanket his body. He was feeling something for Lou and it wasn't just the swollen body part inside his pants. His thoughts had become a twister inside his head. So many questions flashed before his eyes. *Should I spend more time with Lou? Is it too soon after separating? Are there other women I'd like better? Should I become a priest or live in the mountains of Tibet?* Then he started to mumble. "Oh, now I get what Lou meant. *Decidophobia,* Duh." Then Marc sat down and closed his eyes, dreaming about their next date.

SEVENTEEN

Lindsey Warren was not what Marc had expected. She greeted him barefoot, extending her right hand that was covered with a white glove that extended up to her elbow. Her smile revealed a glaring chipped front tooth that Marc couldn't stop focusing on. He tried to look down, but his eyes were greeted by her large buxom chest she displayed through her tight V-neck T-shirt. She had enough cleavage to keep a flagpole erect. When she walked toward him he noticed her limping, dragging her right leg, as her left foot curled inward, pigeon-toed. *Who is this woman?* He thought. *Dr. Frankenstein's assistant, I presume*?

It had become apparent that the lawyer Lou raved about, the one who was going to defend him against Nora and Albert Rankin, looked like a walking disaster.

"Mr. Richards, I'm Lindsey Warren", she said her voice perky. "By the surprised look on your face you must be wondering what you've gotten yourself into?" she said raising her leg, arm and exposing her chipped tooth with a big grin.

He shook his head tentatively, his mouth curling at the edges while he shrugged his shoulders, trying to hide the defeat he was feeling. With his voice cracking he replied. "If Lou said you're great, then you must be," he said cautiously. When he saw her slight grin and pursed lips, he realized that he was not convincing.

Lindsey smiled, revealing her broken tooth again. Marc tried to keep his eyes focused on her eyes, which were a beautiful surprisingly emerald green.

"I normally don't look like this, especially at my office. I was rock climbing at my gym and my partner sneezed and accidentally let go of my tether. You'd think that these 'big mamas'," she wiggled her breasts with her hands like they were Jell-O, "would have provided enough cushion to break my fall. I guess real ones don't have any bounce to them," she laughed, as she kept her breasts bouncing in her hands.

"The tooth, limp, and glove...part of the accident?" Marc said sheepishly.

Lindsey nodded. "Precisely. I see the dentist later today, and my orthopedic doctor tomorrow, and well...my hand got a bad rope burn, but that will heal on its own. I didn't have anything else to wear. I didn't want to scare you, but by the look on your face it didn't work."

Marc had a half-hearted grin before he replied. "Not too scared. But, thanks for clarifying."

She limped back to her desk and put a legal pad in front of her. "Let's get started," she said, her friendly demeanor vanishing before his eyes. She had become serious. "Tell me about your marriage and everything about your wife...Nora, that's her name, and what's brought you to this point in your relationship."

Marc was caught off-guard by her question. He never enjoyed talking about his marriage. Even with Lou, it stirred up too many bad memories. "Where should I begin? I used to think that I loved her, but lately I've been taking a hard look at my life the past twenty-five years. Quite frankly, what I thought was love, could very well be classified as "'Stockholm Syndrome.'"

Lindsey broke out into a loud belly laugh. "I've never heard any husband describe his marriage that way. Very vivid," she said waving her hand for him to keep talking, while writing on a legal yellow pad. "I'd like to hear more."

He had her laughing for the next hour and half telling her story after story. When he finished, he asked her if she had any opinion as to why a woman would treat a husband the way Nora had treated him.

Lindsey pursed her lips, as she combed her hair with her gloved fingers, a concerned expression on her face. "Mr. Richards, if we are going to get you through this divorce with as little discomfort as possible, you'll have to understand that your wife hated your fucking guts since the beginning of your relationship. I only say this with as much objectivity as I can," she said seriously before continuing. "She's loved this Brad character for one reason or the other and used you—I mean your ability to make a lot of money for—another reason. If what you say is correct whatever memories you've had will need to be put aside so you can maneuver through what I envision will be a very challenging divorce. From this day forward you won't have any contact with her. Further, you will stop paying for any of her expenses. Close all bank accounts, credit cards and anything thing that's in joint ownership."

Marc was shocked by what she had said. Not about her hating him, but about not paying for Nora's expenses. "I want this divorce to be more conciliatory. Won't this just make it worse for me?"

"Let me ask you a question. Let's say you keep paying Nora what she wants, will she be any different to you or to be frank, will Albert Rankin be any easier on you? No! But, what I can tell you is, that the more you pay her now, the more you'll pay her in front of a judge. Nora's not going to like you any more or less if you pay her expenses or don't. So I say let the courts decide and let the bitch throw a temper tantrum."

"You're sure?" he said nervously.

"In California, we have what we call *The Judge in the Box.* California is a no fault state and it doesn't matter what she's done or you've done. The family assets are divided up, incomes are evaluated, and for Nora, her income potential is taken into consideration once we have her vocationally evaluated. Then the judge presses a button on his or her laptop and voila we have a settlement number."

Marc seemed puzzled about this *judge in a box*, and about Nora's income potential. She had never worked a day in their marriage. "What do you mean about Nora's income potential?"

"Simple. Since you both don't have any children and since your wife has her Masters Degree in economics, I will have her vocationally evaluated. Then the vocational counselor, who performed the test, would place a monetary value on what she could potentially earn in today's market place if she went to work. The good thing is that you don't have children and any judge in his or her right mind won't allow a woman to just stay home in forced retirement. Once we get the judge to put an income number in her column, it will reduce your alimony obligation. You said she did work before you got married, and she's still keeping current on her Series 7 license? If that's correct, it makes her a prime candidate for a judge to get her off her butt and go find a job."

Marc was beginning to like Lindsey more and more. "So what's my next move?"

"I'll need your last five years tax returns and the same for your corporation. I'll need your corporation by-laws and any other documents you created after you were married. Here's an inventory sheet to help guide you. I'll need a full disclosure of all your assets, both personal and business. Don't try to hide anything. We need to be above board, so the judge will see we are cooperating and not trying to hide any income or assets. Also, Rankin's going to want to distract us with inconsequential nonsense, but we, I mean I, won't let him."

"What's your track record against him?" he asked holding his breath. He hoped he wasn't getting an attorney that does a lot of bragging and can't step up to the plate.

"Great, if we go in front of a judge. Rankin hates going to court, so he'll try to wear us down with expensive requests and expert witnesses that if you're not very strong, will have you screaming uncle and agreeing to a financially devastating settlement. You have to be committed to remaining indifferent. You cannot let the divorce become personal. Listen to me and you'll come out of this with most of your assets and income."

"Won't the judge make me pay her attorney fees?"

"Not necessarily. Most judges hate when one spouse is unreasonable and I will assume that with Rankin by her side and what you've already told me about her, Nora's going to appear that way. Since I'm your attorney I won't let that happen to you. You'll only pay what you're supposed to and will be reasonable when it comes to compromising on the splitting of the assets. I wouldn't worry about having to pay her attorney fees, especially since I know how Rankin operates."

Lindsey looked at her watch. It was time for her to go to her dentist. Marc had to get to his office. He needed to work and keep his mind focused.

Marc left his attorney's office whistling, with a little skip to his step. He was feeling so much better and had so much more confidence. It was a feeling that had knocked at his door many times—only to evaporate after looking through the peep-hole and cowering behind the door, afraid to let it in. He fantasized that for the first time he could put Nora in her place and get on with his new life.

Easier said than done. He skidded to a halt and the whistling stopped. Memories of fighting with Nora—and losing—painfully filled his head.

EIGHTEEN

It had been weeks since Marc had popped into his office unannounced, especially late in the afternoon. Mornings had always become his time—you could set your watch to it. When he didn't show up, his office manager, Bea Stone, a gawky woman of forty-six, a widower of ten years, with a loveable incondite manner, and a friend to all of his clients, ran the office like a top sergeant in his absence.

Bea liked it best when Marc stayed away from the office. She could get more done away from her boss's micro-management style. She had been with Marc for almost twenty-years, or as she tells most of his clients, she was his office wife. He would shiver at the thought of it, praying to God to have mercy on his soul if that ever became an alternative.

It was hard living with Nora, but being with a woman like Bea could push him over the edge.

Marc's other employee, Charlie Barnes II, thirty-four, was named after his father, a drunk, and wife beater. He was frugal and overly cautious in everything he did at the office. Divorced three years, he had finally mastered his "Monk" personality. He was good at the details of his job; however, he was as exciting as paint peeling.

Marc had thought that hiring Bee and Charlie would allow him a chance to be in control. The sad truth was that his decision actually sucked. Having them aboard made it clear that he was trapped in the middle of his accommodating personality. Nora, Bea and Charlie formed the perfect circle that surrounded him inside a disheveled life.

He knew he could never replace his two employees, first, out of guilt and second, out of weakness. He worried if that same inability to take care of his emotional well-being at work was going to transfer over during his divorce. He felt his body overheat, as he imagined those crazy thoughts come alive.

Marc's office had a magnificent view of the Pacific, especially the whitewater that broke against the beach in North Carlsbad. The panoramic views and the large windows brightened up the office. He had paid a higher than normal rent for the location. It was meditative and well-appreciated when trying to get as far away from Nora as possible.

Sunlight and blue ocean water were extremely calming for Marc and made for what he believed was a happy office environment. Who wouldn't like to work in a place that overlooked the ocean?

Walking through the front door at this time of the day, he felt like the secret shopper walking in on some unsuspecting employees. To his shock and dismay, the plantation shutters were closed tighter than a bank safe, making the central office area dark and uninviting. All he could see were the faint desk lamps on his employee's desks that were positioned in front of his closed office door. To make matters worse, it was a rare beautiful sunny Carlsbad day, with blue skies and no marine layer. Catalina Island was a faint outline just north-west, only making his anger worse.

It took Marc a few seconds to adjust his eyes from the bright sunlight to a pitch-black reception area. He could make out a faint silhouette of Charlie reading something, his feet propped up on his desk. As his eyes started to adjust to the darkness he could see that Bea was doing her nails. They were both engrossed in something other than work.

As his disappointment began to boil, he gently closed the office door, his clenched fists resting on his hips. Bea and Charlie were oblivious that anyone had entered his office, let alone their boss. They had not noticed that he was standing there steaming. He dialed his office number and got the answering machine.

"Shit," he whispered. "They're letting the phone just ring. His blood started to boil and he felt his eyes throb. His chest got tight, as his heart pounded hard against his ribcage. He did not want a confrontation, but something had to happen immediately. What he had believed to be his only sanctuary had now become yet another disappointment.

He took a few deep breaths before storming into the general office area. He had no clue what he was going to say, but his brain seemed to have it sorted and organized perfectly for his upcoming reaction. The rage he was feeling was the same rage that flowed through his veins when he threw the knife at Nora and handled the two drunks at the tavern. At that moment he actually believed he could kill someone.

"What are the two of you doing?" He shouted in a voice he did not recognize. He was going postal. "Am I not paying the two of you enough to watch over my business?" Bea started to speak, but Marc raised his hand like a traffic cop. Sarcastically she put her fingers to her lips, turned them, and pretended to toss an imaginary key in the air. Her coy attitude only made Marc angrier.

"It's three-thirty in the fucking afternoon. The answering machine's on. The shutters are closed, and the two of you are loafing around. Is this what's been going on when I call and get the answering machine?" Is this why business has been off lately?" He was like a machine gun with his questions.

Charlie sat up immediately in his chair causing it to rock helplessly back. Then there was a loud crash as his body landed against his credenza. He bounced once and fell to the floor. He immediately bounced up, his hands at his sides—his shoulders hunched forward, his chin on his chest, shaking nervously.

Bea did not flinch. She continued doing her nails, as Marc kept ranting. He walked over to her desk and pounded his fist, coming down hard and tipping her purple nail polish onto her floral skirt.

Her eyes grew wide, jumping up abruptly, her knees catching the edge of her center draw and knocking over her nail polish remover, spilling it over a stack of personal photos she had laid out on her desk. She pursed her lips, her eyebrows raised, as her anger exploded on her face.

"Look what you've done," she screamed. "You're paying for a new skirt." She said running out the door toward the restroom.

Marc had more to say, but it was just him and Charlie who seemed paralyzed by what just happened. His eyes were staring at the carpet like a little boy who was about to be scolded by his father.

"Charlie, look at me," Marc bellowed. At first he did not respond. His shoulders looked like they would fold up and consume his body. "Look at me," he said a little calmer. Charlie slowly lifted his head, his eyes were glassy.

"Mr. Richards, sir...I...don't know what to say. Business has been slow. You've been gone a lot. I have nothing to do. The sun was beating down on us and making us hot. There was no breeze coming in off the ocean...we don't have air conditioning. We thought it would be okay to close the shutters. I haven't had an order from you that I could work on and you've seemed preoccupied lately," he said meekly.

Marc was still boiling, his chest had gotten tight, even though Charlie made sense. It was not in his job description to look for clients. That was Marc's job.

Bea returned slamming the door behind her. "Marc what's gotten into you? Are you all right?"

He seemed lost in thought not reacting to her scolding. His left arm had begun to ache and a pain in his pectoral muscle hit him hard. He couldn't catch breath, as he tried to answer Bea. "I...I...don't...like that..." His chest felt like an elephant was compressing it. He dropped to both knees. Both Bea and Charlie stood there frozen as he was grabbing his chest rolling over on his left side.

All Marc could hear before everything went black was Bee screaming to Charlie to call 911.

NINETEEN

The bright lights were blinding Marc. Strange, unfamiliar faces stared down at him. A woman dressed in a nurse's smock was hooking wires up to his body. Another was inserting an IV into the back of his right hand. He was disoriented and confused.

He tried to speak, but his words came out garbled. "Where am I?" He squeezed out, remembering the pain he had felt in his chest. "What happened?"

"You're at the ER at Tri-Cities Hospital and you've had a heart attack," the young attractive nurse said. "You gave us a little scare, but the doctor, he's the best around…" she said matter-of-factly, winking like Marc should have known what she was talking about, "…was able to bring you back."

His eyes widened hinging on "was able to bring you back". *Where did I go? I remember being at my office yelling at Bea and Charlie,* he was beginning to remember. "Oh shit. Now I remember." He blurted out.

The nurse nodded, deep in concentration, as she completed hooking up the spider web of wires to his chest and legs. "You flat-lined right after the Paramedics arrived at your office. Joe and Sara did a great job resuscitating you before they brought you in," the young nurse said, once again like Marc should have known them. "You're a lucky man. They saved your life. The doctors here just this moment got your heart started again. Now lay still, mister," she said in a playful tone. "I need to get an EKG," she said sweetly, her cool hand was patting his exposed toes.

Marc's mind started to wander with the nurse's touch. *Oh how I love cool hands…Nora's are like hot pokers…another sign she hates my fucking guts,* he told himself closing his eyes tight as another painful chest pain hit him.

He tried to remember what had happened. Lying on his back in a bland room being fussed over did not ease his mind that he was going to be all right. He was very nervous and scared. It was clear to him that his yelling had caused his heart attack. His thoughts ran wild. *Why now, when I'm finally going to get a life? Maybe this is my punishment for waiting so long.* Once again, Marc beat himself up feeling trapped, unable to see any positive alternatives.

The curtained room he occupied in the ER was a buzz with technicians, nurses and doctors. For the first time in his life he was the center of attention. In a sick way he was enjoying all of the compassion these strangers were giving him. How good it felt compared to the crabby attention Nora usually provided.

After what seemed like hours, he was transferred up to the CCU ward. He was being scheduled for an angiogram in the morning. The doctor had given him some good news, ruling out any consequential heart damage. They just had to see inside his arteries to determine what caused his heart to stop.

Marc had finally settled in when Nora marched into his room. He couldn't look at her, biting his lower lip. He felt another sharp pain in his chest. *The warden had recaptured me. This time there would be no escape,* he told himself. "What are you doing here?" He asked despondently.

Nora's face was like white marble, hard and cold. "Don't get testy with me," she said harshly. "I rushed over after my yoga lesson. I had to shower. Bea interrupted my lesson. You know, you need to have a talk with her. She was very rude to me."

Marc turned his head, his eyes beams of fire. He was confused as to why she had come. He knew it was not out of love. "I didn't ask you to come," he said feebly. "I'd rather be alone anyway. Plus my attorney doesn't want me to talk to you anymore. So get the fuck out of here."

Nora did not show any expression or act like she had heard a word he had said. "I tried to find out from Bea, but she did not know," she rambled.

Marc furrowed his brow. "Know what?"

"The life insurance? Has the new policy been issued? How would I survive without it?" she said acting like she almost lost a new dress at a Nordstrom's sale. "Also, you haven't changed beneficiaries on the other life policies since you left…right? They still are in force? Right?" she said crossing her arms across her chest.

If ever he needed an incentive to live, this was it. "Get the fuck out of here and don't come back. What I do with the life insurance is my business," he said, feeling the pain in his chest increase. He tried to press the call-button the nurse had tied to the railing on his bed, but Nora had it tight in her hand.

"Answer my question or else," she said indecorously. Nora had an unseemly demon-like aura encircling her entire body.

Marc's life-line for help was out of reach as the pain in the middle of his chest felt like it was going to explode and splatter all over the room.

Marc was scared, panic cracked on his face. He tried to grab back the call-button, but Nora stepped away from his bed.

"Answer my question, you bastard!" she screamed, her shrill of a voice echoing into the corridor.

Her high-pitched and piercing sound was better than his call-button. Two nurses came running into his room.

"Mr. Richards are you all right?" they said in unison. They both looked at him and then Nora, seeing the nurses call button in her hand.

Barely catching his breath he spit out his orders. "Get her out of here and ban her from returning. She just tried to kill me," he said nervously, as his pain grew more intense.

One of the nurses pulled the button from Nora's hand, breaking one of her long French-tipped nails and placed it back on Marc's bed. She then took Nora's arm and abruptly escorted her out of the CCU. "Do I need to call security, Mrs. Richards?" the nurse said harshly.

Marc could hear Nora screaming profanities at everyone, as the large steel doors closed sealing her outside the intensive care unit.

As fast as his chest pains had come, they subsided when the doors to the unit closed, sealing out Nora's hysterical behavior. It didn't stop the nurse from giving Marc some more morphine to relieve his pain. A warm sensation rushed over his body. Before he fell into a light twilight, he asked the nurse to call his friend Lou Hart. He repeated her number that he had etched to his memory.

His eyes closed slowly and his mind tried to enjoy the quiet and tranquility the narcotic was providing.

TWENTY

Nora couldn't control her agitation. She found herself flustered and paced erratically in front of Elliott Rankin's receptionist. The young perky receptionist tried to calm her down, but there was no reasoning with Nora at that moment. Her voice kept rising, her anxiety at a boiling point demanding to see her attorney immediately.

The receptionist tried to remain as polite as she could. "He's with a client right now. It will be at least an hour. He's just gotten started with her," the receptionist said, her tone turning to edgy.

Nora marched over to the high counter that protected the young girl. "You tell him it's a fucking emergency! Do it now!" she screamed.

The young receptionist held her ground, biting her lower lip. "He instructed me to not disturb him. You'll either have to sit and wait, or walk around the block a few times and calm yourself down. If Mr. Rankin hears you, he'll be very—and I mean very— upset…and believe me…you don't want him upset with you, especially since you're just getting started on your divorce," she said as if she were talking to an unruly child.

Nora, sucked in a deep breath, closing her eyes tightly, deep in thought. She was remembering her last meeting with Rankin when he threatened her about not following his orders. As if nothing had been said, Nora's persona changed, transforming her from a crazed lunatic, to a sweet helpless battered wife before the receptionist's eyes. She picked up her purse and told the young lady in a calm and controlled tone, "Tell Mr. Rankin that I'll be back in an hour. I hope that will work for him?"

Before the receptionist could reply, Nora marched out the door heading toward the elevator.

* * * * *

"Gail, I've got to see you. Something horrible has happened. Marc had a heart attack. He's at the hospital and I don't know what to do about it." she said crying.

"Where are you?" Gail said her tone worried.

"Del Mar. Meet me at Jake's."

"I'll be there in fifteen minutes," Gail said. "You be strong. Is he going to be all right?"

"Fuck! I don't know or care," she barked. Before Nora could say another word, Gail had disconnected the call. "Be all right? What about me and the fucking life insurance? It's mine and I want it," she mumbled as she marched down the hill to Jake's.

* * * * *

Nora was on her second Bombay Sapphire and tonic when Gail had arrived. Gail could tell she had a mean buzz brewing, which only exaggerated her already irritated mood.

"You're late. You're always late when it comes to helping me," Nora bellowed.

Gail gave her friend an icy stare. She held her emotions in check, not wanting to start a fight, especially in a restaurant. "It's horrible about Marc. How bad was it?"

Nora had a puzzled look on her face. "What kind of question is that? Don't you want to know how I'm doing?" Nora said angrily.

Gail seemed confused. "How's this about you? I thought you were distraught about Marc and his heart attack?"

"You're so fucking inconsiderate," she said loudly, causing a few heads to turn in the bar. "Since Marc left he might have taken me off as his beneficiary on his life insurance policies. Maybe he's cancelled them entirely. If he dies before the divorce and my settlement, I could be screwed royally. We all need the money, you know."

Gail rolled her eyes totally taken aback by Nora's comments, especially her attitude. "He can't change anything on the life insurance without your permission," she said calmly.

Nora acted surprised. "He can't? Why?"

"You're the owner of his policies aren't you?" Gail asked cautiously.

"How the fuck would I know?" Nora bellowed. "He's handled all of that since we were married. How would I find out if I'm the owner?"

Gail felt like wringing her friend's neck. Exasperated she responded. "Call your insurance agent and ask. I had Peter make me the owner of his life insurance a long time ago. It helps with probate, and especially if we ever get a divorce, I'll have some bonus compensation if he dies on me."

Nora scratched her head. "I don't know who the damn agent is. It would be so much easier if he would have told me at the hospital. That's all I wanted from him…I would have given him back the blasted nurses call-button if he just told me," she said matter-of-factly.

Gail's eyes had become little slits of contempt. *And I call this bitch my friend?* "You grilled him at the hospital about his life insurance?" said Gail incredulously. You don't think your timing was a little inappropriate? You're a real piece of work, Nora. If he hadn't taken you off, he most surely will now with that bone-head move. You need to start thinking before you speak," Gail said unsympathetically. "Rita and I have been getting you out of trouble for way too long."

Nora's eyes widened at Gail's comments. She acted shocked at what she had heard. "I have to look out for myself. He wanted this divorce; even after all the loving years I've given him. I just want what's rightfully mine." She stood abruptly, almost knocking over the barstool and told Gail she had to get back to her attorney's office.

Gail just sat there shaking her head, a puzzled look on her face.

Nora's mood had instantly changed and with a soft sweet voice she said, "Marc better not die, at least not until I squeeze every dollar out of him," she said smiling.

Gail stood facing Nora. "Have you even thought about what you're doing? How will any of this look? What about Brad? Are you forgetting about him? How will he feel about all of this?"

Nora balled up her fists, resting them on her hips. "Fuck Brad. Fuck Marc. It's time Nora has it all," she said poking her index finger against her sternum.

Gail watched Nora prance out of Jake's, her hands in a prayer position, wishing lightning would strike her friend. "Maybe it's

time to distance myself from her," Gail mumbled, as the server
handed her Nora's bar tab.

TWENTY-ONE

Nora bolted through the parking lot at Jake's, across the community park on the hill by the beach, walking faster and faster, jumping across the railroad tracks, up the hill toward Coast Highway.

It was shaping up to be one of those days when Nora wondered why she ever married Marc after Brad vanished. There had been so many other men, so many other opportunities to secure the life she wanted, but Brad was exciting in a violent sort of way and she was still drawn to him that way, forgetting that he knew so much about her past that could lock her away for the rest of her life. It was all about her right now and thinking was out of the question.

Heading south toward Rankin's office on Coast Highway, she passed her favorite dress shop, fifty-percent off, the sign in the window said. She thought about going in, but deliberated a second, and moved on. She was on a mission and that took priority over some dumb sale. "They close at six. I'll be back," she said in a feeble impersonation of the Terminator.

A burst of confidence had come over her while she marched up to Rankin's office building. From where she didn't know, but a surge of adrenaline was pumping through her veins, giving her the clarity she had lacked moments earlier when talking to Gail.

She decided that storming into Rankin's office and making a scene was the wrong tactic. Like Loretta Young greeting her weekly viewers, she walked through the door, twirling three-hundred and sixty degrees, ever so gracefully, a big friendly smile that showed her newly brightened perfect set of teeth. "Hi there sweetie, I'm back. Is Mr. Rankin available now?" she said ever so innocently.

The receptionist looked surprised at Nora's improved demeanor. "He's waiting for you. I'll let him know you've arrived."

Nora had already taken a cotton-laced handkerchief from her handbag. With lady-like finesse she dabbed her temples and cheeks blotting away the perspiration that had beaded up on her face from her strenuous walk. "Thank you so very much."

Before Nora could sit down, Elliott Rankin abruptly opened his office door, his eyes like molten lava. "Mrs. Richards let's get this over with." His tone was more curt than stern. It was obvious that he had been told about Nora's recent outburst in his reception area.

Before Elliott could scold her, she began apologizing. "I'm so sorry for carrying on earlier. Marc..." she sniffled, "had a heart attack today and I didn't know what to do or who to turn to."

Whatever she said, instantly changed Rankin's mood. A smile grew from ear-to-ear. "I'm sorry for his misfortune, but this is extremely good for us...I mean you. I've seen it before when a husband gets seriously ill, the divorce takes on a whole new composure."

Nora wrinkled her nose, a puzzled looked on her face. "How could this be good for me?"

"People with life-threatening illnesses, especially a man and a heart attack, start seeing their life differently and...well—it brings them to a more realistic state. If I were a betting man, Marc's already calling his attorney and asking her to do whatever we want. He has to take care of himself. I don't have to tell you where his priorities lie now."

"Have you found out who the beneficiaries are on Marc's life insurance policies?" she said nonchalantly.

"I asked his attorney to let me know about that and other items before this happened. Don't say anything about those life insurance policies or Marc's attorney will paint you as the money digging bitch you are," he said seriously. He noticed a guilty look on Nora's face. "Have you done something I need to know about?"

"No," she said without blinking. "I'm smarter than that."

"Okay. Let move on. Now, it's important how the corporation and the remaining assets are vested. The life insurance should have you as beneficiary, so there's no problem there, but I will make sure that you're on as primary."

"We're husband and wife. Shouldn't everything be vested as community property in this state?" asked Nora trying to not sound too stupid.

"It should, however, I've seen some marriages where husbands have given a certain amount of shares in their corporation to their wives. Have them sign a partnership agreement of sorts, which only allows them to claim the value of the shares at the time of dissolution."

Nora turned white as a ghost. "I remember when he formed his corporation. He had me sign a pile of papers. I'm not very smart when it comes to stuff like that," she said coyly.

Rankin shook his head. "That response won't work in front of a judge with your Masters Degree in Economics. Playing stupid won't fly."

Nora started shaking. "Marc's always been a straight-shooter, so I trusted that he was looking out for my best interests. He had told me that I had twenty-five shares of stock in the business. I was flattered at the time, because he said I was now on the board of directors." Nora did not like the expression that formed on Rankin's face.

"Do you have a copy of the papers you signed? Also, the stock certificate he gave you?"

"Is there going to be a problem?" she asked

"I'm not sure. I need to see what you've signed. Marc might not be the meek, trusting imbecile you say he is."

* * * * *

Nora was walking back toward Jake's, thinking about what Rankin had said. *Marc's not that devious. ,*she thought, shaking her head. *I would have seen it in his eyes. He's not Brad.* She got distracted and popped into the clothing store she had passed earlier. "This will make me feel better," she mumbled. "A few new outfits, a visit to the safe-deposit box, and look in at my lovely soon-to-be ex-husband or should I say departed husband." Being a widower sounded so much more sorrowful than divorcee to Nora as she slipped into the fitting room.

A brief flashback interfered with her desire to shop. She recalled Justin, her first love and how he disappointed her by not asking her to the senior prom. His unfortunate accident gave her a lot of attention and sympathy. She liked being the center of attention, especially if she could milk it for a long while.

When she tried to pay for her new items the salesgirl frowned and told her credit card was rejected. "That can't be," she complained. "Try it again." When that didn't work she handed her another credit card. When that didn't work, she stormed out of the store.

On the way back to Jake's parking lot, her face beet-red she started singing. "Marc's gotta die," she muttered off tune trying to feel the mood of the Dixie Chicks song. As she got behind the wheel of her car, she screamed. "Marc you are such a bastard."

TWENTY-TWO

After much finagling, manipulation, and trickery, Lou convinced *"Nurse Ratchet"* to let her in to see Marc. She had no sooner sat down next to Marc's hospital bed when two nurses came into his room.

"Your angiogram has been moved up," the nurse said grinning. "You're the man of the hour."

Marc's shocked look took a backseat to Lou's emotional outburst. "He's having his operation, now?" she blurted out.

The nurse seemed amused. "When we have an opening, patients get bumped up. We had a code-blue on the fellow who Marc's replacing."

"Now?" Marc said nervously. "You just had a plane crash and you want me to go on the next plane out of here? I don't think so."

Lou grabbed Marc's hand and stood shielding her friend, trying to prevent them from taking him away.

The other nurse, in a professional tone said. "We're not explaining ourselves clearly I can see," she said giving her partner a stern look. "The gentleman who was bumped, had a heart attack before going to the cath-lab. An angiogram is a very safe procedure. We've never lost anyone in the cath-lab. You have nothing to worry about, Mr. Richards. Your cardiologist is one of the best we have at this hospital."

The nurse was not very convincing. "Can I have a minute with my friend?" Marc asked. The two nurses walked out of the room chatting to themselves.

"I guess we'll have to finish our little chat later. Will you stay and wait for me?"

Lou tried to swipe at a tear off her cheek without Marc seeing, but she failed. With her voice quivering, she answered. "If they'd let me go inside, I'd be there holding your hand. Should I ask?" she said seriously.

Lou tried to be strong at that moment, but couldn't hold back her tears. "You go get this over with. I want you healthy and strong," she said giving him a wet kiss on the lips.

"Don't get all mushy on me. I'll start believing you really like a clod like me."

Lou smiled. "You can't imagine how much I like you, and we haven't even started getting to know each other yet."

The two nurses came back into the room and pushed Marc's bed out of the room. Lou walked out to the corridor with them.

At the other end of the corridor the doors to the elevator opened and Nora walked out.

When she saw Lou holding Marc's hand, her mouth dropped to her chest. Her eyes were pools of fire, as she ducked around the corner, peeking at Marc. When the woman bent down and gave him a passionate kiss, Nora did everything she could do to restrain herself. *She must be the bitch Rita saw him with the other night.*

"That bastard. He's been having an affair. Oh, he's dead...she's dead...they're both dead," she said under her breath.

TWENTY-THREE

Inside the Cath-lab the temperature felt like a freezer. An attractive nurse had begun to shave Marc, down around the "boys", his first partial bikini shave—right side only. It was cold on the operating table and he tried jokingly, his teeth clattering, to explain what happens to guys when it's cold. The nurse smiled, shaking her head like she had heard that a thousand times before, and kept shaving. He prayed that she could at least see a semblance of his manhood, but he didn't want anything popping up around her sharp razor, so he thought of something else.

 Another nurse started to speak to him, explaining she was giving him a nice drug cocktail and that he would begin to feel light-headed and not to get alarmed. Then the nurse whispered in his ear and asked if he was beginning to relax. Marc had a nice buzz going. He remained awake in a floating sort of way.

The barber of the cath-lab (the nurse) said "Voila". The turtle can come out of its shell," she teased. "But I'd keep the little guy right where he is if I were you. The doctor is getting ready to insert the catheter and you don't want him distracted with a Jack-in-the-box." Marc forced a little grin.

Marc's doctor re-introduced himself. He had seen him hours before in the CCU ward. Marc didn't recognize him with his surgical mask on. In his buzzed state and lying flat on the narrow cold gurney he had to trust that a terrorist sent by Nora was not performing this procedure and was not promised a share of his life insurance. "I must remember to remove Nora as beneficiary to my life policies," he whispered incoherently.

After a numbing shot and a little pressure in his groin area, the catheter had been inserted. A large computer screen was to his left. He turned his head to look at it, his mind floating from the relaxing drugs he had just gotten, hoping to catch up on some emails. He had a wonderful buzz going causing him to become very chatty. "I'd like some of whatever you guys gave me to take with me when I go home. You can't imagine my next few months. I'm going to need a lot of this," he said giggling.

The doctor spoke sternly. "Marc, you'll need to stop talking so I can concentrate while I snake the camera into your heart."

Immediately Marc saw something beating on the monitor. "What's that?" his words came out a bit slurred.

The doctor behind the mask responded, "Your heart. The camera's now up into your main artery. I'll let you know what I find. Please put a lock on all these questions."

During the next forty or sixty minutes, Marc wasn't quite sure about the time, he watched his beating heart and the long snake of a camera gently weave its way through a web of arteries. The silence from the doctor had made him very anxious. He asked what was happening and got no response. *Did he find something? Was I going to die? Will I ever see Lou again?* He chatted to himself. Like a swift kick, his chest pains returned. He tried to speak, but the doctor interrupted him.

"Mr. Richards are you having chest pains right now?"

"Yes!" as the pain exploded.

The nurse asked him what level the pain was.

Marc's voice cracked. "A twelve!"

"Excellent," the doctor said. "At first I couldn't find any blockage or any signs that you have damage to your heart muscle. What you're having at the moment is a coronary artery spasm. It's common during stressful events. For most people who handle stress well, the artery, after a spasm, returns to its normal state. In your case, with all the stress in your life, you and your arteries don't know what normal is supposed to be—cells have memories and yours are not allowing you to return to its normal state."

Marc was totally confused. This stress thing did not make any sense to him. "Are you saying that I didn't have a heart attack?" His voice had sobered up.

"By our initial tests you appeared to have one. By the look of things here, if you did, it didn't damage your heart. My educated guess is that you didn't. Your artery must have had a massive spasm, closing off the blood flow to your heart. When it happened, it was probably totally closed and that stopped your heart. It was a miracle that you did not have any heart damage. And, for the average man with coronary artery disease, I'd see blockage from this problem. But in your case there's no noticeable plaque that needs any intervention. I'd say that you're not dealing with stress very well. You need to make some key life-style changes or the next time you might die."

"I'm trying to do just that. I'm going through a divorce. I can only imagine that my stress is going to get worse for me over the next few months."

"That will contribute to your problem. If you'd like my advice get it over with as quickly as possible before it kills you. But, stress is generally a long term problem that I suspect has been going on for years, maybe even decades. You need to learn to deal with it. I'll bet it's your divorce that's been the catalyst allowing this condition to surface. I'd recommend seeing someone who can help you deal with all of what's going on in your life. I'll prescribe some drugs to calm you down, but you should see a therapist immediately."

"Any recommendations?" Marc asked.

"When I check on you later, I'll have a few names for you and a few prescriptions to take that will keep your arteries open. You'll be on your back for the next six to eight hours. If the silicon plug I inserted is not leaking and you can walk for a while without any complications, you'll be able to go home later today. Do you have someone who can drive you home?" the doctor asked.

"I have a friend in the waiting room. Could you explain all of this to her? I might not remember everything you've said."

"If she not a family member, I can't discuss your case. I'll have everything written out that will explain what I just said. See you later. You'll be just fine if you get a handle on your stress," the doctor said squeezing Marc's shoulder.

Marc was wheeled into a small recovery room and he asked if Lou could come in. The same nurse who shaved him did not object, and within minutes Lou was by his side with her beautiful smiling eyes.

"Glad you made it back," she said cheerfully.

"Me too. Can we get back to what we started to talk about up in my room?"

The doctor's words regarding his stress and changing his life-style kept spinning inside his head. "He looked over at Lou, forcing a faint smile, wondering if having her in his life right now was part of his stress. He knew she was a wonderful woman, he felt comfortable around her, but he didn't think he could handle the distraction.

It was apparent that he wasn't yet comfortable allowing himself to be happy. It was bringing about too much guilt. He thought that getting involved with a woman right away, especially before his divorce was final might jeopardize his health and even piss off Nora more than she already was.

Lou looked more beautiful to him. How was he going to tell her he wanted to cool things off, especially before they really got started? Even though they had only been on three dates, and one that had become intimate, he didn't think it would be a big deal to her. He even thought that if she was a true friend she'd understand what he needed. He was still groggy and couldn't keep his eyes from fluttering closed.

In a light slumber, Marc felt the nap on the back of his neck stand at attention. His paranoia had returned. He was afraid to open his eyes. He was positive someone was inside the recovery room lurking, it was the same feeling he had right before his heart attack. His blood started pumping. He could feel his veins in his neck and on his forehead pounding. Once again he did not feel safe, especially since Nora was fixated on his life insurance.

* * * * * *

Brad could hear everything Marc and Lou had been saying. He needed Lou out of way or she would ruin his plans. He thought of following her and ending it in the parking lot, but Marc was his number one priority and he had to get him alone for his plan to work.

He closed his eyes tight, willing Marc to do something that would get Lou to leave and not return. It was something as boys he was always able to do, to compel Marc to do things he did not want to do.

TWENTY-FOUR

Marc didn't know where to start. He slowly opened his eyes, staring at Lou, feeling uncomfortable about what he was going to say. He kept his voice low, holding back his emotions, feeling himself on the razor's edge of being insensitive.   He couldn't look Lou in the eyes. A short while ago he wanted to spend all his time with her. Now, he just wasn't sure. What the doctor had said about his stress was causing him to rethink his life and his current options. He wasn't sure if it was this life-threatening event that had just happened, or the inner voice that kept telling him to just take care of himself.

One thing that was apparently clear was that he did not feel worthy of having happiness.   What was gnawing at his heart was the fact that he wanted some time alone to think, to figure out what his flashbacks meant and why he had received the mysterious letter in the first place.

Lou just was not going to fit into those plans right now, especially the intimate relationship she indicated she wanted right now. All of it was too distracting.

As he continued staring at Lou, the events of the previous few weeks kept replaying inside his brain. Snippets of memories were beginning to pop up, more vibrant and vivid. Everything was moving way too fast, especially the memories of certain visual experiences. The inner voice kept repeating the words he had read in the letter. The most troubling recall was of three young girls beating a teenage boy to death. His heart attack had gotten him to step back and reevaluate his current situation.

He hadn't told the doctor about the blackouts, the voice, and the dark curtain that had started falling when his stress levels were at their highest. Nor did he tell the doctor that he had time-frames that he could not account for. As he continued his blank stare in Lou's direction he realized how scared he was becoming.

He was watching the concerned expression on Lou's face grow and realized that he was so unprepared to handle Lou's disappointment. But the voice inside his head was telling him that it was finally time to take care of himself.

Lou's eyes appeared sad. She seemed to sense Marc's distance and spoke. "What's on your mind? You seem different."

He tried to grin, realizing that he wasn't hiding his feelings. Lou, for all the years they'd known each other, could sense a problem on Marc's face. She seemed to be seeing something more serious and unfamiliar. She slowly crossed her arms as her body tensed. Her smile lines at the corner of her eyes still formed at the edges, but were slowly turning to sad glassy ones.

"I don't know how to explain this to you," Marc struggled, trying to force a warm, caring smile. "The doctor says that what happened to me today came about from my years of stress. I get coronary artery spasms. When I'm under stress my arteries constrict, preventing the blood to flow to my heart." He tried to act positive, but it was not working. "The good news is that I *didn't* have a heart attack." Lou's facial muscles relaxed and her smile returned.

"That's great news! Stress is easy to control. A little yoga, a little walking, good friends, some great sex and of course eating right. I'm the queen of stress relief," she said happily raising her arm.

Marc pursed his lips, his eyes looking behind her. He realized his approach was not working as he had planned. She was so positive and caring. What he was about to say he knew was not going to go over so well. "You're a great gal," he said cautiously, regretting his condescending tone. Lou at once re-stiffened and removed her hand from his. He tried to rephrase his words, but once said, it's like super glue to a woman. It's there permanently.

"What's going on?" she said cautiously.

Marc swallowed hard, took a deep breath, realizing Lou was watching him like a hawk circling its prey. "Stress is my enemy. I need to learn to deal with it better than I have. Right now my life is spinning out of control with Nora and this divorce. I have to put some things on the back burner and it can't be Nora or my heart right now. Understand, it's not you, it's me. But, I don't want to lose you as a friend. I'm just too overwhelmed right now. Trying to build a new relationship, especially a romantic one." Marc could see the pain he was causing her, sucking in a deep breath. "Just seeing the pain I'm causing you now, I feel my arteries tightening. I can't bear to do this to you. You're a wonderful person who deserves to be treated better than I'm capable of doing right now. I hope you understand?"

Lou nodded, her lips pressed tightly, as she tried to respond. "I have my own opinion of what you might need now, but I won't say. Knowing you as well as I do, this is typical of you," she said sarcastically.

He tried to speak, but she raised her finger to her lips signaling him to be quiet. "Let me finish. This is very difficult for me. We can still be friends, but not while you're sorting out your personal problems. I think it would be better for both of us to cool it for awhile, especially at my coffee shop, until your divorce is finalized." She leaned forward and kissed his forehead and stood. "Don't say a word right now," she said unable to stop the flow of tears cascading down her cheeks.

Marc watched her leave. Sadness had come over him. Even though she was right about him, it still hurt.

Did he really care for her? He wasn't sure, but it was time for him to finally become selfish and try to heal, even if it meant hurting someone he cared about. He reached over to the nightstand by his hospital bed and pulled out the letter. He read it again. He immediately hit his call button. He needed to relieve the pain in his chest.

"I can't do this," he muttered. "Delegation," he nodded.

* * * * *

Marc had been moved from CCU to a Cardiac Telemetry Unit. His cardiologist came by to see him the following morning.

Marc was irritable and tired. He had to spend the night with the roommate from hell. It was an older man in his late seventies or early eighties and a real whack job. By six that evening Marc was already climbing the walls listening to the old man's loud obnoxious voice. His roommate was hard of hearing and kept his TV on so loud that Marc couldn't hear himself think.

Marc had gotten the nurse to bring some ear jacks for the man's TV. Finally a calm quiet enveloped the room.

It didn't last too long as he heard the man's low whisper of help, which sounded like he had become possessed. "Help me. Help me," he cried in the lowest whimper "I need help," his voice got softer almost faint. "Please…come…quickly."   Marc thought the old man was dying and pressed his nurses call button. Two nurses came running in, thinking Marc was having another heart attack.

When the nurses arrived, Marc pointed to the devil through the curtains. They both rolled their eyes, mouthing apologies.

In a polite whisper the nurse said, "he's very ill and going for open heart surgery early in the morning."

Marc tried to feel bad for him, but he had his own problems and didn't need Satan to put him into the grave. He could hear the nurses telling the old man that he had to press the call button for help and not use his TV ear piece for that. They also scolded him for pulling out his IV.

Whatever the nurses had done, hopefully a tranquilizer strong enough to put an elephant down, was keeping him very quiet.

By two o'clock in the morning Marc fell into a nice dreamlike state. It had been no more than five minutes when his crazy roommate turned on his TV at full volume.

Marc's heart jumped out of his chest and his finger wildly pressed his nurses call button once again. She came running in, took one look at Marc, and knew what the emergency was. The crazy old man had tried to insert his IV into the TV thinking it was his ear plug.

By five-thirty in the morning they wheeled the old man out to the OR and peace had returned to the hospital room. Marc leaned back and closed his eyes, enjoying the quiet. Then he heard a tick, tick, tick, tick, ringing inside his head. Then, combined with the ticking, there was now a bright lightning flash inside his closed eye lids.

Marc now had visions of a brain tumor or blood clot exploding inside his head. Once again he pressed his call button. This time the nurse walked in more calmly.

"What's going on now Mr. Richards?" she said coolly.

"I'm hearing a loud ticking in my head. And, when I close my eyes, inside the lids I'm seeing these bright light flashes, something like a strobe light. Could I have a brain tumor?" he asked anxiously.

She tried to contain a giggle, but failed. "First, you're hearing the wall clock ticking. It happens when you go from loud constant noise to total quiet. Your senses focus on the little noises that you couldn't hear earlier. As far as the strobe light, well that's more serious," she joked. "It appears that your reading light is flickering. I'll shut the light off. Why don't you use these ear plugs to block out the ticking noise? You need to get some sleep," she said laughing on her way out.

Within seconds, with the ear plugs in, Marc fell into a deep sleep.

It didn't last too long as his doctor did his rounds early.

"Everything seems to be stable. You can go home later this morning. You said you had someone who could drive you home?"

Shit, he knew he couldn't call Lou. Nora was out of the question. "I'll have someone here," he said. He'd have to call his office manager, Bea.

"Here's the business card of the psychiatrist I told you about. I think you should see him immediately. Also, I made out three prescriptions for you: Zanax to help you stay calm, especially with your divorce pending, Norvasc, to keep your arteries opened and nitroglycerin, when you feel any sign of chest pain. If you have to take more than three within a five minute period, call 911 and get your ass back into the ER. I want to see you at my office in a week to see how you're progressing."

After the cardiologist left, Marc got up for his first walk. He looked at the business card he had given him. It was Doctor Edward Kaplan, Lou's friend. How interesting.

During his walk around the hospital cardiac wings, lapping at least half-dozen men dragging their IV's as they shuffled in their slipper socks, a man in a white doctor's coat walked up to him.

"Are you Mr. Richards?"

Marc seemed weary. The man was holding an envelope. "That's me. You like my stunning outfit?" he said pointing at his hospital gown. The man did not seem to comprehend the humor in what Marc had said. The man's face was serious.

"You've just been served," he said, handing him the envelope. Could you please sign by the 'X'," he said putting clipboard and pen under Marc's nose.

Marc wasn't sure what he was just handed. "Is this my get out of jail card? I thought the doctor said I was leaving at noon?"

After taking back the clipboard and verifying Marc had signed his name, the man finally spoke. "You'll need to be in court on the date stated on your subpoena."

"Subpoena?"

"Your divorce," the man said, spinning around abruptly and marching out of the hospital ward.

Marc found a couch and sat abruptly down jarring his groin area which was still sore at the spot where a catheter had been lodged. It hurt, but not as much as the realization that his divorce was beginning to move at lightning speed. He leaned his head back against the cold leather couch and closed his eyes. The dark curtain had fallen once again.

* * * * * *

Brad had been watching and listening. What the doctor had said to Marc was ruining his plan. He wanted to kill someone. He felt trapped, wondering if Marc would have the strength, even the stomach to hash-up his old memories with a therapist. Then panic struck, worried if Marc's heart would be strong enough to take it? He tore the second letter in half and dropped it into a trashcan.

He had not wanted to do this, but he had no other choice. He was going to have to take matters into his own hands. He saw Marc's eyes flickering and he knew he'd be regaining consciousness. He left the hospital ward as quickly as he arrived.

TWENTY-FIVE

Marc read the date for his upcoming settlement conference. He realized he had only two weeks to prepare for his first court appearance. However, before that date his first deposition had also been scheduled. He was nervous and felt like he was suffocating.

Something was upsetting him and it did not feel like it was the deposition. If it wasn't the deposition, it must have something to do with answering questions that would expose his private life to the world. He hoped Lindsey would make it all go away.

His demons were haunting him and it felt like an atomic explosion erupting inside his brain. He wasn't sure what was going to come at him next. One gnawing question that kept popping up: Is getting a divorce the right thing to do? Exposing his life to everyone was not sitting well with him.

He remembered what Lindsey had told him during their first meeting. *"She's always hated your fucking guts."* He knew, even though it was a startling realization, it was pathetically true. Now, his wretched existence was going to become a matter of public record. He once had thought of writing his memoirs, more a psycho-thriller, and now some court reporter would be ghost writing it for him. His attorney kept telling him it will not be that bad. The Judge is only interested in the objective facts and will not tolerate any drama or finger pointing during the trial.

That did not go over well with Marc, as he wanted to be able to tell the judge what a cruel bitch Nora had been and continued to be. He did not need an objective accounting of his failed marriage. He sucked in a deep breath, lost in thought. *Is this the right thing to do right now?* He was second guessing his decision. He was reverting back to his poor self-image and starting to believe his life with Nora wasn't so bad.

Marc never had close male friends he could confide in or feel comfortable asking for help. Approaching his acquaintances he had met during his marriage would no longer be possible. The wives would be siding with Nora, the "victim" and he would be shunned.

Then there was Lou, but that would not work either at this point. He was on his own and it scared him. If his past was any indication of how he handled difficult matters, it looked like Nora was going to get what she wanted: everything.

Lou was a great example of his inability to be good to himself. Now he just had to leave the hospital with someone and all he could think of was one of his employees. A pathetic realization that only added to the self-loathing he had been feeling.

Bea had come at the precise moment the elderly woman volunteer had come to take him in a wheelchair out of the hospital. His office manager had worn her usual dark flowered dress she favored, wearing no jewelry, her hair pulled straight back from her forehead and wearing steel-framed eye glasses she saw the world through. The only decoration on her dress was a dangling ornament you'd expect to see on a Christmas tree.

"You're looking so much better than when you collapsed at the office," she said, her voice cracking.

Her tone was uneasy. He realized he must have scared the shit out of her. "I'm feeling so much better," Marc said forcing a smile.

"Both Charlie and I have thought it over and we're going to do everything in our power to not get you upset with us anymore. You're a great boss and we both love our jobs," she said teary eyed.

"That will be nice. I'll need to change a few things from my end also." He moved toward her and gave her a big firm hug. She kissed his cheek.

He sat back down in the wheelchair and accidently dropped the subpoena. Bea picked it up and saw it was from an attorney's office. "I know this guy. Is something up with you and Nora?" she asked, her cupped hand covering her mouth.

"We're getting a divorce. We should have done this years ago."

Bea gasped. "I never had a good feeling about the two of you, but never thought divorce was in the cards. No wonder you've been out of sorts lately."

"It will only get better from this point on." He knew it was a lie, but what else could he say at the moment? "My time at the office will be sparse over the next few months and if you and Charlie could be patient, we'll soon enough get everything back on track."

Bea squeezed his hand a little too hard right near where the IV needle had been stuck for the last day and half. "Whatever you need boss, you can count on us."

"That'll be great." He didn't want to tell her what might really be happening to the business. He needed some time to break the news to them.

* * * * *

Bea dropped Marc at his motel room. He was behind schedule on finding an apartment. He called Lindsey Warren.

The next call he made was to Lou's friend Doctor Edward Kaplan. He needed to talk about a lot of things and this guy seemed like a good place to start. Seeing a therapist, to Marc, was being something less than a man, but his cardiologist said he needed to in order to relieve his stress. He felt his chest pains coming back at the thought of dealing with all of his demons. He popped a nitroglycerin tablet and felt the blood rush to his veins and arteries, bringing on a painful headache.

TWENTY-SIX

The week since he had left the hospital had passed by uneventfully. Marc had completed six sessions with Doctor Kaplan and now felt more confused about his emotions. Therapy had not convinced him that all of the shit he was going to have to deal with was going to be worth it, especially dividing up their assets and the chipping away of what little heart he had left.

At his first deposition Lindsey was feeling very confident that it would be a smooth process, providing Marc just limited his answers to a simple "yes" or "no".

"Just keep it short and sweet and you'll do just fine," she had told him at their final prep meeting. "Nothing you say at this deposition matters, except to Rankin. Being overly honest or helpful won't make your divorce go any smoother," Lindsey said sternly. "What he wants to get out of his deposition is for you to make a mistake, give him something to investigate, or convince the judge you're a lying piece of male scum. Just simple yes or no answers will work just fine."

After so many rehearsals, Marc was a nervous wreck. He was feeling like a fresh piece of meat inside a grinder, being processed for someone's meal. He hoped that when the divorce was final, he would not have so much anger and guilt. He wanted to be able to trust another woman and find true love. Nora had left some very deep scars that even his therapist thought would take years to heal.

Over the last week, Marc shifted back and forth about giving Nora everything and starting over, or just staying married and living separate lives. It would be so much easier. Lindsey kept her whip and her harsh tongue on Marc at every meeting.

"You're out of your fucking mind. She hates you. She loves using you. It's your money that she loves and will never give you what you want." Each lecture brought Marc back to his reality, until the next lashing was needed.

Since leaving the hospital he couldn't get Lou out of his mind. He wanted to see her. Kaplan said he should, that he needed a friend like her right now. Lindsey agreed with his doctor's prescription. She was probably becoming tired of being his surrogate best friend and needed time to prepare for her client's divorce. He did not feel ready, and did not call her.

Marc, with every word and every action, seemed attached to Nora like an embryo to the womb. It had become draining to everyone and Marc needed someone like Lou to balance him out. Unlike Nora, Lou's touch was not like a burly carpenter with calloused hands of sandpaper, but more like the hands of a masseuse, soft and cool.

Marc knew he just wanted to be madly in love with someone, anyone, maybe not Lou, but he wanted to experiment. He needed to prove to himself that he could be an active participant in a romantic relationship. He knew it just wasn't going to happen until he was divorced and Nora was out of his life forever.

The day had finally come and Marc was falling apart sitting with Lindsey in Rankin's reception room. *"Goodbye Earl"*, by the Dixie Chicks was still playing while they both waited for the deposition to get started. Lindsey was humming the words.

"I just love that song," she said smiling. "Had a few guys in my life I could have done that to."

"What's with your kind?" Marc said. "Is every guy a bastard to every woman?"

"My kind?" she giggled. "Oh relax and don't have a tizzy-fit. It's not often enough us girls have a song we can chant. You're one of the good guys. Nora's a real moron for fucking up your marriage."

Marc shrugged his shoulder and shook his head. At that moment he felt like he was about to make the worst mistake of his life.

The large conference room at Rankin's office was impressive. A large oval mahogany table filled the room. Sixteen executive high-back soft leather chairs were evenly placed around the table. Marc wondered how large a legal team Rankin was bringing in to grill him. Expensive original artwork decorated the walls. He wondered how many husbands had paid for them.

Sitting at the far end of the room was a heavy-set woman setting up some equipment. Marc assumed she was the court reporter who was going to memorialize every word that he said. Next to her was a laptop that was being plugged into her machine. On a chair immediately to the laptop's right were four banker boxes that were stacked on the floor. His heart started racing as he wondered what information Rankin had already accumulated.

Lindsey must have heard her client's heart throbbing. She leaned over and whispered in Marc's ear. "Just relax. This is Rankin's home field and his MO is to intimidate. We've not sent him enough paper work to fill one of those boxes. Just relax and let's see what he's up to."

"It was easier practicing at your office. I'm scared shitless right now," Marc said trying to act brave, but his trembling voice gave him away.

"Just keep to what we've practiced and don't answer any questions until I have had a chance to hear them and make my objections to them for the record. I will tell..." she said emphatically... you to either answer a question or not. Also, let him finish asking his question. You can't assume you know where he's going."

Marc's heart would not stop pounding against his ribcage, even with Lindsey's reassuring words.

Rankin had kept both of them waiting for over forty-minutes before he and Nora pranced into the conference room. He had a politician's smile, while Nora looked like a mother lion on the hunt.

Nora wore her most sexy dress, revealing her cleavage that was exaggerated by her Victoria Secret push-up bra. She always looked great in red and today was no exception. While she still had a great figure, her anger had taken its toll on her facial muscles. She showed some noticeable wrinkles and dark circles around her eyes exposing the stress she was having. Marc was surprised that he was not feeling sorry for her. He felt a slow grin forming on his face as he stared at Nora.

"One sweet victory for my side", he said to himself.

Her broken nose seemed to have healed and the black and blue rings around her eyes had disappeared. Marc could still hear the crack of cartilage against his fist. A tranquil smile grew on his face, as he stared blankly at his soon-to-be ex-wife. *Satan's Mistress had arrived.* .

Nora seemed to sense what Marc was thinking, her special radar she had over him made her nostrils flair. She started poking Rankin's arms, while whispering something in his ear.

Rankin looked over at Marc, then panned his eyes toward Lindsey. "I hope you can control your client," he said raising his voice. "I can see his violent hostility toward my client. Tell him to stop staring at her. She's in a very weak and frail state since he brutally beat her."

Marc felt his blood begin to boil at Rankin's remarks. "Weak and frail state," He blurted out before Lindsey could respond. She grabbed his arm, squeezing it tight.

"Let me speak, Marc," she said calmly. "Elliott, let's keep the theatrics for when you're on the record, unless you'd like to postpone the deposition until little frail Miss Nora," she said in a very good southern drawl, "is strong enough to listen. You did tell her that she has to keep her bitchy mouth closed during this entire process?"

Marc felt a surge of adrenaline flow through his veins. Lindsey was a street fighter and he liked that.

Rankin exposed his overly white teeth, his incisors growing by the second. "Just keep your boy in line so we can get through this smoothly."

Lindsey did not respond. She leaned over and whispered to Marc. "He has to complete this deposition today or he can't take it to court next week. He's between a rock and hard place and wants to get you to storm out of here. Just stay calm and answer his questions with simple yes or no answers like we practiced."

Lindsey had the final word. "I didn't hear your answer to my question," she said curtly. "I hope you've instructed your client that she's only here as an observer and will keep her big mouth shut throughout the entire deposition?"

Nora was about to throw her water glass at Lindsey, when Rankin grabbed her arm. "She knows that. Can we get on with this?" he said a little flustered.

The deposition began with the normal formalities and then Rankin came after Marc with both barrels.

The deposition ended six hours later. Marc thought he had done a great job, until Lindsey scolded him in the parking lot.

"I thought we agreed to just yes and no answers? Why did you feel you had to expound on almost every question? We don't look like a confident team when you don't let me object first to Rankin's questions."

"It's not easy listening to his questions and their slant that I'm some form of horse-shit. I just thought showing the judge my cooperative side would go in our favor." Marc could see that she was angry and held his breath for the next barrage of verbal abuse.

"Did you see the laptop next to the court reporter? Rankin already has his own copy of the deposition. I'll have mine in a week. I'm not going to have enough time to review it before our first meeting with the judge at family court. I don't like being surprised," she said squeezing his arm firmly, digging her nails in hard enough to leave a mark.

Marc puffed out his chest and spoke. "We'll be all right. Rankin did not ask all of the important questions about my business," he said grinning. "He and Nora are in for a big surprise."

Lindsey had a puzzled look on her face. "Is there something you haven't told me or disclosed to Rankin?"

"I'm not sure. I gave you everything I had about my corporation, but I don't think Rankin understood how it's been set up. Let's go back to your office. I'll explain it to you there."

TWENTY-SEVEN

Nora sat with Rankin waiting for him to speak. She tapped her long fingernails on the mahogany conference table incessantly.

Rankin grabbed her hand hard. "Stop that," he barked harshly. "We did very well today. Marc's falling apart. I think if we make a reasonable demand, this divorce might just be over without any effort on my part."

Nora beamed with delight. "I'd like that. You'll save me lots of billable hours," she said.

Rankin shook his head. "Read our agreement. I get a third of what we settle for, even if it happens within the first month or three years from now. My expertise is invaluable. A divorce like this should take a few years and unless you want to drag it out, you'll be paying me what I deserve no matter how long it takes," he said unable to hide the smirk that popped on his face.

Nora's expression changed as she realized this was a good thing. She would still get what she wanted, only sooner. "If I was going to spend the money anyway, it really doesn't matter. Won't Marc have to pay me back for my attorney fees anyway?"

"It's possible. I'll be pressing the judge for it, as long as you follow my orders. We need you to come across as the victim here. If Marc steps out of line in any way, you get on the horn and tell me. I want every conversation memorialized. Once we can show the judge that he's the animal you say he is, it will help sway the subjective part of the overall settlement. I have no problem with you pressing a few of his buttons before our settlement conference with the judge…if you get my drift?"

"That's right up my alley," she said proudly, her index finger pressing on her cheek.

"Just don't get overly confident."

"After seeing Marc today, he's going to give me everything I want and a lot more," she said smugly. "Knowing him as well as I do, I don't think he'll show that nasty side again. He's ready to rollover and play dead."

"Just record everything. If he hurts you again, it might make it impossible for you to work for an awfully long time," he said with a wink.

Nora bit her lip and closed her eyes tight. She furrowed her brow which wrinkled her nose as she tried to squeeze out a thought. She started nodding like an idea had entered her brain. "I know exactly what I have to do," she smiled eerily.

Rankin stood ready to leave the conference room. "I'll fax over our demands for Marc. You'll need to review them and sign by all by the highlighted areas. Don't delay. I want his attorney to have them by the end of the business day today."

* * * * *

Nora left Rankin's office and her feet never touched the ground. She called Gail and told her the wonderful news. Gail seemed aloof about it. Nora didn't notice, as she kept talking.

Next she called her cosmetic surgeon. She had his cell phone number. "I'd like to schedule the work you told me about. I'm coming into a large sum of money. I'll need you to make me a hot attractive number. You know what guys want now. I'm back on the market and want to find a nice sugar daddy."

TWENTY-EIGHT

Lindsey Warren seemed distant, in a pissed-off sort of way. At the moment it did not seem to matter to Marc what she thought. He just wanted his divorce over.

Inside his body he felt a stranger was materializing, a stranger who at first was unrecognizable, but now this new person seemed familiar and he knew at that precise moment he was going to enjoy getting to know and love the new Marc.

He realized that further dealings with Nora and her attorney would only put him in the grave. The new Marc Richards wanted everything done and done now, but he would not throw the baby out with the bath water. A new cold-hearted toughness was exploding out of him.

With confidence he spoke. "I know what you're going to say," he said trying to seem indifferent. "You are going to say I blew it. I should think of settling. Whatever arrangement we can get from Nora and Rankin..." his attorney raised her hand like a traffic cop, stopping Marc from saying anything further.

Lindsey leaned back in her chair, her arms folded behind her head. She had a smile on her face. "Marc, my initial reaction was to kill you for going against my orders. I've had time to review your corporation by-laws and if I do say so, whoever drafted these documents was a genius. I think they'll hold up in court."

Marc had a puzzled expression. It had been fifteen years since those papers were drafted and he had really forgotten every detail of how his corporation had been formed, except for the one important thing that made getting a divorce financially easier. That was the true intention of the buy-sell agreement and it all stemmed from what Nora wanted back then.   He was delighted that Lindsey had figured out what he already knew. He smirked, feeling like a kid who had been caught with hand in the cookie jar. "You really think under California's community property laws it will work?"

"Was Nora made aware of what she was signing?" Lindsey asked.

"It was set up this way because of what Nora wanted back then. Everything was explained to her by our corporate attorney and signed in front of the notary. Nora loved the idea. Not by being on the board, but that she had her own personal income from the business and a stupid title. I really believe she wanted it set up that way, hoping that some day she would be back with this Brad character she always bragged about. In fact, she liked it so much that she pestered me to divide our personal assets up so that she had her own property that she could pay for from her separate account and I could pay for my property from my separate checking account. I believe now it was her way of not having a connection to me. I always felt used and abused by her, but now…well, it's fitting for what I've been through."

Lindsey raised her eyebrows in amazement. "But you did co-mingle some of your income to pay for her stuff didn't you?"

"Our CPA pays all of our bills. I confirmed with him the other day that over the last fifteen years, he's been writing checks from each of our accounts and applying them for our own separate property. It's as if we were a married couple, under the same roof, living singularly separate lives. If this arrangement holds up in court, what's my worst case scenario?"

Lindsey scratched her head, acting a little baffled. "I'm not totally sure. I'll have to have a forensic accountant audit everything, and confirm what your CPA told you. If what you're telling me is correct, Nora's only claim is against your business or any joint funds that did not get included in your initial split. By the courts interpretation, she's been making a living and supporting herself all these years and it might turn out that you won't have to pay any alimony. Based on your buy-out agreement, you can stop paying her an income and buy her out for only $50,000." Lindsey seemed very excited. "I've got to be sure we find all of her bank accounts and that the two of you don't have any co-mingled funds. This could end up being the easiest divorce I've ever seen."

Marc couldn't contain his joy. "Nora's been such a jerk all these years. She felt that she was controlling me, but her arrogance bit her in the ass," Marc let loose with a loud belly laugh. "Take a closer look at the corporation agreement. You'll find that a bigger chunk of her ass has been bitten off. In addition, most of my savings has accumulated from my parents' estate that was held in trust during my years living with my aunt and uncle, as well as what I saved from my salary. I never co-mingled any of that trust fund."

After two hours of reviewing the family assets, Lindsey's legal assistant brought her in a fax from Rankin's office.

"This is a laugh," she said. "Rankin's becoming shoddy. He's made a demand that's a pathetic joke," Lindsey said, sliding the fax across her desk for Marc to read.

Marc's eyes grew wide with disbelief. "I guess he thinks Nora knows what she's talking about. He couldn't have looked at all the financials we've sent him."

Lindsey knocked fists with Marc. "Rankin has a big ego and probably thought he didn't need a forensic accountant to check things out. If you approve, we should reject their demand and go to court next week. We don't need to spend the money to depose Nora. We can always do it later if the judge wants to review everything. This might be the shortest divorce and division of assets I've ever done," she said. She sat up straight in her chair, the grin on her face gone. "We shouldn't be too overconfident. The judge still has discretion in all settlement matters and could rule that the set up of the family assets and corporation was not with Nora's full knowledge or best interest."

"Oh, but it was. I shouldn't be responsible for her ignorance…well her stupidity?"

Lindsey leaned forward. "Within the law, especially contractual law, there is a theory of what a reasonable person would have done when entering a contract. Nora is not a reasonable person and if she's smart, will use her unsavory wiles to sway the judge."

Marc's heart sunk into his stomach. A big knot had lodged in his throat. "Does that mean we could have a big expensive fight on our hands?" His voice was strained with breathless desperation.

"Let's cross that bridge another time. We should enjoy these feelings while we can. There are some things that are out of our control. See you in a week at family court."

Marc had one last item he wanted to discuss with Lindsey, but decided to wait for another time. He was wondering what would happen to Nora if he decided to leave the business and have her buy him out? He already knew the answer. His new feelings of being in total control were like a drug and he liked the euphoria he was experiencing.

Marc sat in his car, his adrenaline pumping wildly through his veins. He was breathing hard; the guilt that had been a regular part of his life with Nora, had magically evaporated and was replaced with an uncontrollable need to get even. As his heart pounded, it brought on his black curtain. His chin fell to his chest. A smile grew slowly, as his last thought was to kill her.

TWENTY-NINE

As Brad stretched his arms over his head, his fury was building. All he could think about was Nora and how she was trying to get him out of her life. He pulled out of Lindsey Warren's parking structure and headed to Marc and Nora's house. He wanted to confront the bitch.

Her car was parked in the driveway. He coasted to a stop around the corner and cut across a vacant lot to the back door by the kitchen. He stuffed the Garrote in his back pocket before he entered. Surprise was his objective.

He could hear music blaring, making it easier for him to slip inside unnoticed. He looked around, panning the rooms on his way toward the stairs to the bedrooms. An eerie laugh spilled out from his lips noticing the clothing trail Nora had left on the steps to her bedroom. As he got closer, he could hear two female voices giggling.

He understood Nora's need for female intimacy, remembering his first experience with her and her friend Rita back in high school.

Even though Nora had always been a spoiled brat—Brad loved her animalistic passion she had for wild sex. He missed it terribly. He thought about what he had come there to do and he knew he had to remain vigilant.

On the large king size bed Nora's head was between two long slender thighs, her buttocks up in the air, exposing her perfectly shaven vagina, like an orchid in full bloom. The other woman had her eyes closed, her body undulating slowly in rhythm to Nora's tongue.

Brad could not control himself and was getting caught up in all of the excitement, stretching the Garrote tight. He couldn't catch his breath. He was once again caught inside the world of Nora. He couldn't contain his unrest any longer—his erection was bursting through his pants. He slipped the Garrote inside his pant pocket and said in a deep burly voice, "Is there room for one more?"

Nora did not seem startled by Brad's presence. It was as if she had known he'd show up for the party. She craned her head toward him. "Is that you Brad?" she said smiling. "Unless you've forgotten, I think there's a wet place for you to hook yourself up to," she said returning back to what she was doing for Rita.

Brad was naked and sliding inside of Nora. He spoke softly. "When we're done, we need to talk about Marc. You've got to start being nicer or we're not going to get control of his money" he said, grabbing her hips tightly and pounding hard inside of her.

All Nora could say was, "Uh huh," not missing a beat.

* * * * *

When the three of them were done, Brad laid out his plans for Marc. Rita had her job and left early to get started with Marc.

THIRTY

Right after Nora had seen Lou and Marc at the hospital she had hired a private detective to locate the woman and find out everything about her. It was not too difficult. There was a sign-in sheet for all persons entering the CCU. After some flirting with "Nurse Ratchet" who was on duty then, the P.I. was able to get Lou's full name. He then entered her name on Google and within seconds had her home and her business addresses. Then, with a few more key strokes he got directions from Mapquest to both locations.

Nora looked over the digital image of Lou that was attached to the email from her private investigator. She was surprised that Marc's new girlfriend was more his age than the last slut he had and did not look anything like her. Lou was annoyingly different. She seemed nice.

Ashley had looked more like Nora, whereas, Lou was extremely feminine, in a Diane Lane sort of way. She was slender, and very attractive. What Nora had noticed at the hospital was that Marc's new whore had a cocky confident air about herself and seemed very attracted to Marc. Women knew the look.

Nora's blood had started to boil, her anger ready to explode. She did not like competition, especially someone that might sway Marc away from her. "You money grabbing bitch," she shouted at the computer screen. "You'll never see a penny of MY money." Nora couldn't contain herself.

Knowing Ashley had resembled her in looks, hair color, and body build flattered her at that time. She rationalized that Marc had just wanted another Nora, only a younger version. But, Lou was different. Her mannerisms and assurance showed a special quality that said "I'm a keeper".

Nora's nostrils were flaring. She was coming out of her long dumb blonde hibernation and unleashing the violent women that had been asleep for over twenty-five years.

* * * * *

Later that same day, Nora was two houses down, sitting low inside her Red 530I BMW when she spotted her target walking on the sidewalk. "Miss Louise Hart, you don't know what you've gotten yourself into," she muttered. She shut her laptop as Lou approached her house carrying two plastic bags of groceries.

"If you think you'll have Marc after our divorce, you're mistaken. I might not have him, but no one else will either," she said with a chilling fury.

Nora's face had become twisted—her veins were bulging ready to pop out of her face. The transformation had begun. She was back at high school, once again upset at seeing her boyfriend with another cheerleader. She wanted to call Rita and Gail for their help again, but this time she was going to handle this slut on her own.

Once Lou closed her front door, Nora jumped out of her car, slipping her revolver into her jacket pocket. She walked briskly across the quiet street.

THIRTY-ONE

Nora walked with the calm of a tiger stalking its prey. She eased her way around the side of Lou's house, being ever so careful to not attract attention. But, that was impossible.

Her outfit, a black and yellow striped turtleneck blouse and black leotards she had left the house wearing, as well as the black and blue discoloration from her broken nose that faintly outlined her eyes made her look like a wounded raccoon . Something you would have seen on an old Batman TV show. Nevertheless, Nora was in her own world, a real gangster ready to make a hit.

Turning the corner toward the backyard, she heard a woman's giggling voice and a man's belly laugh. The sounds drew her to an open window. She crouched down, close to a crawl, inching toward the window. She rose slowly, allowing her eyes to peek over the windowsill. In her excitement her foot slipped, causing her to slam her chin on the window's edge hard enough to draw blood.

"Shit," she whined, biting her finger. She pressed her hand on her chin and felt her warm blood oozing between her fingers. She attempted one more look, as her curiosity got the better of her. She thought if it was Marc, she might just kill two birds with one stone. Then no need for a divorce or dividing up of their assets. She was amazed how well she could think under pressure.

Rising ever so slowly again, her fingers dripping with blood— she tried to not injure herself again. Like most of her well thought out plans she was startled by the burping of pipes and the powerful spray from the sprinklers that had turned on at the most inappropriate time. She was soaked instantly.

With mascara dripping down her cheeks, her black and yellow blouse soaked, and her flip-flops making a squishing sound, she darted back to her car.   Nora was a sight to be seen. Inside her car she looked in the rearview mirror.

"Fuck," she screamed pounding the steering wheel with both fists.

"Look at me. My chin might need stitches," she wailed.

"This is all Marc's fault," she cried.

Nora slammed her foot on the accelerator, fishtailing away from the curb. Another constipated idea squeezed out of her brain. "I guess I've got to go to plan B since this didn't work so well," she said incoherently.

* * * * *

Lou had heard a bang by the back window when the sprinklers went off. Then, she and Dr. Kaplan heard the squealing of tires out front.

She shrugged her shoulders. "We have some crazy teenagers living in the neighborhood," Lou said.

Dr. Kaplan looked at his watch, preoccupied, and not paying attention to Lou. He wanted to say something to Lou, but did not know how to form the sentences so she would not close down on him.

"Marc has a problem," he said seriously. "It's worse than I first thought."

Lou's smile faded, as her expression turned to concern. "Problem? What kind of problem?"

"I can't be specific. I must press upon you that you do not have contact with him, until I can treat him a little longer," Kaplan said. "I thought at one time that you might be good for him while he dealt with this transition, but I don't think so now."

Lou shrugged her shoulders frowning. "He wanted to cool it anyway, so that won't be too hard."

"Don't call him until I've had more time with him."

She understood that Marc needed his space to deal with his health and Nora, but why couldn't Dr. Kaplan just tell her what was troubling him? "Does the problem have to do with his health? Is his heart worse than he's led me to believe?"

Kaplan sighed with frustration, not wanting to cross a professional line. "You're trying to take advantage of our friendship. I can't allow that. He's my patient now. Trust me that he's in good hands, and leave it at that." He regarded her with equal measures of tenderness and irritation. He tried to avoid her eyes, his chin on his chest. "That's the best I can offer you now. You'll have to accept it for the time being."

Lou had become sullen. "I guess I have to?" she replied.

THIRTY-TWO

After putting a band-aid over the cut on her chin, Nora had one of her great ideas playing out perfectly inside her brain. She lived in the "now", like she has always done, without taking time to think about how her rash actions would impact everyone around her. She had already forgotten her botched attempt to shoot Lou. Brad was sitting on the couch mulling over what she was asking him to do.

"You have to do it. It's our only choice to get Marc to see the light and give me all of his money," Nora said.

"I've hit you before, but not like you want me to do right now. Not that I haven't thought about it," he said grinning. "You can be such a bitch, you know," Brad smiled slipping on the black leather gloves Nora had handed him. He knew her plan had too many holes in it, but his pounding headache would not allow him to think clearly. However, letting his aggression loose on her was going to be very meditative.

Nora, like she did with Marc, had always known how to press Brad's buttons so he'd do her bidding. Her violent and depraved actions tied them together. And, like Marc, he was powerless to her demands.

He stood slowly, glared at her, his anger toward her building. He realized that if he released all of his rage, the beating she wanted would probably kill her. With what he had seen of her lately, the thought that having her dead might not be a bad idea. He was beginning to believe he could bring back Marc's memories without Nora's help. He could pin all the murders on her, Gail and Rita with all the evidence he had saved over the years. For that to work he needed Marc's memories to return and that was not going to be easy. Lost within his thoughts, he shrugged his shoulders and refocused on Nora.

He approached her and without warning hit her ribcage hard with his gloved left fist. Then another powerful blow with his gloved right fist, which by the look on her face, had brought a searing pain that had to have rattled her teeth.

She looked in the mirror thinking twice about him hitting her on her almost healed face. Without hesitation both of Brad's hands sprang up with lightning speed impacting her cheek bones, almost causing her to pass out.

Brad had had done this before in high school for Nora. The first time had been when she did not like her math teacher and decided to accuse him of raping and beating her. Setting up the evidence with the teacher's DNA had worked perfectly. Her teacher was arrested and sentenced to fifteen years for the brutal sexual assault to a minor. He died in prison three weeks after his sentencing.

Brad's adrenaline was pounding through his veins, bringing on a searing headache. He had to leave immediately or he'd have to kill her. Without saying good-by, while Nora was in the bathroom, he was out the door, on his way to Marc with Rita to carrying out the rest of their plan.

She lifted her wet blouse—her skin had already turned pinkish. She knew that the two bruises would turn black and blue within an hour. Her cheeks were another story. They had broken skin that oozed with blood. When she returned to her bedroom all she found were the bloodied gloves Brad had used lying on the carpet. She picked them up and hid them in one of the hundreds of shoe boxes in her walk-in closet. She was pleased with herself. She had sustained a good beating and was moving along well with her plan…no Rankin's plan. She waited almost an hour before calling for help.

She reached deep down into her lungs and started screaming while dialing Gail's cell. Before she could blot her wet eyes, her friend answered.

"Gail," she howled. "Get over here. Marc attacked me again. I think he broke some ribs…shit my face is cut from his fists. Fuck, he wore leather gloves. I look horrible."

Gail tried to ask a question between Nora's loud sniffling. "What was he doing at your house?"

Nora took a quivering breath allowing her enough time to come up with a believable response. "He...he...he...called wa...wa...wan...wanting to see if we...we...we could resolve the divorce amicably."

Gail contained her doubts about Nora's story, but knew this was not the time to grill her about what really happened. "We should get you to the ER and you should call the police again. I think a restraining order is what's needed,' Gail angrily barked. "He's such a bastard. I never knew you were living with such an animal."

"I can't begin to tell you. Can you drive me to emergency? I'm too shaken to drive," Nora sobbed.

No sooner had Gail hung up, Nora dialed Rita. "Did you get it done?"

Rita said without any emotion, "He doesn't even know what happened. What had you put in his tea?"

"Never you mind," Nora said calmly. "Are his hands bruised enough to look like he beat me up?"

"Yes. I just hope nobody saw me helping him down to the beach."

Nora blew her a kiss through the phone. "Gotta go. Gail's coming to take me to the ER. I'll call you after Marc gets locked up."

* * * * *

At the hospital a cute doctor was finishing up bandaging Nora's cuts on her face. Officer Monroe had taken enough digitals of her bruises, while Officer Perez filled out the police report.

Perez, stared at her partner. "I wonder what Mrs. Richards did to provoke her husband this time," she said sarcastically. "He better look worse than her or he's sleeping in lock-up until the D.A. throws the book at him."

Monroe was speechless. "Let's go pick him up. I'll personally cuff the bastard," he said angrily. "No one, especially THIS woman, deserves such a beating."

Nora could simultaneously listen to three separate conversations in a noisy restaurant, so picking up what Officers Monroe and Perez were saying was easy. She leaned back on the ER gurney, an evil grin curling across her lips.

Gail noticed her friend's wicked smile. "What's up Nora? You're scaring me."

Nora put her finger to her lips. "Nothing you should worry yourself about. It's between me and my attorney."

THIRTY-THREE

Marc had been passed out in his car for almost three hours—his hands were trembling—as if he had come slowly out of a dream. He could smell Nora's perfume. Had she been inside his car? He wondered.

He drove to his new studio apartment, off Coast Highway, just south of Leucadia Boulevard. The one room had a large picture window, which viewed the whitewater breaking on the sand. On a clear day he had the most spectacular orange and pink sunsets.

The apartment was sparsely furnished with a Murphy bed, a beat up couch, an art deco dinette table and two metal chairs with red plastic seat cushions. The walls were bare, except for the peeling paint, a poor man's version of a faux finish paint job. There was a small refrigerator with a motor that hummed all night long, in symphony with the dripping faucet that completed the makeshift kitchen.

Marc thought the studio was perfect. It paralleled his life at the moment. Exhausted, he flopped down on his sagging couch trying to focus on the ocean below. His thoughts bounced around from Nora, the upcoming court hearing, his constant angina, and Lou. As he sipped a cup of his favorite hot tea, he felt lightheaded, unable to keep his eyes opened. He had not been home more than fifteen minutes when he was once again being wrapped in his familiar black curtain. His tiny world had become very quiet once again.

* * * * * *

Marc wasn't sure how long he had been out. He awoke lying in the sand, the tide soaking his jeans. He was confused and disoriented. He didn't know how he got there. He sat up sliding back away from the pounding surf. The sky over the horizon had an orange glow. He realized that sunset had just past.

He felt very nervous not knowing how he got down the long wooden steps to the beach and what happened during the last five hours. He tried to stand but his legs were rubbery. He wiped the wet sand from his hand on his pants. When they were cleaned he noticed his bruised knuckles and dried blood.

He opened and closed his hands. They felt like they had hit something or someone. He felt his cheeks. They had scratches on both sides. An uncomfortable déjà vu consumed him.

He briskly walked up to his apartment avoiding any eye contact with the other people sitting on their beach chairs drinking and enjoying the remnants of the sunset. Fortunately, no one seemed interested in him. He was able slip up the beach steps back to his studio unnoticed.

He looked in his mirror. He did not recognize the face that stared back at him. He had not seen that look since Ashley disappeared. His heart started pounding, blocking out all thoughts. He was now in a panic thinking about Lou.

He dialed her cell and got her voice mail.

He did not leave a message.

He dialed the coffee shop and reached Jesus, her bus boy.

"Hey, Jesus, it's Marc Richards."

"Si, senor Richards. Miss Lou is no here right now. She's no show up today."

He felt bile burning in his throat. "Has she called in sick?" He asked, already knowing the answer. Lou was missing.

"Si, she called early this morning. She's got, how you say…24/7 flu?"

He felt relieved. He still had his doubts since she hadn't answered her cell. "Jesus, thank you. When she calls in tell her I was asking about her."

His first thoughts flashed to Nora, but she did not know about Lou. He was not about to ask her. He called Doctor Kaplan. He knew he needed to finally tell him about his blackouts.

Marc could not stop shaking. His little studio apartment was closing in on him. Never had his body trembled as much as it was at the moment. Horrible things were spinning inside his head. His mind was foggy with memories of things he had done during his blackouts.

Without a second thought Marc was on the phone to his therapist. He felt desperate and in dire need to talk to Dr. Kaplan.

The doctor was delighted to hear from Marc and was able to see him immediately.

Unlike previous sessions that took almost thirty minutes to open up, Marc jumped right in and told Dr. Kaplan about his recent blackout, but did not think it prudent to tell him about the other ones that were coming on more frequently. He brought up the voice he had been hearing for the last few months. He showed him the scratch on his cheek and his bruised knuckles. He was not prepared to tell him the details about the other blackouts he's had, at least not at the moment.

Kaplan seemed to regard him with equal measures of tenderness and frustration. Marc could see in the good doctor's eyes he knew there was a lot more that had to be told.

"That's all you can remember? Kaplan said, combing his fingers through his hair. "The blackout could be related to your heart and the pressure you've been under. You are taking blood pressure medicine, which has been known to cause similar reactions." Marc sucked in a deep breath knowing that it wasn't the blood pressure medicine. The blackouts were not a new phenomenon, which Marc was not able to fully talk about until he figured them out. He still did not know if he could fully trust Kaplan.

"It's all I remember at the moment," Marc said evasively.

"Blackouts are not something that happens out of the blue. You're sure you haven't experienced others before?" Dr. Kaplan asked.

Marc had now become edgy by Kaplan's probing. He was feeling invaded, struggling nervously to keep his secret hidden. Nevertheless, at the moment, the doctor was the only person he could talk to.

"I can't be sure," Marc said warily. "When my parents died, that day…it was a hit and run…I…really don't remember much about it, only what the police and Nora—she was one of my close friends back in high school—had told me. I might have had a blackout then. I can't be sure."

Marc thought hard about telling Kaplan about Ashley, another blackout situation, but thought better of it until he knew that Lou was okay. If Lou was missing and with his scratched cheek and bruised knuckles he'd turn himself in.

He looked at his bruised hands and realized that if Kaplan suspected he had committed a crime he would be obligated by law to report him to the police. He knew that he had to refrain from being too chatty.

Just hours earlier, he was feeling on top of the world. His divorce looked like a slam-dunk. He was rounding that mysterious corner and could see a bright light at the end of his dark tunnel. He wondered how everything evaporated so quickly.

He found this ironic in a fatalistic sense. His emotions felt like a grinding wheel was being used to file down his new found stability. His emotional soul was feeling raw. However, now with his memories starting to return, he was beginning to see things a bit more clearly, and he had begun to overflow with guilt and sorrow.

Marc was now frantic about finding Lou and seeing her smiling eyes once more. But, Nora kept creeping inside his head, a warning that something bad had happened. It was the same feeling he had when Ashley disappeared.

"Hey doc, tell me something," he said despondently. "Why's there a place inside my heart, a chamber, where light can't reach, where a calming silence can't be achieved?" Marc's eyes fluttered closed, waiting for an answer.

Kaplan nodded before he responded. "That's a very astute observation on your part. Let's see if I can say this delicately enough. You've not had a lot of experience with people, I guess. Nora's been your entire world, and a very dark one to boot. She took control of your life during your formative years and began molding you into the person she wanted you to be. Based on what you've told me in our previous sessions, you've not had a chance to discover who you really are. So," Kaplan said pressing his hands together and bringing them to his lips, "you don't have any other reference point to compare your life to. Most men and women are not anything like Nora. You're a good man who's been afraid to venture outside of his marriage. Nora's been emotionally abusive for twenty-five years or so and it's left many deep scars. I don't want you to give up on yourself just yet."

He knew, like Lou, Doctor Kaplan believed differently about him, but nevertheless he felt the way he felt, and nothing at the moment would change that.

"How can I give up on something I haven't really started?" he moaned, as the self-pity slowly oozed out of his mouth.

"Oh, but you have. You've taken the first step. You started your divorce," Kaplan said with conviction. "You've stood up to Nora in ways you never thought possible. That's a really big step forward," said Kaplan.

"I tried this once before and it backfired on me then. I lost someone very dear to me."

Kaplan seemed puzzled. "Were you trying to leave Nora when your parents died?"

"No. Not really. We were just friends back then. She just jumped right in taking over. I was young and thought that was love. It felt good back then. Once we got married, though, our problems began. As I look back on things that I can still remember about that time after my parents died, Nora's actions were not as loving as I thought. I've realized that she's always been abusive to me. I just never saw it that way at the beginning. As her cruel actions toward me escalated and she rationed out the amount of intimacy we would have, I started looking for some needed tenderness and passion. Then, without really looking too hard, I found someone that made me feel…well like Lou makes me feel now, and pursued that new relationship. Now, in hindsight, I should have asked for a divorce and moved on back then. Maybe I would have had some real happiness?"

Kaplan just nodded. "I understand how you must have felt back then. What you did was normal and healthy. You were taking care of yourself. I am curious. What happened when you tried to divorce Nora the first time?"

Marc was taken by surprise by the doctor's question. He did not want to get into the Ashley thing just yet. He just wanted to locate Lou. "Can we talk about that at our next session? I'm just not ready to open up that can of worms." He stood, gave Dr. Kaplan a strong man-hug and left.

Marc was in his car speeding back to his apartment.

THIRTY-FOUR

Marc closed his notebook, one of the four he had written in since his Aunt and Uncle's death. Social Services back then had suggested that he keep these journals to help him deal with the tragedy of losing his entire family in such a short period of time. Lately his writing was more a recap of his dysfunctional marriage with Nora and offered no real insight to his past or his missing memories.

   He mechanically gripped the edges like spring-action clamps. His brain had begun exploding with thoughts, mostly confusion, of what he had read. It was hard to fathom that the words on the pages had come from him. It had been a while since he read them, but the passage about when he remembered his first blackout, to his surprise, had started months before his Aunt and Uncle's accident.   For Marc those notebooks were pieces to a troubling puzzle that still now, twenty-five years later, remained unsolved.

   Reading his words seemed stranger than fiction. They were beginning to make some sense of what the mysterious letter was about. In fact, there was a pattern that a good detective would see in a heartbeat, except Marc was not a detective and couldn't connect all of the dots.

   Marc looked out of his large picture window watching the sun playing peek-a-boo with the clouds. The humid air had a luminescent quality, catching particles of light and suspending them in the weightless haze, reminding him of how he felt the night his Aunt and Uncle, his legal guardians, died.

   In his memory, he was able to see Nora and a police detective talking. He had been sitting on the steps of his porch, weeping with his head in his hands. He remembered how much his hands smelled from gasoline and did not understand the significance back then.

After Nora had finished talking to the detective she had come over and sat down next to him, crying uncontrollably. "I'm so sorry," she had said unable to catch her breath. "I told the detective you were with me at the time of the accident."

Marc looked up. "I don't remember that," he said shaking his head. "Everything's a blank. It's as if every memory has been erased," he said confused.

Nora had stopped crying and gripped Marc's arm tightly. "You smell from gasoline. I don't know where you were, but you need to tell the detective that you were with me between 7:00 P.M. and 11:00 P.M."

Puzzled, Marc said. "But...I don't remember anything. I can't lie to the police." His voice was cracking with sadness.

With a cold, menacing tone Nora said. "You'll do what I tell you to do, say what I tell you to say, or you'll get arrested. Right now you're their number one suspect. Your neighbors have already told the police about the argument you had with them. One said they heard you shout that you 'wished they were dead' right before you stormed out of the house. That was around six."

Marc dropped his head, resting his chin on his chest. "I just don't remember fighting with them or saying those words."

"Trust me. You do know how much I love you, don't you? Right now my only concern is protecting you and keeping out of jail," Nora said, kissing him on the cheek.

Marc looked at Nora's face, his eyes filled with tears. "I don't know how I could ever thank you enough for helping me like this."

"Marry me. Then I won't be able to testify against you," she had said coldly.

Suddenly, Marc was startled back to the present by a loud crash against his living room window. A seagull had hit the glass, breaking its neck against the reflective window pane.

* * * * * *

Marc was excited. For the first time he had tiny glimpses into his past. He was remembering the first time he had seen Nora. It was at a local high school hangout he frequented. Nora had all the guys' heads turning when she walked in.

She gracefully climbed on a stool next to Marc. She just sat there acting like he did not exist. Then she turned and smiled. To get a beautiful girl to even notice Marc was an oddity, but there was something about her that captured Marc's heart. She seemed familiar, someone from another time and place.

Nora seemed to sense Marc's isolation around his new school buddies and introduced herself. At first he acted like a blithering idiot, unable to say a word, let alone his name. When she touched his hand, electricity shot through his veins. His heart had started pounding loudly inside his chest, drowning out her words. Her touch was seductively familiar.

"I'm Nora Williamson." Marc just nodded, his pounding head was echoing so loud it was drowning out her words.

He cupped his left ear and leaned closer. He became overwhelmed by the seductive perfume she was wearing, again it smelled familiar. He backed away abruptly, feeling awkward. Marc's lips moved, but nothing came out. Now his face was glowing with embarrassment, feeling very foolish.

Nora smiled sweetly and put her hand on the middle of his chest, her eyebrows raised. "I'm not going to bite. All I did was introduce myself. I didn't ask you to marry me."

Marc still couldn't speak. He just nodded his head, hoping he'd not faint.

"Let's start over. Hi, I'm Nora Williamson. I just moved here from Phoenix," she said pressing firmly on his rapidly beating heart. "Before you faint and I have to call the paramedics, I'd like to know your name," she said cutely.

He took in a deep breath. "Marc Richards," he said nervously. "What a coincidence. I'm from Phoenix also," Marc said surprised he was even talking about himself. "My parents died a few months back and my aunt and uncle are allowing me to live with them while I finish high school," Marc's faced got flushed. "A great way to introduce myself...sorry."

"I've been told worse. I didn't mean to make you nervous. I hate coming to a new place alone, but my girlfriend seems to have stood me up," she pouted.

Marc had started to calm down and felt more settled. What he said next surprised even him. "I would have thought you'd be meeting your boyfriend here."

She furrowed her brow. "I wish. I haven't been in town long enough. My old boyfriend, his name was Brad went missing. The Phoenix police are still looking for him."

"I didn't mean to pry."

Nora patted his hand that was resting high on his thigh, her pinky almost touching his groin area. She looked deeply into his eyes and smiled. "Know any nice guys I could meet?" she said continuing to rub his thigh ever so seductively.

Marc rolled his eyes, raising his arm in the air. "Not taken. I haven't found anyone who's worth making an effort for…until now," he said not believing how bold and confident he sounded.

"I would have never guessed," Nora said in a slow drawl. "You have a caring face that any nice girl would want to have as a boyfriend."

They talked for the next two hours, totally oblivious to the noise and chatter around them. Marc took her hand and asked her if she'd like to go somewhere a little quieter.

She smiled, happily squeezing his hand with an affection he had never felt before. "I'd love that. What about your friends…?"

"They're not my friends, just high school buddies."

Nora acted surprised. "High School? Just how old are you Marc Richards?"

Marc had a puzzled look on his face. Was Nora older than him? "I'm eighteen. Is that going to be a problem?"

Nora shook her head. "Nope. I've always liked my guys a little younger. My Brad was about your age."

"Can I ask how old you are?" said Marc.

"It's not polite to ask a lady her age. Let's just say I'm a few years older. We can go back to my apartment and get to know each other better."

They wasted no time ripping off their clothes, bumping into every piece of furniture on the way to the bedroom. Nora introduced Marc to a world of sexual intimacy he'd never forget. She had an uncontrolled hunger for sex. Little did he know that it would soon end once they said their "I do's".

He remembered wondering what Nora had seen in him that first night, but she kept her calendar open for the next four months, allowing them time to get to know each other more intimately. Sex remained wild and passionate, always finishing with long loving cuddles. As far as Marc was concerned, Nora was perfect. He did not need to search any further for the woman he wanted to spend the rest of his life with.

* * * * *

When the blackouts first started, the missing timeframes were short. With each new blackout, though, the missing minutes started to turn into hours. He was re-reading his words inside his notebook and trying to understand the confusing puzzle they created. Even the beginning periods of time with Nora were slowly being erased with each episode.

Then, a flashback exploded inside his head. He vividly remembered a dinner that had gone bad at his Aunt and Uncle's home. It had started when Nora had an emotional outburst toward his Uncle. Something about her age and or something to do with taking advantage of Marc was brought up.

Nora had become very angry, which only got Marc's Uncle to escalate his rage toward her even more. Marc's Aunt tried futilely to calm things down, but when Nora also lashed out at her, chaos ended the wonderful dinner Marc's Aunt had prepared.

Marc recalled trying to defend Nora, but his Uncle was seething, and nothing Marc could say or do mattered.

Marc's Uncle kicked him out of house, yelling and chasing his nephew and Nora to her car.

It took Marc hours to calm Nora down. He had never seen such rage and hate in anyone before. While he wanted to defend her, he remembered how scared he was of the woman he loved.

He recalled that the next day he visited his aunt. She hurt him the most by not accepting Nora's side of how his uncle had insulted her. Her words stung like a swarm of killer bees.

"There's something strange about that girl," she said. "I don't trust her. She's coming between us. She's not good for you."

The flashback was becoming very real. He could feel his blood boil and rage toward his Aunt escalate. He heard the words he had screamed at her.

"You just don't want to see me happy," He started yelling like an out of control teenager. "I don't think anyone I'd bring home would be good enough for you. And, my Uncle Jim…well…he's a piece of work," Marc said sarcastically. "I wish my parents were still around Aunt Betty," he sighed. "They would have never asked you to take me in if they knew how mean you'd be to me."

He could see the hurt in his Aunt's eyes. He saw her bite her lower lip before responding. "You're making a horrible choice. How do you even remember your parents anyway," she lashed out. "Are you just guessing? I'm very hurt by all of this. One day you'll see how right I was and it will be too late. Now go before you hurt me anymore than you've done today." Marc's heart ached seeing his Aunt lift her apron to her face sobbing.

He could hear his horrible words, *I wish both of you had died instead of my parents.* Marc finally realized it was that one defining moment, the blowout at this Aunt and Uncle's house that was the last time he had seen them alive.

A month after Marc's guardians died, he and Nora were married in Las Vegas. Two strangers acted as their witnesses, and Elvis conducted the marriage ceremony. That was the day Marc's prison sentence began and he discovered the term "married/single".

He closed his notebook, completely drained and distraught. Now the coincidences pointed at him. The thought that he might have had something to do with his Aunt and Uncle's death, or even the disappearance of Ashley, had him gasping for breath. He had to find Lou.

THIRTY-FIVE

Officers Monroe and Perez were standing in the archway to Marc's apartment door. They did not appear to be making a social call.

The color had drained from Marc's face, and his legs felt like rubber. He felt guilty and rightly so. He had bruises and scratches on his face that he did not remember how he got them. His knee-jerk thought was to blurt out 'I didn't do it'. Feeling the painful scrapes on his knuckles, he casually slipped his hands into his pants pockets. "Hey, officers, what's up?" His attempt to act nonchalant did not impress them. He saw Officer Perez lightly swinging her handcuffs in her hand, a frightening scowl on her face.

"Can you tell us where you were at around one this afternoon?" Perez asked, her emotionless tone told him he was in big trouble.

Marc started grinding his teeth. His jaw had become tense. He tried not to stammer, but he was very nervous. "I was asleep on the beach?" he responded sounding more like a question than an answer.

Officer Monroe spoke. "You're not sure, or you were asleep on the beach? Which is it?"

The lump already in his throat felt like a baseball. He didn't know if he should ask for a lawyer or still be as casual as he was trying to be. By the look on their faces, he was not doing a good job either way.

"All I remember was that I was having some herbal tea, *Midnight Slumber*. It's a great herbal tea, really relaxes me. I've been drinking it for years. It's better than coffee to take the edge off. Really puts me in relaxed mood—"

"Just answer the damn question," Officer Perez barked.

Marc felt another rush of jibber-jabber-jibber-jabber exploding inside his brain. He took a deep breath, expelling the toxic air that was numbing his brain. He must have sounded like a balloon leaking air. "One minute I was on my couch, the next I was waking up five hours later on the beach. The tide almost swept me away." He shrugged utterly puzzled at his behavior. "Why are you asking me?"

He held his breath hoping that they were not going to give him tragic news about Lou. *Shit, what happened during those five hours I was out of it?* he wondered.

Officer Perez did not answer his question. She forcibly spun him around, yanking his arms behind his back roughly. He felt the first cuff lock tightly around his wrist, then the other. She was obviously pissed off about something, because it hurt like a son-of-a-bitch.

"What the fuck's going on?" Marc yelled, struggling.

Officer Perez first read him his rights and ended by stating that he was being arrested for assault and battery on his wife. She put the digital camera viewing screen in his face. Nora's bloodied and battered face was staring at him. He couldn't focus on the pictures, as officer Perez had the camera pressed up against Marc's nose.

"This is how your wife looks after you beat the living daylights out of her. What you need is a good ass-kicking and I'd love to volunteer," Perez whispered in his ear. Marc tried to keep his head down, as he was escorted to the police car, trying to hide his face since this was his first opportunity to meet and greet his new neighbors, who were all on their patios holding cocktails and watching all of the excitement.

He was breathing hard, trying to remember what had happened to him. His heart was pounding powerfully against his ribs. His angina returned with a vengeance.

Marc stumbled and fell to one knee. He curled up in fetal position on the driveway, trying to use his knees to stop the pain in his chest. It felt like an elephant had just stepped on his lungs. He couldn't breathe, and then he blacked out.

THIRTY-SIX

Once again Marc woke to a team of hospital personnel attending to him.   His left wrist still had the handcuff on, but this time the other half was securely clipped to the hospital side rail.

"What happened?" Marc asked. His throat felt like he had swallowed a pound of gravel.

"Good news is that you did not have a heart attack Mr. Richards," a pretty redheaded nurse said. "The doctor feels it was another anxiety attack."

Marc looked at the nurse, then at the handcuffs rattling them. "Good news, if there could be any good news at this point of my day." The nurse shrugged and left the room.

Officer's Monroe and Perez replaced the nurse. Perez was holding a notebook. "We need to finish what we started at your apartment," she said curtly.

It all came flooding back to Marc. He was being accused of beating Nora. They once again showed him the same photos before he blacked-out, but this time the camera was not pressed up against his nose.

He was scared.

He did not remember anything from noon to five and it gave him doubt about his own innocence.

Maybe he did hurt Nora?

Maybe during his blackouts he's doing things, horrible things, he just doesn't want to remember. His face turned white as the bed sheet, as a slide show of memories exploded inside his head. First it was his Aunt and Uncle, then Ashley, and the really confusing flashback of three young girls beating to death a teenage boy. He was scared. Then, Lou filled his brain, but he did not know where she was, so he hoped there was a happy resolution to her whereabouts. Now with the photos of Nora's battered face and torso staring him in the face, he was having doubts about his innocence. He really did not know at this point. Could he actually be some kind of sociopath? What he did know was that he needed a lawyer.

"I'm not going to answer any of your questions without my lawyer being present. Get me a damn phone," he ordered.

Officer Perez was ready to hit him. Her face twisted with disgust. "A lawyer isn't going to help you. Cooperate with us and maybe the DA will go easy with you," she said.

Marc knew that his asking for a lawyer made him appear guilty. He was confused, somewhat puzzled, and frightened. All he knew was that he needed someone on his side and officer Monroe and Perez did not look too chummy at the moment. "Just get me a phone and get the fuck out of my room. I feel more chest pains coming on just looking at the two of you," he said defiantly.

Over the last few weeks Marc had felt a radical change come over him. Old memories had started to return with a vengeance. He was beginning to have doubts about who he really was. At times he felt like two people were fighting inside his body trying to get out. He felt very guilty at the moment.

He looked at the two officers trying to act calm, but it wasn't working. "Can I have that fucking phone, now?" he said to Officer Perez. "I want to exercise my right to remain silent."

THIRTY-SEVEN

"What evidence do they have that you did what Nora is accusing you of? Lindsey Warren asked noticeably irritated.

"They showed me photos of her battered face and torso. The problem is…I can't account for five hours…the time Nora said I attacked her. I woke up being soaked by the surf. My hands are bloodied and bruised," he said frustrated waving his knuckles at the phone. "It looks like I had hit a brick wall with my fists and that Nora was that brick wall," Marc said, his voice strained. "Lindsey, I can't fuckin remember anything," he yelled back into the phone.

Lindsey blew out a loud breath of air. "Don't say anything to anyone until I get there. I'm going to call a friend of mine. He's a great criminal attorney. It sounds like you'll need him more than me at this point. I'll try to postpone the arraignment with the Judge. What we don't need is to be on the defensive right now."

Marc didn't like what Lindsey had said. "A criminal defense lawyer? That's for real criminals."

Lindsey sighed. "Oh brother, do you ever not worry? If you're innocent, then you have nothing to worry about. You're innocent, right?"

"I think so. But, there were times in our marriage I wanted to kick the shit out of her, but I never acted it out." His morning ritual of staring at Nora popped into his head and with it came rushing back the picture of him holding a pillow over her face. A cold sweat had begun to run down his back. *Who the fuck am I?* he thought.

"I don't want you talking to anyone about your lost five hours. Knowing your wife, this could be a setup."

"You really think she's capable of letting herself get hurt like that, just to win our divorce?"

"I've seen crazier things from angry women. It becomes a game of just punishing their spouse, no matter what the physical or financial costs will be. Just sit tight and keep your mouth shut," Lindsey said. "Anything else before I hang up?"

"Can we still proceed on with the divorce?"

"Right now you have to try to stay out of jail. If not, Nora might be able to take control of all of your assets. I don't have to tell you what that would do to you."

Marc swallowed hard, trying to control his breathing. He was feeling the dark curtain coming down again. "Please help me, Lindsey. I've been having blackouts since my last year of high school. First my Aunt and Uncle die, then my lover Ashley goes missing, and now this. I'm scared. I don't know who the hell I am anymore," he said desperately.

"Hang in there. I don't believe you could have done this, even if you're having blackouts. I'm going to call a P.I. I've used him on a lot of my cases. He's great and can get at the root of what's been going on. Stay calm. Ask the doctor for one of their wonderful hospital cocktails and take a nice nap. When you wake I should have things under control."

Marc should have felt better hearing her confidence, but he didn't. He hung up the phone and called for his nurse.

* * * * *

Albert Rankin couldn't stop rubbing his hands together. What Nora had told him about her altercation with Marc was the best news he had heard all day.

He had just finished reading all of the documents Lindsey Warren had sent him. The way the assets had been vested by Marc, and how the corporation had been formed, would leave Nora with virtually nothing, which would leave nothing for her attorney. Now, with the possibility of Marc going to jail for a long time, he was drafting up a motion to give Nora power of attorney over the corporation and all of their community property. He couldn't stop rubbing his hands together, realizing how close he came to not getting a single penny. He had to make sure Marc went to jail.

* * * * *

Nora, Rita and Gail seemed pleased with themselves, their giggles exploding into downright laughter. "This is good shit," Gail wheezed.

"Rita puts it together," Nora tried to explain with a gagging cough. "She mixes the stuff with so many additives that the high is terrific," she said passing the joint to Gail.

"Err," she, she said, choking. "I feel too good to give a shit right now."

Nora grabbed the roach clip from Gail's fingers and sucked in a long drag. These brownies are the best," she said stuffing one in her mouth as she slid off the couch. "Marc's going to be so fucked." She pulled on Gail's arm causing her to roll on top of her.

They both were on the carpet laughing hysterically.

THIRTY-EIGHT

Martin Bailey, the criminal attorney Lindsey had recommended was making Marc anxious. He was way too serious and making him uncomfortable. He wanted someone more sensitive and this lawyer was anything but that.

Marc's aunt and uncle had talked down to him.

Nora talked down to him.

Almost everyone he knew talked down to him. If they weren't treating him as if he didn't exist, people constantly interrupted him when he spoke, and Bailey was no exception.

Marc decided he had to put his foot down. "Lindsey," he said sternly. "We need to talk...privately?"

She looked at him confused. "You can talk in front of Martin. Nothing you say will leave this room."

Marc was determined to have his way. Right now he was feeling very insecure and wanted to bury his head and pretend his nightmare was over. "Just have him leave the room. I want to talk you alone!" he said coldly.

Martin Bailey shook his head, acting a little put out, throwing his hands in the air, as he walked toward the nurse's station.

Lindsey was noticeably upset, her fists on her hips. "What's up Marc? Bailey's here to help. You're being rude," she snapped.

"I don't like him. He's treating me like a child. Don't you have someone that I can feel comfortable with?"

"He's the best chance you have of staying out of jail. There's no one better. Stop acting like a baby. Your being too sensitive. You do not need a friend right now. You need a cut throat attorney that knows how to get even the guilty set free. That's your number one priority right now."

"Does he have to talk down to me? I hate it when people do that," Marc whined.

"That's his style. It works for him and it will work for you. Do you think the District Attorney will talk nice to you at trial? Consider this good practice to get you ready. Now deal with it and get over it. I don't want you in jail, or Nora controlling your company and personal assets. Now, can we get on with this?'"

Marc still didn't like being pressured, but he did trust Lindsey. "Fine," he reluctantly agreed.

Bailey was dressed in a sport coat and jeans. He had a Tiger Woods golf hat on and acted very rough around the edges, nothing like what Marc envisioned a criminal attorney to be. He held his breath waiting for his attorney to speak, unable to guess what would come out of his mouth next.

"Mr. Richards let me be frank. The bruises on your wife, as well as the scrapes on your knuckles don't look very good for you. A judge will immediately side with the battered wife in situations like this. Everyone's going to believe that you put a good beating on her," said Bailey, as if he were making his opening remarks to a jury. "Also, I don't like that you can't account for your whereabouts for five hours today. That's disturbing and will make our case more difficult. It'll be hard getting bail to keep you out of jail. I'm hoping to get a judge to agree to a restraining order and letting you out on remand, possibly with an ankle bracelet to monitor your whereabouts."

Marc was shocked by Bailey's remarks. "You sound defeated already. I thought you were supposed to be the best."

Bailey slapped his forehead hard. "What was I thinking? I should show some confidence in your case." He said   "You're in deep shit," he said sarcastically. "But, nothing I haven't dealt with before. So stop whining and relax. Just let me do my job."

Marc rolled his eyes, waving his hand for him to continue. "Just get this over with. I'm scared shitless as it is, so what's a little lack of confidence from my attorney going to really do to my fragile emotional state?"

Bailey was noticeably frustrated by Marc's behavior. He rubbed his index finger and thumb together pretending he was playing the smallest violin in the world. "Do you always feel sorry for yourself?" Bailey snapped. "A judge will see right through that and not listen to anything you have to say in your defense. Being a victim works well for women, but for a man, well, it's not very believable, especially after the injuries your wife has. No criminal case is a sure thing for either side. The district attorney still has to prove that you battered your wife. So far Mrs. Richards doesn't have any witnesses. The police can't find anyone in your old neighborhood who saw you or your car earlier today. If your blackouts are for real, then I can explain that your bruised hands are from you falling down near the jetty by the beach. Reasonable doubt goes a long way when a jury is trying to convict an outstanding citizen like you."

"Do you really believe what you're saying? This isn't some hype that will keep your retainer full?" Marc asked sarcastically.

Bailey raised his eyebrows, a puzzled look appeared on his face. "Tell me now, so I won't get sideswiped during your trial. Did you beat the shit out of your wife? Even if you did, I can still get you off. Lindsey's told me what a real piece of work she is and that she probably needed it anyway."

Marc didn't know how to respond. He hesitated, gathering his thoughts before he spoke. "I can't believe I could do anything like that to anyone, let alone Nora. He shook his head slowly combing his fingers through his ruffled hair. "Honestly, I can't remember what I did during those five hours."

Bailey clapped his hands. "That's okay. I'm going to have your doctors run some additional tests. It's possible you have a disorder called 'Vasovagal Syncope'. With your recent heart problems, it's a likely conclusion. When you sit or stand blood settles in your legs and abdomen. It results in less blood to the heart. Blah, blah, blah, but in a nutshell, when this happens your blood pressure drops and voila you black out. I'll let the doctor give you the medical explanation."

Marc seemed both confused and surprised. "Is this condition serious?"

"It can be if you're doing recreational drugs. Are you?" he said matter-of-factly.

"Never have, and don't plan on starting anytime soon. But a stiff drink sounds real good right now. Does that count?"

Bailey ignored his remarks. "I'll have the doctor run a full blood panel, checking for any drugs in your system. We'll get to the cause of all of this. Don't fret. I'm as good as Lindsey says," he boasted, playfully elbowing Lindsey in her ribs.

THIRTY-NINE

Marc spent the next four days in the hospital being subjected to hundreds of tests. His nerves remained frayed and overloaded with worry. The doctors were not telling him anything, which only made him more anxious.

He had left Lou five text messages, three voice mails, and two other messages at her restaurant. He struck out each time. He desperately needed a friend to talk to. At least he knew that she was okay after talking to Dr. Kaplan. He just didn't understand why she wouldn't even call him to see how he was doing. He knew he had told her he wanted to cool things for a while, but after all of his messages he expected her to call.

Marc's mind struggled to stay positive. It would drift toward the more morbid topics and he'd rally his resolve to think of more pleasant things—unfortunately, nothing seemed pleasant to him while being handcuffed to a hospital bed. He'd close his eyes tight and struggle to remember anything that would trigger his memory to come back, either before the blackout or while he was sleepwalking in it. Like everything lately, he was a total blank.

Then from out of nowhere, something had started to change inside of him.

It felt strangely familiar and at the same time frightening. Yet, it was something he was having trouble resisting. Something inside his mind was taking over and it was not his paranoia.

Self-preservation was now his only thought. Without it, Nora, her attorney and the police would lock him up and throw away the key.

Marc felt the stranger growing inside him, a new assertively strong man that would do anything to survive. He wanted his new life to materialize and he was determined to do whatever it took to make it happen.

If Lou wanted to abandon him, then so be it. His out of control thoughts were telling him he never should have believed that someone like her would care for a person like him. He had to remain strong and diligent in his defense. No more being the victim. "Screw Lou and screw Nora", he mumbled yanking the handcuffs, frustrated. Marc Richards will now become a TNS type of a guy. *I will TAKE NO SHIT…not from anyone from this day forward"*, he mumbled.

Images sitting inside a courtroom, in front of a female judge and her ruling in favor of Nora, were flashing inside his head. It was a slideshow that had him frightened. Even though Nora rescinded her original statement that he had tried to kill her with a knife, his attorney had said that the judge would have the initial report in front of her. While juries are supposed to be objective and hear only the facts, judges are human and can have preconceived notions about a case. Having the new photos of Nora's battered face and ribcage was not going to help his defense. While it was circumstantial evidence, it was a perfect visual aid to a sad conclusion to his marriage.

* * * * * *

Martin Bailey had made a surprise visit to Marc's hospital room. He had shunned his Tiger Woods golf hat and had his hair pulled back in a ponytail. He wore a navy blue Armani pinstriped suit, with Ferrigamo shoes. His silk tie was solid pink. Marc smiled. "I guess you can look like an attorney after all," he jested.

He wheeled in one banker box on a metal luggage cart, a big smile on his face. "This shouldn't take too long," he said calmly.

Marc tried to erase his down in the dumps look on his face, but he wasn't feeling so confident at the moment. "You look way too happy this morning," Marc said oozing caution out from between his lips.

Bailey was pulling notebooks out of the banker box. Each had labels that Marc couldn't read. He had one legal pad with a red felt tip pen, ready to write. Martin seemed somewhere else as he went through this ritualistic organizational exercise, ignoring his client for the moment.

When he was finished, he leaned over and whispered in Marc's ear. "You lied to me. Your blood work came back positive for Marijuana use and a few other exotic drugs. Never lie to me again," his tone was biting and cold.

Marc's eyes grew wide with disbelief. He was pissed. "I've never used any illegal drugs in my life, especially Marijuana. Those tests are wrong." Bailey slipped the blood work results in front of him.

"It doesn't really matter. I know for a fact that this judge does a little puffing after a long day on the bench. However, it could be the reason you're having blackouts and that's all I need to make my case before her."

Marc shook his head. "I can't lie if she asks me about this. Those tests are wrong and I won't admit to using dope."

Bailey sighed. "You won't have to. She has my motion to release you on your own recognizance. Since there's no history of any domestic abuse or any drug use and since the district attorney has no concrete evidence proving you were anywhere near your home or in the presence of Nora at the time of the alleged attack, you don't pose a flight risk. Just sit back and relax and let me do my job."

* * * * *

Bailey was right. The judge did not throw Marc in jail. In fact, she told the DA to either come up with solid evidence, or any evidence that even implicated that Marc Richards was the one who attacked his wife, or drop the case and refile. The DA shrugged his shoulders shaking his head.

"Your honor, I'm dismissing the charges against Mr. Richards until I have the evidence I need to bring him before you again." He handed the judge a warrant to search the Richard's house. "If you'd be so kind as to sign this warrant, I have officers waiting at the Richard's house right now to look for any evidence related to the attack. We have not had a chance to re-look at the crime scene. There are few inconsistencies with Mrs. Richards' account of the attack. I need additional time to check out her story further."

The judge had a puzzled look on her face. "Do you believe that Mrs. Richards filed a false police report? If so, I hope to see her in front of my bench very soon," she said sternly.

The DA seemed baffled at her question. "We have not considered that, but I will look into it immediately," he said nervously.

* * * * * *

It did not take long for the forensic team to find the bloodied gloves Nora had hidden in her closet. The police were checking her cell phone records at the time of the attack. They discovered she had made two calls before calling 911, almost an hour after she said Marc had beat her.

FORTY

Marc was still dripping with insecurity. He was a constant wreck. His mind would not give him the space to think or even feel positive. One thing for sure, he could feel a personality change taking place.

The Marc he once knew had been pushed a bit too much by Nora and that person was drifting slowly away. His brain was convincing him that under any circumstances he could not live with Nora. His mind was seeing scenario after scenario and each one pictured Nora totally out of the picture.

He was in quicksand and felt he had to make a rash decision to save what little freedom he still might have. With Nora alive, he knew he'd never get a moments peace.

His memory was still in the toilet. But, not to even know that he smoked pot, made his head spin. At one point, a few weeks ago, he liked the stranger who was blooming before his eyes. Now, under so much pressure to stay out of jail, so much stress about his blackouts, he wasn't even sure who he was or what he was about to become. Since reading his journal entries describing his past, he was beginning to believe that Marc Richards never existed. He was a lost soul with no past and an uncertain future.

The voice inside his head kept getting louder and clearer. He felt that someone was lurking in the shadows and it had him thinking he was going insane.

All he wanted was some peace and serenity.

He knew that recreational drugs were being used by a large part of the population, so what was the big deal, even if he did not remember doing it? But, it was a big deal to him.

He tried to reason with Bailey, but his attorney brushed off his complaints as no big deal in the entire scheme of things of keeping him out of jail. He even eluded that he was relieved that his client had a dissolute side that was hidden by his anal exterior.

Marc recalled how Bailey had acted when the District Attorney dropped the charges against him. Bailey had put his arm around his shoulders, giving him a hard squeeze. "Don't take this marijuana label use so seriously. If you know that you've not taken it, then so be it. I really don't care. The criminal charges have been dropped and you'll be getting my final bill within a few weeks. Great doing business with you, Marc, and good luck on your divorce."

Marc wanted a stiff drink to help him to feel better, but he opted to buy a new set of golf clubs instead and wait to have his well deserved drink when he got to his vacation home in Palm Desert at the end of the week.

In the meantime, he took a brisk beach walk in downtown Carlsbad. He knew that after a few days of fresh ocean air he would desperately need some golf therapy. He had four days before the first divorce settlement conference, which gave him enough time for a short respite from all of his stress.

* * * * *

He was off to Palm Desert to his two-bedroom single level condo at Shadow Dunes Country Club. It overlooked a double fairway with two lakes and waterfalls with dancing fountains. It had become his little slice of paradise, his refuge away from Nora. She had always hated Palm Desert. Too much heat that made her sweat and a dry desert sun that could make her look like a wrinkled prune. Marc was happy for those small blessings every time he made it to the desert alone.

Highway 79 to Palm Desert in the early morning couldn't be expressed in words. Once out of the overgrown city of Temecula, the countryside was blanketed with purple and yellow wildflowers, blooming from the wet winter the desert had experienced. He was an obsessive-compulsive person, especially when he drove long distances. He always needed to know the mileage from point A to point B, which drove Nora crazy, but it provided him with something to think about while he drove and that in itself calmed him.

He knew he had only eighteen miles before he reached highway 371 and the panorama would become even more pristine. The next leg of his journey was twenty-one miles, which would bring him to his final descent on highway 74. Once he made the right turn he would instantly feel his tensions peeling away.

Before he made the last few miles down the hill, he would always stop at Vista Point and say a silent prayer, giving thanks for the serenity he would soon experience. He never got bored gazing at the breathtaking valley that was surrounded by the Little San Bernardino's (Chocolate Mountains to the locals) and Santa Rosa mountains.

He hadn't been to his little hideaway, that Nora quick-claimed to him, in almost nine months. It was a godsend that Nora hated the heat of the desert and had never set foot in his hidden paradise. All he had was his own peaceful memories to go to. She loved the mountains, so she had a small cabin in Big Bear. One of the many examples that reminded him of the married/single syndrome he had been imprisoned in.

* * * * *

No sooner had he opened the front door of his desert home and dropped his bags, his cell rang.

"Hey Marc, Chip Campbell here," he said like he was a long lost friend.

"Say What? Do I know you?" Marc said irritated from the guy's lack of formality.

"Your attorney Lindsey Warren hired me to help with your divorce. Is this a bad time?"

"I'm out of town for a few days. I can't talk to you now—it's not a good time."

Chip did not take the hint, ignoring Marc's impatience. "No problem amigo. I've done some preliminary work on Nora's background that you might find interesting. I can be in Palm Desert in three hours so we can go over some interesting stuff I've found so far," he said.

"How the fuck did you know I was in Palm Desert? I didn't tell anyone where I was going."

Chip laughed. "That's what I do. Your cell has a global positioning chip…I have a receiver that can pinpoint your location within a half a mile if your cell is not turned off. Oops, I guess you didn't turn that puppy off did ya?"

Marc's temper was starting to boil. "I don't know who you are or what you're up to, but this conversation is over"— Before Marc could hang up, Chip interrupted him.

"I think you'd want to hear this before dismissing me. Let me finish. During my initial background check on you and Nora, I discovered you owned a condo in Palm Desert."

Marc raised his voice—his agitation with this guy was growing by the second. "Do you know what the fuck I'm wearing?" He barked.

"I'm not that good," he replied chuckling. "I do think we should meet," he said his tone more serious. "You'll for sure need what I've found out for your divorce. I can shred everything I found, but trust me, what I have will shock you!" he said emphasizing the last six words.

He had piqued Marc's curiosity perfectly. He looked at his golf clubs and then his watch, it was still early in the morning. He shrugged his shoulders. "It's eight-thirty and I have a T-time at nine thirty. I'll be done at one. Meet me at the clubhouse for lunch. We can talk then," he said.

"Let me have directions—"

Marc didn't let him finish his sentence. "If you're that good, you don't need directions. Be here at one," he laughed and ended the call.

What could he have on Nora that is so important? He thought.

* * * * * *

Lou listened for the tenth time to Marc's message. Her heart was breaking at the desperation she had heard in his voice. She wanted to call him, to be there at the hospital, but Doctor Kaplan had said to stay away. "It's for his own good right now," he had told her.

"That's a load of bull," she muttered to herself. She dialed his number anyway, but on the first ring, she hung up. "What if Kaplan's right?" she moaned.

FORTY-ONE

Marc's round of golf had been uneventful. He had too much on his mind to relax. With every swing of the club he looked up, not because he wanted to see where his golf ball was going to go, but because he felt the prying eyes on the back of his neck. Every plantation shutter slat, every bush, every palm tree stared back at him.

The other three golfers in his foursome did not notice his peculiar state. Each missed shot, each ball that went out of bounds or into the numerous water hazards throughout the course, did not resemble his true abilities as a golfer, just proved to Marc that the paranoia he was feeling was killing his golf game. The round only took three and a half hours, but to Marc it had seemed like a life-time.

He had not been waiting long before Chip pranced into the main dining room of the clubhouse. Marc's curiosity about what he had said he found out about Nora had him interested. While his future Ex was a real bitch, as far as he knew, she had no questionable past that would have any relevance to the divorce or his life. If anything, she had been a hard woman for so long, covering whatever sensitivity and capacity for empathy with a carapace of self-importance, but that would have no bearing on the outcome of their dissolution.

The hard truth about Nora is that she had set up the most auspicious conditions within their relationship, promising passion, dangling the sexual carrot and submitting to his desires with an obligatory attitude. Mercy fucks were humiliating, but a guy thirsty for any degree of passion, would take what morsels are given to him.

What in truth transpired almost daily was a series of combustible issues that continuously led to a marriage engulfed in wildfires. Marc had learned to bury his head hoping that some degree of probity would be restored within his relationship with Nora. He knew he should have left after his first month of marriage, realizing that the passion he so craved was being saved by Nora for someone else. He had a suspicion it was for her boyfriend before him, Brad, with no last name.

Nora never said why Brad had left her or what caused them to separate or if Brad was even alive living near-by or in another State. The ex-boyfriend had been put on a pedestal and everything Marc attempted to do passionately for Nora never measured up to what Brad would have done.

Nora was the queen of 'victimness' and when it came to giving of herself to Marc she was just too depressed to be nice. This resulted in a mean emotional attitude toward her husband.

He used to believe that marriage should be viewed as sacrosanct and divorce a last resort. Marc attempted to see his diverse and pathetic marriage as a mélange of experiences that two people had to traverse through, in order to build a successful relationship, even working through her wounds that had been caused by Brad leaving her.

Marc wanted, at the beginning of his relationship with Nora, to experience the kind of love he projected toward Nora to be returned in equal amounts. But what he received were moments of passion, mixed with pain. As he had done for over twenty-five years, he just avoided the awful truth, the sad reality that the woman he married would never give him the love he deserved. He thought he knew Nora as well as anyone and any new information would probably be old news about a sad life.

What Chip Campbell had for him he believed would most likely be a waste of his time. Nora had always been too concerned about how others saw her. She continued to work hard at keeping that image intact. She remained the diligent one, the consistent one, the mean spirited one, everyday and every moment of Marc's life.

When Nora's violent behavior erupted in their bedroom he rationalized that it had exploded from his renascent character that was unfamiliar to her. Now he had jumped from their merry-go-round relationship and was running away, while she was still going around in circles looking for someone to comfort and cater to her needs. He believed for that reason and that reason alone, she was pissed about the divorce.

For Nora, her beauty was her basic pleasure that she had become immune to, unable to see how truly beautiful she was on the outside. It was that unhappiness about her appearance that got intermingled with what little soul she had left. It had made her a bitter and unattractive woman. If ever the day would come that she did not have her beautiful façade, Marc knew that her world would cease to exist and it would be totally over for him to be able to leave her. She'd work the guilt, pressing the right buttons on Marc, tapping into his loving heart, and trapping him inside a loveless world forever.

That thought had triggered a bad memory. It was ten years ago when she was in a car accident and was hurt pretty badly. His heart just ached seeing her in such pain and all alone. Could something like that draw him back to Nora out of guilt? He shuddered at the thought.

Marc had finally understood that this malaise of Nora's was what made her unwell spiritually and emotionally. Her ill spirit forced her to seek immense wealth through lavish expenditures, filling their home with a false beauty that was only pleasant to the eye, but not very real to the heart. Her lavish desires were her appetite, not her food for her soul. She was on a mission to accumulate everything she believed she wanted, even her outer beauty and now with the likelihood of her being divorced wanted every penny she could squeeze out of their marriage.

Having the time away from Nora had provided Marc enough time to reflect and see the unhealthy environment his marriage stewed in. He now saw how pitiful Nora had grown.

Whatever Chip had discovered about her would not surprise him. He had seen it all. If what this detective had would help him emotionally cut the umbilical cord that Nora had him tethered to, he'd welcome it.

Chip had interrupted Marc's drifting mind with a boisterous hello. "Nice to finally meet you Mr. Richards," he said smiling broadly.

"It's Marc. Have any problems finding this place?" he teased.

"The wonders of Map Quest," he said proudly holding the directions he pulled from the internet. "Couldn't get anywhere without it," he said waving them in Marc's face.

Marc was not impatient by nature, but wanted to have the meeting over with so he could get back to relaxing. "Let's order lunch now," he said waving for the waiter to come over. "Then you can brief me on what was so very important that you had to drive out here today."

Chip did not appear fazed by Marc's agitation and opened a blue manila folder sliding two, eight by ten photos under Marc's nose. "You recognize these women?" he asked.

"This one's my wife," he pointed. "That's my wife's friend Rita and yoga instructor." Marc seemed puzzled. raising one eyebrow. Then Chip put two other photos in front of him.

Chip smiled. "Do you know this woman?"

Marc was losing his patience. "This is my wife's best friend Gail. What's so important about this? I could've given you these pictures."

"I'm sure you could have, but did you know that these two ladies have known your wife for almost thirty-five years?"

Marc shrugged his shoulders uninterested. "So, what's the big deal? Nora's kept up with lots of people she's known."

Chip's expression grew serious. "I believe Nora's not who you believe she is. Her birth name was Rebecca Morgan and Rita, her yoga instructor's birth name was Blanche Ruiz. Gail's birth name was Carla Shortz. When people change their identities it's because they're hiding from a past they don't want anyone to know about."

Marc was still confused at what this had to do with his divorce. "Why should I care what any of their names were?"

Chip was combing his hair with his fingers, frustrated by Marc's lack of comprehension. "You're missing one important point here. None of these ladies had legally changed their names. You married her believing she was Nora Barkley, right? If so, then she falsified her marriage certificate. Your marriage could be null and void. That would mean, and understand I'm not a lawyer, but I would guess you'd owe her nothing."

Marc was nodding his head slowly, now digesting everything Campbell had said. "Are you sure you've checked out every source, every county record on this Rebecca whatever her name is?"

Chip nodded. "I'd like to dig further, to see if anyone or any authorities are looking for all three of them. "But the extra costs go beyond what your attorney authorized me to do. If you…let's say, approve an advance of five-thousand dollars, I could wrap this up in a week or so. It could be the best investment you've made in a long time. The three of them in my experience…well, they're connection doesn't seem Kosher. My gut tells me they're hiding from something and it might be the police."

The thought of not owing Nora or Rebecca Morgan anything was very appealing to Marc. It was the most exciting news he had heard in a long time. "If you can do what you say, then go for it," he said excitedly.

Marc thought of showing Chip his mysterious letter. He had been avoiding returning to his aunt and uncle's home and now having someone else look into it might kill two birds with one stone. "I received this letter a few weeks back and don't have a clue what it means. Could you check into it and get back to me?"

Campbell read the letter, he licked his lips, as he rubbed the fresh stubble on his chin. "Consider it done. This could tie into what I've already found. You don't know who sent this to you, do you?"

Marc acted evasive. He wasn't ready to tell another person about his memory loss and his flashbacks. "Not really. I suspect it's someone from my past. Just check into it and get back to me."

Chip remained calm and cool. "While this is just preliminary stuff, there's something that's just not right about these three ladies and now with this letter, it could be some kind of warning. Just watch your back until I get back to you."

Chip was cracking his knuckles. Excitement beamed on his face. "Soon all of this will be behind you."

"Great. Let's be clear with our arrangement. If you find out anything before then, I want to be the first to know. I'll talk to my divorce attorney and see if she can get a postponement of my upcoming settlement conference."

During lunch they talked about golf and Chip's escapades with women. He had never been married and thought that qualified him as an expert in marriage, love, and sex. He had a Magnum PI sort of look about him, but bragged way too much to make his stories believable. After two hours they had exhausted every subject matter. Chip drove back toward San Diego and Marc took his golf cart back to the condo.

Marc needed to talk to someone and thought of Lou. He was upset with her about not returning his phone calls, but he put those thoughts in the back of his head and dialed her cell anyway. He once again got her voice machine. "Lou, its Marc…again. I'm so worried about you. I've been calling for a week. Why won't you return my calls? I need to see you. Call me on my cell. We really need to talk," he begged, his voice cracking.

* * * * *

Lou saw the caller ID and hesitated. She wanted to take Marc's call, but had just finished talking with Doctor Kaplan. He was adamant that she keep her distance from Marc. Even that it did not make emotional sense to her; she respected her friend and wanted Marc to get well.

FORTY-TWO

Marc was sipping his hot cup of coffee. He did not have his favorite tea with him. He pressed his head back into the soft cushion of his dark brown wicker lounge chair, his vacant eyes staring out over the two lakes and lush green fairways that he called his backyard. He tried to experience that spiritual moment, as the sun rose over the mountains and the pink and orange colors reflected off the calm lake, but this morning he was stymied.

He called Kaplan, to see if he had heard from Lou. He at least wanted to know if she was talking to anybody.

"Marc," he said in a calm monotone, "I've spoken to her. She's agreed with me that she shouldn't see you until we can do a little more work on your emotional state and your stress levels."

Marc was stunned. "So you're the one having her ignore all of my calls? Who the fuck do you think you are?" he shouted.

"It's all for the best while we work together. I won't be able to figure out where your blackouts are coming from if you're distracted. This is an important time for you to take care of yourself. You've never been alone before and you'll need to learn to stand on your own."

"I'm being isolated, because you think it best? That's bull-shit."

A quiet came over the phone as Kaplan thought of his answer. "Look, I feel you're vulnerable right now and need your space to resolve your issues with your wife. In my professional opinion it's not healthy to use a new relationship to lean on. Lou has her own problems and wouldn't be able to give you what you want anyway."

Marc's blood was boiling. He could feel the veins on his forehead ready to pop. "Are you seeing Lou professionally also?" Marc barked. "Did Lou really agree to this?"

Kaplan took in a deep breath before he replied. "She's in agreement with me," he said, concealing his little white lie.

"Really?" Marc was fuming. "You tell her I really don't need her. I'll take care of myself on my terms," he said, as an unfamiliar anger started to grow. "Look doc, maybe, I need my space from you also," said Marc realizing that Kaplan wasn't someone he could trust at this time. He was just a businessman who took money from patients for listening to their problems. Marc sucked in a deep breath, his emotional state on overload. "I'd rather see a prostitute than you. At least I'd find some emotional and physical release, which is what I really need right now." He flipped his phone shut without saying good-by.

Marc had thought he had found a friend in Lou and that she cared about him. At that moment, as his disappointment consumed him, he felt the dark curtain come down and everything went black.

* * * * *

Brad, was swollen with pride with Marc's intensity to stick up for himself. His adrenaline was rushing through his veins at warp speed. His heart couldn't stop racing thinking that finally Marc would be capable of returning to the violent man he had once been. He needed that from Marc. It made them the perfect team.

Even though Marc's memory was unable to see his past, to see what he really was, Brad knew that it was just a matter of time before Marc exploded out of his cocoon. Once that happened it would open the door for Brad's return. They were once unstoppable and they needed each other to handle Nora and her friends.

Brad was now remembering the first time he and Marc found their unbreakable bound. They were both five years old comparing their black and blue marks on their arms and ribcages. Their father's physical abuse had brought them closer. Marc at first was a little too nice for Brad's liking, but soon their personalities began to blend into one.

As the weeks turned into years, Brad and Marc had learned to watch each other's backs, becoming stronger and intimidating, putting fear into anyone who wanted to hurt them. If Marc couldn't hurt one of the boys at school without getting into trouble, he and Brad would cause them other pain by killing the boy's favorite pet. It was not until they met Rebecca Morgan (Nora) in eighth grade that Marc and Brad's violence reached new heights. She was two grades ahead of them, but that didn't seem to matter. Rebecca was in control and began molding the two different personalities to help her achieve her sadistic goals.

It had not bothered Marc that Rebecca liked Brad's personality better. Marc was shy and not into girls that much. They were friends and shared everything. When Rebecca got jealous, Marc would become the enforcer and Brad the executioner. Like a one-two punch, they were relentless.

Once, when Rebecca thought that the head cheerleader at her High School was fooling around with Brad, the girl was found under the football bleachers naked, her face and torso slashed and sodomized with a baseball bat. Even though, Rebecca and her girlfriends did the deed, Brad and Marc had brought her there and were accomplices, which was held over their heads as leverage by Rebecca. The cheerleader survived, but had not returned to finish her senior year.

When Rebecca introduced Marc and Brad to her friends Blanche Ruiz and Carla Shultz, they had become the most feared group at their schools. Rebecca was the ringleader. She was the craziest. Brad never really trusted her, but she liked the same wild sex he did and he allowed her to feel the power she imagined. It made her happy and when she was happy, she made Brad very happy.

Rebecca's had a sadistic plan to help Brad with his abusive parents. Her method took a drastic turn when she crashed her car into Marc and Brad's parent's car, critically injuring them. Brad was shocked at what she had done. Without thinking Rebecca convinced Brad to end his abusive parent's life.

She knew she had to get Brad to act immediately or he'd chicken out. In a caring and loving tone she said, "This is a great opportunity. Your father's been abusing you for so long and your mother just doesn't care for you anyway. I'll take care of you. You can count on me." She moaned as she watched Brad nervously sink into one of his blackouts, leaving her to do his dirty work again.

When he regained consciousness, Rebecca told him how brave he had been. "You took a deep breath and without a second thought you put your hand over your father's mouth. At the same time you pinched his nose with your other hand."

She told him excitedly how the surprised look on his father's face had given him for the first time some needed relief. As her words sunk in he had another blackout for a minute or so.

Brad did recall when he woke up again that his mother and father were both dead. He looked at this father with cold eyes and didn't feel anything, but seeing his mother with the shocked look on her face brought a profound sadness that made his heart ache.

Brad stepped away from the car. He turned toward Rebecca who was smiling. "What just happened?" he said confused.

Rebecca put on her best poker face and replied. "You did what you should have done a long time ago. Now it's over and you are free."

Brad scratched his head puzzled at Rebecca's words. "Are you saying I killed both of them?"

Swiping a tear from her cheek Rebecca said. "I'm afraid so."

"Then, you know that I cannot stay around here. I'm going to have to leave." He said.

"Why? No one's going to know what happened. There are no witnesses. I'll get rid of my car and say it was stolen at the party."

"I am not concerned about that. What about Marc? He'll never forgive me for doing this. I cannot have him disappointed with me. He'd never understand."

Rebecca slapped Brad hard across the face causing another blackout. Now she was running out of options. Her great plan was now falling apart. She moved him to the curb so she could think before the police and ambulance got there.

She was shocked that she might be left holding the bag on the murders. She looked over at Marc who was lying by the curb not moving. Brad was gone.

She checked Marc's pulse. He was alive and she thought of a great solution to her problem.

Mustering up all the strength she could find, she moved Marc's limp body into his parent's car and left him at the accident.

When Marc came to, he was surrounded by medical personnel, his mind a blank about what had happened. He was told his parents had died and he had a concussion. What the doctors did not know is that Marc's memories were gone. He did not know that the two dead people were his parents or that Brad had ever existed.

When a detective tried talking to him, about the accident, he got frustrated and bolted from the ambulance.

As he ran, his memory scattered behind him on the streets. He'd glanced back over his shoulder checking to see if he had been followed, but all he noticed was that with each stride another memory floated away, emptying his head until he did not have a clue as to where he was running toward.

He wasn't sure how long he had run or where he had ended up, but the stress caused him to collapse. He lay unconscious on the street. But the next thing he knew, he was back on his front porch, his head in his hands and the detective once again trying to talk to him about the accident.

Marc's brain felt like it had been erased. All he heard was a faint buzzing sound inside his head. He knew his name and that was about it. He couldn't remember anything before the accident. Who his friends were or any of the abuse his parents had inflicted on him. Brad was a non-entity.

Social Services took control of Marc and got in contact with his aunt and uncle in California and they became his guardians. Soon Marc was in a new high school in California and would be graduating in a year.

* * * * *

Months later, Marc was sitting at a local high school hangout when he met Nora. He liked her instantly. There was a strange familiarity to her, which he thought meant they had met in another lifetime. He thought he was being romantic, unaware that he had known her as Rebecca Morgan.

* * * * * *

Marc was startled awake by a distant train whistle and found himself sitting on his Palm Desert deck looking at the golf course, feeling like he had just come out of a bad dream. He was feeling very alone, just like he did the night his aunt and uncle died.

He remembered the first night he had met Doctor Kaplan and how angry he had gotten at Lou. His thoughts then drifted to the two women he had defended at the tavern that night. He looked at his contacts page inside his Smart Phone, went to the category labeled "New Women" and found only two name, Samantha and Lisa, as well as their phone numbers. He did not have their last names, but that didn't matter.

He was unsure of who to call first. They were both beautiful and very outgoing. He tried Samantha's number and got her message machine. He did not feel comfortable leaving a message. He then tried Lisa and she picked up on the second ring.

"What time do you need me," she said playfully, not asking who was calling.

Marc was perplexed by her greeting, but thought that maybe she put his number in her cell and recognized his name. "Hi, it's um, Marc Richards, the guy that defended you and your friend Samantha a few weeks back?" he said sheepishly.

"Oh, Marc…yes, I remember you. How's my big strong hero doing? Is your divorce moving right along?" she asked cheerfully.

"Let's just say it's moving. I was wondering if you'd like to have dinner with me some time." He tried to sound casual and not too desperate, but his heart was racing wildly.

"I'd love to. How about tonight?" she said. "I'm not working for a few days and would love to see you. I do owe you for coming to my rescue."

His heart sunk. No way was he leaving the desert. "I'm in Palm Desert for a few days at my condo. I needed to clear my head."

Without any hesitation Lisa's response, surprised him. "I love the desert. I can come out and spend some time with you if you'd like. I love Palm Desert, it's so spiritual."

Marc took a deep breath, trying to think. He had never had any woman, especially one as gorgeous as Lisa, come on to him that way. He licked his dry lips and wiped the spittle from the corners of his mouth. He cleared his throat. "If you'd really like to drive out here, I'd love to see you. My place is big enough, so you'd have a place to crash," he said innocently.

She giggled. "You're really new at this, aren't you?" she teased. I think we're going to get along just fine."

In three hours he was going to have the first woman at his condo retreat.

* * * * *

"Nora, Marc's getting closer to finding out about the three of us. We can't let that happen," Rita said. "I just spoke to Brad and he told me about the PI."

"I'm sure we're okay," Nora said calmly. "Marc's never been that smart. He's nothing like Brad. When he finally figures things out, it will be too late and he and Brad will be a team again."

Rita sighed. "His PI knows about the three of us. He's been asking a lot of questions. Marc's given him permission to dig a little deeper. If Marc's divorce attorney discovers who Rebecca Morgan really is, you won't have a leg to stand on during your divorce. You signed you marriage certificate as Nora Barkley. You do remember the real Nora Barkley is dead. You're using her social security number. And, besides falsifying your marriage certificate, there's a murder we're all involved with."

Nora remained silent, letting her shallow breaths escape through the phone line before she replied. "The real Nora Barkley had no family, friends, or anyone who knew she existed. I'm the real Nora Barkley. Don't worry about it. All my birth records, photos, and family I once had were destroyed long ago. Marc's PI is going to run up against a brick wall and we'll be safe as a bug in a rug," said Nora.

Rita's tone showed her frustration. "This is not the same as when Marc's aunt and uncle found out about your past and wanted to expose you then, or when his mistress Ashley recognized the real Rebecca Barkley who attended Edgewood High School. We all lived in West Covina, California and can't afford to be exposed. Those little glitches were all handled swiftly. I'm just not so sure how we're going to handle this PI. It's serious. We could finally be put in jail for a long time."

Nora sighed, her irritation building. "You worry way too much for my liking. If you feel uncomfortable, then do something about it. I just don't want to be bothered with this problem right now. You talk to Gail and handle it. If she agrees with you, then make Marc's private investigator disappear.

FORTY-THREE

While Marc waited for Lisa, he thought about what Chip Campbell told him. He couldn't believe that Nora's real name was Rebecca Barkley. But, it had a familiar sound to it. He grabbed his laptop and did a Google Search, but came up with nothing. He looked through every state, and still no one with that name popped up.

Frustrated, he was about to get off the internet, when he tried R. Barkley and got four hits. One was in upstate New York, another in Chicago, the third one was in West Covina, California, and the last was in Seattle. He printed up the four pages to check out later.

His thoughts shifted to Lisa's arrival. He knew he was in uncharted territory and felt nervous. He started second guessing himself and could hear Dr. Kaplan's voice in his head.
"Maybe you should just deal with your divorce and your blackouts before you get involved with a woman?" the doctor had said. He shook his head knowing his sexual urges overruled any advice he was given.

Then he heard the voice in his head again. "You're driving me crazy. You're not going to marry this woman. Just have sex and go on your way. We do need it, you know?"

Marc was not as puzzled about the voice, as he'd been before. Today it felt like a long lost friend. "I guess you're right," he said, looking around to see if anyone was listening. The memory of Lisa sitting on his lap at the tavern had him excited. Then he was feeling the violent side he had exposed that evening and his excitement about Lisa quickly evaporated. He did not want to believe he was capable of showing a brutal side without any blackouts.

Marc felt he was swimming inside his whirlpool of troubles, doubting once again if getting involved with a woman was the smart thing to do at this time. He knew the D.A. had dropped the charges against him. He knew that the D.A. was only doing that until he could find the evidence he needed. His paranoia was running rampant.

He thought that it might be possible that the District Attorney could find out about the barroom fight if he interviewed Lou and Doctor Kaplan.

What if he talked to Eddie the bartender?

"Oh shit, I could be fucked," he mumbled.

He instantly changed his thoughts back to Lisa. He forced himself to fantasize. He was sure of one thing—he deserved to ravish a beautiful body or be ravished by one. She sounded like she was going to be a willing participant. Then he started to think that maybe he misinterpreted what she had said. Maybe she's just coming out as a friend. He tried to hold on to the fantasy a little bit longer. Lustful thoughts seemed like a smart drug at this time.

Again the voice spoke. "You dumb fuck. You're driving me crazy with all this wavering. Take a deep breath and try to remember who you really are. It will make things a lot easier," the voice said.

Marc stared at a distant point on the wall deep in thought. "Can you tell me who I am?"

The voice just sighed. "You wouldn't believe me if I told you. It would be so much better if you'd figure it out yourself. Then everything would become perfectly clear."

Marc wrinkled his nose, now getting very impatient. "Just leave me alone. There's nothing to find out."

"You're wrong," the voice argued. "But, have it your way." The voice was gone, leaving Marc with just a faint ringing in his ears.

Marc shrugged his shoulders, feeling a bit weird about the conversation he had just had with himself, but he would be going into divorce-hell soon enough and wanted a nice distraction to mask how confused he was. He wanted someone warm and caring to talk to like Lou, but apparently that was not going to happen. Lisa would have to be his surrogate Lou.

He couldn't stop picturing himself with Lisa. He was panting out of control when the doorbell rang. He felt his face go flush realizing that Lisa was at the door. He took a few deep breaths, which still did not lower his heart rate. He stood, pulling out his shirt from his pants to hide his excitement and opened the door. His legs felt like rubber. A nervous twitch had just started just below his left eye.

She was more beautiful than he had remembered. His nose took in her fragrance. He did not want to forget to ask her what perfume she was wearing. If things worked out today, maybe a future gift for her birthday?

Lisa had the biggest and warmest smile he had seen in a long time. Her ocean blue eyes were like beacons of passion that melted his heart. Her long blond hair was back in a ponytail exposing her high cheekbones and full lips. Marc couldn't suppress the strange wanton desires exciting his body. *Stop staring you pervert!* he shouted to himself. *She might not like doing what you're thinking.*

He totally lost it when his eyes fell on the cropped tight T-shirt she was barely wearing that said: *THESE ARE REAL.* When she raised her arms to hug him the t-shirt lifted just high enough to expose the lower portion of her bare breasts, revealing a glimpse of her nipples.

Marc saw her lips moving, but couldn't hear a word she was saying. His heart was pounding so loud that his ribs hurt.

FORTY-FOUR

Lisa lifted Marc's chin with her soft hand forcing him to make eye contact. "That's better. Are you going to give me a hug or what?" she said playfully.

Marc stepped in close. It ended up being more of a stumble, knocking his chest hard against her firm supple breasts. He then awkwardly hugged her tightly to steady himself. With the gracefulness of a pickpocket she slid her hand past his waist and gently gripped his erection. "You seem really happy to see me," she teased, pushing him back, breaking his strong hug. She kicked the door shut with her foot. "You want to do our talking later?"

It happened too fast. Marc had not time to think clearly or second guess himself. They started stripping off each other's clothes, tripping over their feet on the way to his bedroom.

Lisa sat him down on the bed, kneeling. "Just relax," she said in a soft whisper. "This is your reward for being such a gentleman the night we met." She had slipped off his pants and then his bikini briefs with the grace of an ER nurse, which he had a lot of experience with lately.

She pushed his chest back forcing him to stare at the ceiling. She had undone her ponytail and starting dusting his thighs with her long silky hair. Then her head started to slowly oscillate her long blonde hair across his exposed stomach and groin. This went on for a few minutes, while her hands massaged his throbbing manly part. Without warning, as if this was her normal routine, she slipped her large lips around his throbbing erection and drew it deep into her mouth. Marc gripped the sides of the bed holding on for dear life. His body was tingling in ways it had never felt before.

He was having faint memory of Nora having done this once when they first met twenty-five years ago, but it didn't come close to what was being done at the moment.

Lisa was good at what she was doing. She knew how to keep him on the verge of climaxing. It was as if she could sense when he was about to explode and would slow down her rhythm, allowing Marc's urge to climax to subside. When she was confident he had control of himself, she then resumed what she had been doing, but this time slower, focusing on the most sensitive spots with her lips.

Marc had lost all sense of time. His eyes had been closed tight and his toes curled almost to the point of cramping, until he could no long restrain himself. An explosion on a scale of eight point zero went off inside her mouth. When he thought it would have been over, it wasn't. Lisa kept moving her lips up and down until he felt four more aftershocks shoot through his entire body like a surge of electricity.

He had to beg her to stop. His body couldn't take any more of what she was doing. He needed air or thought she did and gently lifted her head.

With the most sensual look he had ever seen, she smiled and spoke. "Did you like it? You tasted like a cherry lollipop."

Marc was speechless. He didn't know what to say. He swallowed hard.

"How the hell did you do that? I've never experienced anything like that before. You were great. Did you take a class in that?" He couldn't stop rambling.

She innocently shrugged her shoulders. "I just know what men like and I like giving them pleasure. I hope that doesn't bother you?" she said, her voice showing a nervous edge to it. She saw a puzzled look on Marc's face.

Who cares? He thought. *She has a past and a life.* "Are all women like this?" He asked regretting asking such a stupid question. "What I mean is that I haven't been with many women in my life and the ones that I have been with would never do anything close to what you just did. Don't get me wrong, I loved it, and would love it again, but don't you need something for yourself?"

Lisa touched his cheek. "Aren't you sweet? Not too many of the men I know care a shit about what I want. They see my boobs, my lips, and other parts and just want me to satisfy their personal fantasy. I could tell you had one about me before I got here?" she said. "I just thought I'd deal with it first before we attempted to get to know each other," she said frankly.

Marc instantly felt embarrassed, maybe because she was right, or that he was acting like the men she had just described. "Guilty as charged. But, you didn't give me much of an opportunity to participate. How about some reciprocity?"

"You really want to do that? It's not necessary. We can just cuddle and talk. That's all I really need," she said unconvincingly. He could see a pain in her eyes as she spoke.

Marc, without saying a word, led her up to the bed and laid her on her stomach. He gently undid her bra and slipped off her jeans and panties.

He straddled her letting his hands gently glide over her upper back toward her neck. He proceeded to give her a gentle massage, adding a little sensual touching, as he came close to the inside of her thighs. Like he was handling a fragile piece of ceramic, he spread her legs apart and began rubbing her inner thighs, lightly touching her. She started to moan. Her butt was undulating slowly, allowing his hand to slide underneath to her stomach. This went on for a while. Marc could feel her impatience and her wetness.

He rolled her over and continued the massage, only changing the stroking from his hands to his tongue. She spread her legs as if she was yawning and held his head between her thighs. Marc was surprised how sweet she tasted.

"You taste good," he muttered. It did not take her long to climax.

Marc had thought she was done, but she pressed his head hard signaling him to continue. She was not at all like Nora. She had six more body quivers. Then she had him enter her where she proceeded to climax again, and to Marc's surprise so did he.

He had never known what it would be like to have a mutual orgasm. He loved it and only hoped that he could experience it one more time before he died.

"Was I mistaken or did we just—" She put her finger to his lips.

"Marc, before you say anything, let me speak first. I've never met a man like you before. But, my life is very complicated. I'd like to continue to see you, however you need to know what I do for a living," she said, as a deep sadness consumed her tone.

Marc's eyebrows raised in a puzzled look. "What could you do for a living that would stop me from seeing you again…?" then it hit him. "Oh, you're one of those," he said shocked. "Was that what you and Samantha were doing at the tavern that night?"

Lisa turned her head, unable to look at Marc. "No. It was our night off. We just wanted to act like normal ladies for one night…and then that jerk came over…then you defended us. It was the first time that any man saw me and Sam as nice respectable women. I liked the feeling and was so happy when you called today. I had been thinking about you ever since that night."

"So you do this…what we just did with other men and charge for it?" Marc asked—his voice had too much judgment in it.

Lisa's confidence had evaporated. Her eyes had become glassy. "It's just a job that pays me enough so I can take care of my little girl. I'm going to get out of this profession soon. I just need a little more time to save enough money," she explained her voice cracking with embarrassment.

Marc slid away from her and propped himself against the headboard, his arms folded across his chest. He felt his anger rise. "The first time I find a woman with such passion and she ends up being a whore. I have a wife who's emotionally abusive. I have a female friend that won't return my calls and now this. Could it get any worse?" He was totally oblivious to Lisa, as his harsh self-centered words exploded out of his mouth.

Tears had begun rolling down Lisa's cheeks. She started sobbing uncontrollably. "You might think I've had choices in my life, but I didn't. I was really young when I got pregnant. My daughter's father was in the military and died in Iraq. We were only married for less than a month. I had no means of support. From your viewpoint it might seem like a poor choice and maybe it was, but it has provided me with a fortune of money that I would not have been able to earn working in an office."

"You had choices. Does your daughter know what you do?" He asked sternly.

She stared at him with contempt. "I'd never let her know. I make her breakfast every morning before she leaves for school and I'm home with her after school. I tuck her into bed at night and read her a story. I only work on the weekends as an escort for lonely rich men. Yes, sometimes sex is involved, but nothing like what we just did," her tone was biting. "At least I've made a choice in my life. What have you done? By the sound of it, you haven't done much."

Marc felt a wave of anger coming over him.

His head felt light.

He was seeing circles.

He thought he was having one of his blackouts.

He put his head in his cupped hands and started massaging his scalp with his fingers. The bedroom started spinning, everything went pitch black.

He didn't know how long he had been out, but Lisa was dressed and putting a cold wash cloth on his forehead. "You gave me a scare. I thought you passed out, but you were just frozen in a blank stare. It happened so quickly I didn't know what to do. I was going to leave and call 911 when I got on the road, but I couldn't leave you under these circumstances."

The fog had lifted from his eyes and he pulled himself up, leaning against the headboard again. "Thanks for staying," he said. "I've had blackouts lately. I don't understand them. I had so many tests done and all they had come up with is that I'm using Marijuana. I've never used that stuff in my life."

Lisa's expression reflected doubt at what he was saying. "Unless someone switched your blood work, those tests are pretty accurate."

"I'm telling you I've never taken weed or any other illegal drug in my life," his voice rising with irritation.

"Maybe someone is giving it to you without your knowledge."

"I either eat out or cook for myself," he said defensively. "It's impossible."

Lisa took his hand in hers and brought it to her lips. "I could help you figure it out," she said in a sweet whisper.

Marc didn't respond. He had the matter of being with a whore to deal with. Oops, she's an escort. "I just don't know. I'm a little mixed up right now. I have my divorce settlement conference in a few days. I have my blackouts that are driving me crazy. I don't think I can deal with any other distractions right now."

Lisa spoke in a soft caring voice. "We could just be good friends. It sounds like you need at least one right now. If you can handle what I do for a living, it might work?" Her shoulders were hunched and her eyes were unable to look at him. She seemed sad and vulnerable at the moment, which was a weakness for Marc.

He tried to respond politely, but his brain and tongue were not in sync. "I've never been with a prostitute before or had one as a friend. Can one of your Johns be a friend also?" he said his tone a little too sarcastic. He regretted his words the instant they spewed out of his mouth.

Lisa looked up, her eyes moist. "I didn't come here to charge you anything. I just wanted to have a good time and enjoy a guy that treated me like a lady. But, I guess I'll always be seen as a whore," she said sucking in a deep breath, not wanting to show Marc anymore of her fragile emotional state.

Marc wanted to speak, but nothing flew into his head. He watched her bounce off the bed and storm out the door. He had just realized that best experience of his life had come and gone in a heartbeat.

"Who am I to be such a prude?" he whispered. He didn't know what had come over him. He jumped out of bed and pulled his jeans on and bolted for the front door. Yanking it open, he almost ran into Lisa who was just standing there crying out of control.

"I forgot my car keys," she said her head cupped in her hands. "I was afraid of coming back in."

Marc pulled her close burying her head into his chest, his arms wrapped around her. "Maybe we could see how this friendship stuff might work. If you'd like to stay…I'd still love to have some company," he said kissing her tears.

The next three days had been glorious. Lisa was a bright and sensitive woman and she talked about her life. They had moments of uncontrolled laughter mixed with deep rooted crying. After each talk, they exposed their emotions that brought up their more sultry desires. After a day of learning about each other, something more serious than a friendship had begun to surface.

A lot of Marc's questions focused on her escort services. At first she was not comfortable talking about it, but eventually they had an understanding and a plan for her to quit. For the first time in his life, he was able to talk freely.

Marc was beginning to learn that friendship required a lot of understanding and a ton of non-judgmental feelings. It was hard, but he felt it was worth it so he could explore a new and exciting side of himself.

Lisa did not need his help, but appreciated that he wanted to be there to see her through her situation. She returned that same care to him, which was very refreshing.

She left a day before his settlement conference. As soon as she was out the door he was missing her. He was determined to go with this new type of friendship and let it run its course.

FORTY-FIVE

Spending time alone had never before been a problem for Marc. It had always been his most favorite time, those precious minutes he treasured without Nora. When Lisa had left, though, it was the first time he actually could hear the eerie silence that had always been inside his heart. She seemed to have connected with something magical and it was creating a yearning that he did not know he needed.

He did not think he could talk to Lou about Lisa even if he wanted to. She was not returning his calls. His only choice was to call Doctor Kaplan.

That had proved to be another mistake in a long list of mistakes he had been making since walking out on Nora. After a much needed session over the phone, Marc was once again confused.

He had thought that his therapist would have listened, done what all therapists do: not speak, but grunt out sounds that made the patient keep talking. The moment he had made the phone call and had opened his mouth to Kaplan, he had realized he should have kept it shut. From feeling good, he had sunk to feeling as if he had just cheated on a lover. Marc was beginning to wonder if Kaplan was the professional he really needed.

Doctor Kaplan, during their phone session, controlled his feelings, but Marc could tell the doctor wanted to yell at him. Then without warning, Kaplan without any reservations lashed into Marc making him feel uncomfortable about himself and his actions. Marc couldn't finish talking about Lisa, before the good doctor was chastising him for not calling him first before he invited her to see him.

Marc was baffled to say the least. *Did he really think that under the circumstances, those lustful ones, I'd be in the right mind to rationalize and stop what I was doing? Why would any healthy man use logic at a moment like that?* Marc pondered.

Kaplan's words did not come across as an understanding therapist, but more like a parent who disapproved of their child's choices.

Marc remembered how loud the doctor sounded through the phone. *"What the hell do you want from me?"* He was noticeably pissed at Kaplan's condemnatory tone. He kept playing their conversation over and over inside his head. *"You're here to help me, right? Right now you're acting like my father, who you know was an abusive bastard."*

Marc then remembered the long silence at Kaplan's end before the doctor replied. *"I'm sorry. I can see how I was sounding like your father. I was shocked and dismayed at what you told me. You sounded like you're falling for this prostitute? Did I read you wrong?"* The doctor's words did not make Marc feel any better.

Marc felt manipulated. First he's been scolded. Then, he was treated with understanding. *How can he flip flop so easily?* He thought. Isn't trust supposed to be important for a patient-therapist relationship?

Marc never let Dr. Kaplan respond. Marc answered the question for him. He felt assertive when he had spoken. *"Right now we have none. And, for your information, Lisa's different. She's unlike any woman I've ever met."*

Kaplan had kept scolding his patient. *"Marc, you've told me the same thing about Lou."*

The doctor's last comment infuriated Marc. *"That's different. Lisa ignites a flame inside of me that I never knew existed and it is not just sexual. Lou is sweet and very nice, but she doesn't do what Lisa does for me,"* he said with conviction.

Then Kaplan sighed. *"You've been deprived for so long of any mature female contact and you're grasping at any affection that's given to you. You'd respond the same way if Nora pressed the right buttons. I'd recommend that you avoid any emotional relationships at this time. You're too vulnerable."*

Marc didn't like what he had said. It sounded like psycho-babble. Marc's carnal side was craving what Lisa offered and not seeing her was not going to be an option at this time.

He kept arguing with the doctor. *"I can't believe you don't want me to have any female friends. I'm horny. I won't be celibate. I like making mistakes. That's how I learn,"* he had said.

It was now a full blown argument and Kaplan wanted to win at all costs. *"I don't think it's such a good idea at this time. You've made enough mistakes with Nora and see where it's gotten you."*

Marc was feeling as if he was in one of his no-win fights with Nora. *"That's a low blow. What kind of a fucking therapist are you? Aren't you listening to me? Don't you have a clue what is right for me now? It might have taken me a long time to figure out that my marriage sucked, but I'm learning now."*

Marc could hear Kaplan sigh. He knew he wanted the last word, which he tried to get. *"Maybe in a few months, when you're stronger, and we have a handle on your blackouts, then I could support your desires. Right now I'm concerned that a problem with either Lou or this Lisa could have you crawling back to Nora begging for her to take you back."*

During this heated telephone session, Marc did not believe that Kaplan had his best interest at heart, and did not feel good about what he was suggesting. He remembered trying to end the call with one final statement. *"I think it's time for me to go with what makes me feel good. You can't understand what's going inside my heart right now. I need friends, especially intimate friends that can make me feel happy."* Nevertheless, Dr. Kaplan had more to say. Marc felt like he was being harassed by a car salesman after he had said no a dozen times.

Kaplan had kept pushing his point. *"Then you should give Lou a call. She's more right for you than that woman,"* he said coldly.

Marc would have strangled the doctor if they were face-to-face. *"That woman's name is Lisa. By the way I've been calling Lou and you're the one who told her not return my calls."*

Marc could not believe how Kaplan kept begging for him to take his advice. *"Look, I think if you give Lou a call this afternoon, she'll talk to you. Please Marc, don't pursue this prostitute. It will only put you in a dangerous spiral that will hurt your chances of getting better."*

"Damn it, her name's Lisa," he had shouted, frustrated at Kaplan's critical attitude. He flipped his cell phone off.

Marc glanced in the dresser mirror and could see his contorted face changing before his eyes. He did not recognize the face in the reflection. He knew that if Kaplan was sitting in front of him, he'd have his strong hands around his neck squeezing the life out of him. What he was seeing scared him.

* * * * *

Marc still wanted to speak with Lou, knowing that it was Kaplan that kept her from returning his calls. He waited an hour to call Lou, hoping that Kaplan would call her immediately and tell her to speak to him.

His facial muscles had returned to a calmer state and he then decided to dial Lisa instead. He was craving to hear her voice.

Her phone only rang once and a young girl's voice answered. "This is Melissa, who may I say is calling?" she said in a perky voice.

"Melissa, my name is Marc Richards. Is your mother home?"

She yelled, her voice high-pitched and squeaky, "Mommy, it's for you. Nice talking to you Mr. Richards."

What a nice little girl he thought. It didn't feel like he had called an escort's house. He heard heavier footsteps approaching the phone.

"Thank you sweetheart, you answered the phone like such a grownup lady. I'm so proud of you," Lisa said with a loud kiss. "Hello."

"Hi, it's Marc. Remember me?" he joked.

"Remember you? My heart hasn't stopped fluttering since I left you. What's going on? I'm surprised you're calling so soon."

"I hope I'm not being too pushy. I just wanted to hear your voice. I just wasn't sure if I had dreamt about the time with you…hearing your voice has reassured me that you're real and what happened was real."

Lisa laughed. "That's sweet. But you don't have to call me, I'm not that clingy. I can wait until you want to see me again."

"You don't think I'm stalking you, do you?"

"No, silly. I'm just not used to having guys calling my house in the middle of the day. It will take some getting used to, but you can keep calling whenever you'd like. I like hearing your voice."

Marc thought really hard on how to phrase his next words. He prayed that his brain and tongue were going to cooperate. "I know with you working nights—" she cut him off abruptly.

"I just work Fridays and Saturdays. My Sundays are for me and my daughter. So ask your question now?" she said pleasantly.

He swallowed hard trying to get rid of the lump in his throat. "I…I just wanted to see when we might be able to do a nice dinner together?"

"This weekend I'm busy, but…" there was a long silence before she spoke again. "I'm going on a picnic Sunday with my daughter's soccer team. I'd love for you to come and meet my daughter. The kids will be playing most of the time and we can sit under a nice tree and talk. You'll see the real me. I'm a great mom and love everything about it. Think about it. I know this kid thing can be quite scary."

Marc felt uneasy. He wasn't sure he was ready to meet her daughter. His thoughts flashed to the wild and funky sex with her mom. It just didn't feel right. "Maybe some other time. Call me when you have some time alone and we'll do dinner," he said sounding a little hurt.

Lisa did not respond right away. The long hesitation had him thinking he said something wrong. He wondered if he had hurt her feelings. "Did I say something wrong?" he asked breaking the silence.

"No, nothing like that. I just allowed my feelings to get away from me for a second there. I guess having you meet my daughter is going way too quick with our friendship. How's next Tuesday for dinner? You choose the restaurant."

"Tuesday sounds great. How about Vigalucci's at Tamarack and Coast Highway, say around eight?"

"That will work. See you then. I miss you Marc," she said, then the phone was disconnected.

He spoke to the dial tone. "I miss you too."

As soon as he had put the phone in its cradle it rang again. "Hi, did we get disconnected?" Marc said happily.

"I don't think so. Marc, it's Lou," she said pensively.

He was surprised to hear her voice. "It's about time stranger," he tried to sound friendly, but his voice rang with betrayal.

"I feel so bad not calling you back. I was worried sick about you. Doctor Kaplan told me that you couldn't speak to anyone in your condition. I was scared for you and didn't want to do anything that would harm your recovery."

Marc wasn't buying her bullshit. She knew what was right and what a friend was supposed to do for another friend. "I find your excuse unacceptable. Do you even know what I was going through? First, I didn't even know if you were all right. After my blackout I thought something horrible happened to you. Kaplan's an asshole and should not have tried to control me or you."

"I'm so sorry. You're right. I should have known better. Please forgive me?" she said in the most sincere voice.

It was hard for him to stay mad at Lou. She had been there for him for the last five years. "I guess so. Do you want to meet me for a drink or dinner or both?" he asked.

Without any hesitation she replied. "What time do you want to meet today?"

He smiled. It felt good talking to her. "I'm driving back from my condo in Palm Desert in about an hour. We could meet at Meritage in Encinitas, say eight-thirty. It might be busy on a Friday night, but we could drink at the bar until they seat us. See you then. I've missed you."

"I've missed you too, Marc."

* * * * *

Nora was furious about what Brad had told her. "Marc's becoming such a bastard," she shouted over the phone. "If he thinks he can hook-up with a whore that has a kid and a bitch that owns a fucking restaurant, he got another think coming. Just no fucking way will this happen. When you find out where and when he's meeting those two bitches…I want to know," she screamed before slamming the phone into the its cradle.

FORTY-SIX

The night's sky was illuminated by the rays of the full moon, bouncing off the Pacific Ocean at Moonlight Beach. It gave Marc time to contemplate the three women in his life, as he gazed out on the whitewater that pounded the sand. Some people like disorganization in their lives and some like things put in a perfect place. For Marc, the new Marc, he seemed to like complicated women. His mind ebbed and flowed like the ever changing ocean, as he thought of Nora, Lou, and Lisa. He felt bewildered and overwhelmed, trying to make sense of his life. But it was the blackouts that scared him most of all.

More and more he was beginning to believe he was another person with some form of amnesia. The voice inside his head did not seem to be a friendly one.

His inner voice was making it hard for Marc to be decisive. Even attempting to walk through new doors, take on new relationships, Lou and Lisa, it was not easy for him. He kept second guessing himself. Should he divorce Nora? Should he let his relationship with Lisa flourish? Or should he stick with his friend Lou, who had proven to be someone he could trust? He wanted everything. The divorce, Lisa and Lou, but knew that would be impossible.

Divorcing Nora was inevitable and had to happen if he was to begin to enjoy his life. He fully understood that a loveless relationship was not an option. Attempting to choose either Lou or Lisa, well, that was going to be difficult. At the moment he was being lulled to sleep by the crashing waves. "I shouldn't have to decide who to see, or who to share my lustful cravings with," he muttered, wondering if that was the voice talking.

Marc had never understood the *Harry met Sally* philosophy: That friends can't be lovers too. The decision had been made. He clapped his hands. He was going to go with what feels good and let his life just unfold in front of him.

He glanced at his watch. He had fifteen minutes before he had to meet Lou at the Meritage Restaurant. He felt sure of himself and would just go with the flow of the evening and see where it would lead him.

The bar was packed—a solo barstool had his name on it and he claimed it. Brian and Jacinto, the longtime bartenders, were performing their magic, especially with the ladies. Both bartenders made great Lemon Drops, but Jacinto was the showman, pouring two shakers simultaneously into two martini glasses without spilling a drop, and at the same time able to flirt with his two gorgeous customers. Marc knew that the show would become a memory when the martini touched the lips and its sweetness brought a satisfying smile to one's face.

Meritage was a neighborhood restaurant that had the best happy hour bar and food, all at half-price, and a five-star food menu to die for. While the bar was full, there were enough tables available for dinner, so Marc wasn't too worried he and Lou would not be able to be seated.

Marc sipped his gin and tonic, a little manlier than a lemon drop, even though he loved Lemon Drops. He was becoming a bar-fly, on the make, and had an image to create. And, foo-foo drinks would not cut it right now.

Coming through the door was Lou. She was not as pretty as Lisa, but she had a regal refinement about her. He had almost forgotten how beautiful she looked. The tight red jersey dress she had painted on adhered to every curve on her body perfectly. Her femininity oozed from every pore. Seeing her reminded him of why he liked her. He was now more confused. *How am I going to juggle two women?* He thought

"Hi sailor. New in town?" Lou teased, her smile exploding on her face.

Marc couldn't speak at first. His mouth felt like it had cotton balls, as he attempted to reply with the same bravado as Lou. "You...you look great," he finally said. He couldn't stop staring at her dress. "Wow, you look fantastic in that dress." He blushed, as his mind flashed back to Lisa and how she had dressed when they met in the desert.

She cutely said, "This old thing. I'm way too fat to even wear such an outfit."

Marc rolled his eyes. "Yeah, right. Why can't women take a nice compliment without responding with a negative putdown? A simple thank you would work well in this situation," he joked.

Lou smiled, while her face turned red. "I guess it's a girl thing. We women see our beauty in sections of flesh and imagination. We imbue our imagination with our longings and dreams and come up with our emotional insecurity of not looking our best. Plus we want to hear the men in our lives convince us that we're just so perfect."

Marc laughed at her explanation. "Blah, blah, blah. I don't get it. You must have a funhouse mirror you're using to check yourself out, because there is no way you have any fat oozing through that dress," he said without hesitation.

Lou pursed her lips before she replied. "Look here," she pulled at some imaginary extra skin on her hip. Now look at my Gila Monster arms," she continued—her arms rose at ninety degree angles, and then she proceeded to flap her loose triceps muscles wildly. "See what I mean?"

"Oh, brother. That is not a pretty picture," Marc said, trying to hold back his laughter with his hand. Everyone at the bar was now staring. "You've made your point. That visual is forever etched on my brain," he moaned.

They were seated rather quickly. "That's a great trick you have there to get a table. We should try it again sometime when we don't have reservations somewhere. I've never seen so many men frightened. All you had to do was a high-pitched wale and you would have cleared the entire restaurant."

Lou's face turned bright pink down to her neck. "Just trying to make a point," she said humorlessly.

That's what Marc liked so much about Lou. The way she could laugh at herself or was it her self-confidence…maybe both. He wasn't really sure. "Let's agree that when I compliment you, you just say thank you. Can you promise me that?" he begged, pressing his hands together.

Lou had a sheepish grin. "Does this mean you're not mad at me anymore?"

"It's hard staying mad at you. Let's just forget about what happened and move forward."

Marc's eyes drifted from Lou's to a gorgeous woman hanging on an elegant gentleman's arm. She was dressed in a slinky sundress, just cut above her knees and low enough to reveal enough cleavage to get his heart racing. There was something familiar about her body. Her face was silhouetted at first, until she was inside the dining room. Marc blinked a few times to focus. What he saw surprised him. It was Lisa.

Lisa instantly saw Marc and gave a casual wave. Lou craned her neck to see what he had been drooling over.

"You know that woman?" she said, a hint of jealousy in her voice.

"Yeah. Her name's Lisa. She's a new friend," he said. An ounce of embarrassment spilled off his tongue. "She was one of the women I met during my little altercation at the tavern."

Lou's eyes stared at him. "I can see that she's a little more than just a new friend. You're smitten with her aren't you?"

Marc felt his face flush. He felt guilty, like a kid caught with his hand in the cookie jar. "I've spent time with her," he said sheepishly. "You wouldn't return any of calls. What was I supposed to do? Does it really matter who I have as friends?" his voice rising a bit.

Lou's body had become rigid. She was noticeably upset. "I have no say over who you see or date," she said sarcastically. "I don't understand why you're being defensive?"

Marc was feeling his blood boiling and his anger building. His good feelings were starting to evaporate. The voice inside his head was taking over. He couldn't believe what he had said next. "We've been friends for a long time and now that we've become intimate you want to control me?" he said, instantly regretting how his words had come out. But, he couldn't control what came out next. His emotional bucket was overflowing. "I've been imprisoned for twenty-five years with a controlling bitch of a wife and don't want any part of that anymore. I can't for the life of me understand why women can't allow their friendship to grow into an intimate one?" His voice was echoing past their table, making heads turn in their direction. He was feeling like a monster was about to pop out of his skin and attack everyone in sight, including Lou. He tried to get control of himself, but it was not working too well.

Lou's eyes grew wide with horror at his tone. "I didn't know you thought of me that way." Lou bit her lower lip, her eyes had become glassy. She looked at Marc with contempt. "Don't ever raise your voice to me again," she said holding back her tears. You did it once before and I forgave you. Not this time. I just don't know who you are right now. You have a lot to learn about women. I promised myself that I would never sleep with a married man or for that matter, one going through a divorce. The fallout can be unbearable. I made an exception because you seemed like a nice guy, but I can see that was a mistake. I'm thinking that Dr. Kaplan was right about not seeing you. You have a lot of baggage to work on right now and I don't have the energy to deal with all that!" She was now sobbing, blotting her eyes with the tablecloth. She pushed her chair back harshly, tipping it over. "I've got to go," she said, then turned and rushed out of the restaurant.

Marc turned toward Lisa, shrugging his shoulders embarrassment cracking on his face. He felt sort of sad about what he had just done, but not totally. Lisa had a shocked expression. Her hand was cupped in front of her mouth.

Marc dropped his head unable to look at anyone in the restaurant. Then in the background came a loud clapping. He turned his head to see where the applause was coming from. Nora was standing up at her table, cheering her husband's performance.

"See what happens when you leave me Marc Richards?" she bellowed. "Are you going to beat her like you beat me when I didn't do what you wanted?" she yelled, raising her arms above her head. "See what that bastard did to me," she shouted, lifting her blouse revealing her discolored torso.

Marc felt sick to his stomach. He felt mortified. He knew that it was Nora's same baseless story, but he still had no memory about that incident. Even though it was a false report, a fabrication by a sick mind, it didn't matter to all the people at the restaurant. He looked guilty. He once again exposed his violent side to Lou for a second time and hoped Lisa did not believe Nora's false accusations.

A cool hand lifted his chin. He looked up to see Lisa's smiling face. "You should leave," she said calmly. "I guess that's your wife. She's setting you up. If you stay here any longer it's going to get worse. There's nothing you can do to make this situation better. Call me later. I'll be done around eleven. We can talk." She leaned down and kissed his cheek.

"Thank you," he said, his voice cracking. He thought it would be hard seeing her "working", but she had such a caring loving smile that none of that mattered.

* * * * *

Nora pranced over to Lisa and whispered in her ear. "Stay away from him. You have a nice little girl that won't do well in foster care, you whore bitch."

Lisa had turned white as a ghost. "You stay away from my daughter or you'll be sorry," she said with an even tone. It took her by surprise that Marc's wife even knew about her or that she had a daughter.

Nora smiled menacingly. "Just fair warning. Marc's all mine and will always be mine. So fuck off and leave him alone. He's confused enough."

Nora made a phone call to Gail and Rita while sitting in her car furious at Marc for all he was putting her through. "I have something for us do tonight." She barked out the address and closed down her cell.

FORTY-SEVEN

It was past midnight and Lou could not stop crying. "What a jerk I was," she mumbled to herself. She had lost all track of time.

She knew about her jealous side and wished she had controlled it. As with her previous husbands, she ended the relationship at the first sign of infidelity. Real or imagined, it did not matter. She thought Marc was different. He had a good heart and she just stepped on it, scraping her feet on his vulnerability.

A loud pounding on her front door put a smile on her face. "Marc," she called out, happy he might be coming over to talk. Without looking through the peep-hole, she opened the door, only to be pushed back roughly by three attackers all wearing ski masks, all dressed in black.

One of the attackers kicked her hard in the abdomen, while another clobbered her with a gloved fist. She fell on the tile floor, banging her head, the impact rattling her teeth. Lou, for the first time in her life, was terrified. Her heart was racing wildly, trying to figure out how to survive.

Without warning and with callous abandon, the three attackers let loose with a barrage of punches and kicks, directing their blows on her face and body. The searing pain was devastating, it was not allowing Lou to think straight or protect herself. She felt her warm blood forming a pool around her hair. It was at that moment she realized she was going to die. She tried to lift herself up, but a heavy boot pressed against her throat. She couldn't breathe, gasping for air. She tried opening her eyes hoping to catch a glimpse of who was beating her to death, but with each strike she closed her eyes tight. Her head ached and her eyes had become glassy, filling with blood with each blow. She tried to look for a scar, or the color of their eyes, anything that could help identify them to the police, but the barrage was non-stop.

Her eyes had now become swollen, affecting her ability to see. She did notice one of the attackers had excessive amounts of black mascara, outlining the eye sockets of her mask, as if she had rushed putting on her makeup. Another attacker was taking off one of her gloves. She was complaining about her broken fingernail. The third attacker must have notice Lou staring at them and with a menacing grin, kicked her hard on the side of her head.

That final blow brought unbearable pain over Lou's entire body, and then numbness blanketed her. Lou gave into the realization that there would be no hope of living through this attack. She was unable to feel her legs or arms. It did not take long for the pain to subside and the room to get dark. She thought of Marc and whispered a good-bye to her friend. An eerie silence filled Lou's head and then it was quiet.

One of the attackers opened a zip-lock baggie and dropped its contents over Lou's twisted body. The attacker with the broken fingernail brought the phone over and pressed Lou's curled finger on the keypad and dialed 911.

"Help," the attacker said in a low gravely pained voice and stopped talking.

One of the other attackers whispered. "That's enough. When the police don't get a response, they'll dispatch a patrol car and find her body. Let's get out of here. We've done what was needed. Marc will have to explain himself once again to the police."

FORTY-EIGHT

Chip Campbell had been with LAPD for thirty-five years before starting his own PI agency. It was not the same as the great detective work he had once done, but it paid the bills and kept him out of trouble.

Most of his cases were about cheating spouses, or tracking down deadbeat dads. But, this case was proving to be more interesting and showing great potential for real detective work again. He had turned up more than he had expected about Nora's past. Her real name, Rebecca Morgan, had been tied to an unsolved murder thirty years ago, when she was still in high school.

The West Covina police file was extensive and the detective's report showed the murder of a Brad Stevens, an All-American high school quarterback was Rebecca's Morgan's (Nora's) boyfriend. The violent murder was still unsolved and listed as a cold case. Back then there was no DNA testing, so all they had was the burnt body of a young male with Brad's build.   No one had looked at the file during last three decades. Chip was surprised that there was no dental records on file. He was caught off-guard that Steven's file had a medical report that showed he had been suffering severe blackouts prior to his brutal murder. "Interesting," Chip said. "Not sure what it mean just yet, but it must mean something or the detective would not have written down."

Back then, Rebecca Morgan was the first suspect the police looked into. She had threatened Brad in public on numerous occasions. Screaming that she'd never let him leave her. She had motive and the rage to commit the crime, except that she was with her two friends, Rita Thomas, who back then was Blanche Ruiz, and Gail Sparks, who was really Carla Shortz. With Rebecca's alibi, the police ran into a dead end.

Chip had searched the unsolved crime files of the FBI, using certain keywords and discovered that two years later at the University of Davis there was a similar unsolved murder connected to Nora, Rita, and Gail. This time it was Rita's boyfriend. Again, the three of them all confirmed their whereabouts the night of the murder. They once again had perfect alibis.

Campbell was now chomping at the bit, when he discovered that Gail had accused her psychology professor of rape, similar to what Nora had done back in high school, and the professor turned up dead after the jury had found him not guilty. The police looked at Gail as the prime suspect. Again, the gang of three covered for each other.

Studying the case file a little bit more, Chip could see that the FBI agent felt he was on to something and kept the case opened. The file was sketchy, with lots of holes in it, but Chip believed he was beginning to see why the three of them had to disappear and change their identities. Apparently, the agent was beginning to tie in the other two murders, just like he was, but before he could do anything about it he died in a freak car accident. This was too much of a coincidence and made Campbell nervous.

Chip suspected that Marc's Aunt and Uncle's death and Ashley's disappearance had to be connected to Nora and her friends. Proving it and tying them into the other deaths would be difficult, but not impossible, he thought.

He called a friend at the FBI and asked him to check out the three names, hoping he'd find more on Rebecca or Nora and expose her for who she really was. He wanted to proceed cautiously, realizing that the three women were like a pack of wolves, vicious to the core, with an uncontrolled thirst for blood.

He hoped that the puzzle pieces would start fitting together after he got more of the facts about Marc's aunt and uncle's death and Ashley's disappearance. He did not know what significance the unsigned letter Marc had given him would have on his investigation, but if past experience told him anything, he just needed to find the one major puzzle piece and the entire case would become clear.

Chip Campbell bit his lip as he remembered his sordid past as a detective. The pounding rain on the window in his small living room was triggering too many memories he had tried to bury. The weather outside mirrored his feelings, bringing up the blackness and desolation he had felt after being dismissed from the Los Angeles Police Department.

Fighting back the urge to put his fist through his wall, he watched a couple covering their heads with a newspaper, running for their car along the deserted sidewalk. The night his wife had left him, after the scandal that rocked the LAPD, had been the day the worst rain storm in Los Angeles history hit. His head had begun to throb, thinking of how his desire to put away the bad guys had changed his life and had ended his marriage.

During his first years as a new cop, he was naïve and gung-ho about solving crimes within the confines of the law. As he matured and got promoted to detective, he could no longer watch guilty killers and rapists get off with just a slap on the wrist. He started to think outside the box, becoming creative with his evidence, and making sure the scum he arrested went to prison for a long time.

A cold sweat soaked his shirt, as he felt the urge to do whatever he could to put the three women away for life. But, this time he was going to do it by the book.

He heard his fax machine working and rushed over. The first file on Nora was printing up. "Shit, I knew it," he said slapping his leg. Then the next two files spewed out and he had to sit down. His case had just gotten bigger and more dangerous. He wanted to call his friend at the Carlsbad police department. He'd need his support, but it would have to wait until he had more concrete facts and convincing evidence. He did not want to be out of the loop and knew if he reported his findings too soon—it would become a police matter. Campbell wanted to solve these cold cases and get some needed retribution.

Chip called Marc and got his answering machine. It was six-thirty in the morning and he was surprised Marc wasn't home. "Marc, we need to meet immediately. I don't want to discuss it over the phone. Be careful and watch your back. What I've found out about your wife and her friends is bone chilling. Your life could be…no…most definitely is in danger," Campbell said nervously. "I'll be at the Armenian Café in Carlsbad by nine. I have a shit pile of stuff to show you."

FORTY-NINE

Rita and Gail had been sitting in front of Marc's apartment for an hour monitoring his phone when they heard the call from Campbell.

Rita looked at Gail, her face white as snow. "Do you think Campbell really knows?" asked Rita.

Gail shrugged her shoulders, fear etched on her face. "Something has that ass-hole scared. Whatever he has, we have to get it before he shows it to Marc. I don't think Brad's coming back anytime soon and there's no telling what Marc would do with the information. We had this before when Marc realized we killed his Aunt and Uncle and he slipped into a terrible rage. When Nora hit him with the baseball bat and he was knocked out, we were lucky he lost his memory. What if this information brings him back to that day, he'll kill all of us," Gail said, sucking in deep fast breaths.

Gail was making Rita pace in circles. For the first time she was showing signs of nervousness.

Rita was a cold, vicious and vindictive human being, never frightened, never scared, but the thought of being exposed, igniting Marc's rage, put her in a spiraling panic. "Here we go again, moving, and I was becoming comfortable living by the ocean." she said frustrated. She slipped back into the car and pounded the steering wheel hard, lost in thought.

Gail slid her back against the passenger door and crossed her arms across her chest. "I've not seen you this way in a long time. I'm not ready to pack up and leave again. I like my new life. There's got to be another way."

"Right now I can't think of any," said Rita. "We made a promise a long time ago that if we had to leave town, we'd all go together. If Nora decides that we're leaving…then we're leaving. You don't have an option," Rita said her tone threatening.

Gail turned white as a ghost. "What if we kill Campbell before he sees Marc? Then all of this will go away? Don't you think it's worth a try?" she pleaded.

"Maybe." Rita dialed Nora and filled her in on what they had heard. The profanity from Nora resonated inside the car. "I'm not leaving until I'm ready to leave. There's too much unfinished business to attend to. If you're sure he knows, then dispose of Campbell and everything in his apartment. We can't go anywhere until my divorce is final and I have Marc's money."

Rita hesitated before responding. She knew not to object when Nora made up her mind. She was not ready for one of her vulgar lashings. "We'll head over to Campbell's and check it out. If he's not there and with Marc…are you ready to dispose of your husband if it comes to that?"

Nora expelled a long breath. "Let's cross that bridge after you've dealt with Campbell. First I need to find out if I'm the primary beneficiary on Marc's life insurance, then that decision will be a no brainer.

Rita moaned. "You know we've saved enough money. You've been skimming money from your accounts for over two years. Let's not get too greedy. We can't keep acting as our alibis. The police have computer programs now that can show patterns and then figure out that we've done this before" Rita said, her voice showing signs of exhaustion. Gail grabbed the phone from her.

"Nora, I don't want to leave. I'm happy here. I've got a kid and a good husband—" Gail's eyes grew wide with fear hearing Nora's menacing scream.

"Look, I say when we leave or stay. You know what will happen if you don't come with us. There's no choice. We can't have any loose ends. You're in way too deep to be left on your own. You don't have a choice," said Nora coldly.

Gail face had drained of color listening to Nora's threat. "Don't threaten me. I've been loyal to both of you. Why would I jeopardize our safety? It's time we thought of another solution instead of running away. We're heading to Campbell's now and we'll let you know what we find."

"Let me talk to Rita," she said coldly.

"What?" Rita said her tone edgy.

"Watch Gail closely. She might be a liability. Don't let her be on her own. I want you killing Campbell and destroying his apartment."

"Yeah, right. I'll call you when we're finished.

FIFTY

Nora bit her lower lip hard, drawing blood, trying to control a blood curdling scream. She felt sick. She peered through her kitchen window trying to see through her watery eyes. "This can't be happening again," she murmured. It took all her concentration just to stay calm. Yet the events of the past few weeks kept intruding, taking her mind back to a time she had wanted to forget.

Her memory transported her back to her standing on the roof of her childhood house remembering the first time her uncontrollable temper flared. In her arms was her mother's Persian show cat: the animal that got more attention than she did. Without any hesitation, she snapped its neck and tossed it in the air. It dropped on the driveway like a sack of potatoes.

Listening to her mother's screams had given her a personal sense satisfaction. She pretended to be interested in her mother's grief, but the look on her mother's face, her fear showed that her mother knew that her daughter was sick.

Her mother a whore and crack addict wanted to send her away, but had plans for her when she got a little bit older.

Nora's cell rang, bringing her back to the present. It was Marc. She smiled as she answered. "Marc, sweetie, I'm so glad you called. I've been thinking about you. I miss you so much," she said seductively.

Marc sighed hopelessly. "Cut the crap. I don't know what kind of game you're playing, but you better stay away from my friends. Our marriage…our life…if any rational person could call what we had a life, is fucking over," he shouted with a temper that Nora had not heard from him before. It was getting her excited. He was reminding her of Brad.

Marc ignored her. "I know you have a past that you and your friends want to hide and it doesn't matter to me. You'll get what you deserve from our divorce. Just be a good girl and not complicate the process. Stay away from Lisa or you'll be sorry," Marc said coldly.

"Marc, there has to be something I can do? I want you back. I can change. I know I can. I've been a bitch for so long and you deserve better from me."

"You've got that right."

"I need you now more than ever. I didn't want to tell you this, especially with your heart problem, but I saw my doctor yesterday," she paused sucking in a deep emotional breath. I have breast cancer. I start radiation next week and chemo after that. I'm probably going to lose all of my hair and be hideous. I'm so sorry to do this to you. When I saw you with your new girlfriend at Meritage, well I just fell apart. I don't think I can handle this alone?"

Needless-to-say, Marc was shocked by her news. "Sorry to hear about your cancer," he said with a sincere sadness in his voice. He was feeling himself being beamed back to her. His head was spinning out of control. Like a whirlpool, she was sucking him down with her. "I don't know what to say. How long have you known?"

Nora sniffled loudly. "I've been feeling weak for a few years, thinking it was a hormonal thing. I couldn't control my mood swings and you suffered for it. I'm so sorry."

"Answer my question. How long have you known you had breast cancer?"

"I was afraid to go to the doctor. I waited too long. The doctor said something about stage-four. I'm not sure. Maybe we could go together and you can ask her what it all means. I get too nervous and scared when my doctor explains things to me. I just block out her words."

"Something just doesn't make sense here. You've not appeared sick. This isn't one of your manipulative games you've put me through over the last twenty-five years?"

Nora tried to contain her anger at his accusation. "Could you just come over? I don't feel comfortable talking about this over the phone."

"Maybe. I need to first digest all of this. I have some serious trust issues with you. I'll call you back later. I'm meeting a friend for breakfast and won't make any commitment to you just yet.

Nora stared into her phone, listening to the dial tone. She knew he was suspicious, but was confident her performance was stellar. She checked the magazine on her Beretta. It was loaded. "He'll be here," she whispered. "What's a poor girl to do, but defend herself from a wife-beating bastard like him?"

FIFTY-ONE

The sun was just rising, igniting the sky with an orange glow, as Campbell bounded out of his apartment. Today was unlike other mornings when he left his home. Instead of panning his surrounding, looking for danger, trying to see if anything was out of place today, he had too much on his mind, positive things as he rushed to his car.

The eastern sunrise was exceptionally bright, illuminating the dark blue sky, with tints of oranges and pinks that was not engulfed by the typical early morning marine layer.

He was heading toward his garage squinting unable to focus, his tired eyes struggling to adjust. A few loud car horns and one siren from an EMT bus drowned out the approaching footsteps. Just as he reached his garage door a sharp burning sensation shot through his lower back. He thought he had pulled a muscle or his sciatica was acting up. He reached back to massage away the burning pain only to feel a warm wetness seeping through his Hawaiian shirt. Surprised to see blood on his hand he turned around quickly only to be confronted by two hooded attackers. He tried to block the first blow, but the second attacker was faster and thrust a sharp object through his ribcage puncturing his heart. Campbell's eyes grew wide, terror exploded on his face and he fell like a ragdoll on his driveway. It was over quickly.

Rita opened his briefcase and pulled out all the manila folders he had, while Gail searched his pockets for his apartment keys. "We need to see if he made duplicates."

Rita nodded while she searched his attaché case. "Good idea. I'll drag him into his garage and you check out his apartment.

Remember to put on your latex gloves." Rita was remembering what Nora had said about not trusting Gail, but she had to drag Campbell's body into the garage. It was a simple assignment. It was something Gail could complete.

Gail was inside his apartment searching his desk, checking his computer files, frustrated she didn't find any of the files in the computer's index. "Was he that disorganized that he did not make copies?" she muttered sweeping his papers and junk off of his desk.

She was startled when his phone rang. She stopped and held her breath, as if the person leaving the message would hear her breathing.

"Chip, Marc here. Got your message. I'll be at the Armenian Café in forty-five minutes. I have to get cleaned up. Stayed out way too late last night talking with a friend. Can't wait to see what you've found."

Gail gave the apartment one more look through and returned to the car. "No copies or any files on his computer," she whispered. "Marc's in for another surprise. He called confirming his appointment with Campbell." Gail giggled.

Rita pursed her lips, her brow furrowed in puzzlement. "You did erase Marc's message?"

"No. I didn't think I had to."

Rita was deep in thought. "Don't you think it should be erased?" Rita asked. "The machine has a time imprint."

Gail swallowed hard. "He said that he was with a friend talking last night. Maybe it will alert the police that Marc, yet again, is connected to what happened to his friend Lou?" she said, her voice cracking.

Rita shook her head, disgusted with Gail. "Did Marc say what friend he was with, you moron? If he wasn't with Lou then he might have an alibi."

Gail wrinkled her nose, deep in thought. "I'll go back and erase the message"— Rita grabbed her shirt sleeve.

"Let's get out of here. We need to talk to Nora. We can always come back later. Just our luck that Marc was with that Lisa bitch."

FIFTY-TWO

Marc had been waiting for two hours at the Armenian Café, sitting outside on their patio under an umbrella trying to remain focused and clear. He was starving and couldn't wait for Chip any longer. He knew what he wanted to eat. He liked opening up their unusual menu, the 8 ½ by 11 photo of a buxom belly dancer that always gave him a laugh, which he needed that at the moment.

Nora's cancer had become a distraction. He called Chip's home phone and cell four times, nervous that he was late. Marc's two sunny side eggs with hash browns had come quickly. With a little extra aggression, he destroyed the perfectly cooked yokes and with his fork and rye toast he mashed all of his food together hoping Nora was watching. "One for my side," he mumbled. Chewing his food he started to think about what Campbell had told him.

Chip had said his life might be in danger, but from whom? Not Nora. She was way too frail to be dangerous. Could it be Gail and Rita?

Marc drifted back to last night at Meritage. Was it just a coincidence that she turned up last night? Then to have the news of her cancer at this time was not making any sense. It seemed surreal. He knew he needed to see what Campbell had uncovered before he saw Nora.

Marc realized that beginning a new life after such a long and tumultuous marriage would not be easy. He never imagined that his normally calm demeanor would be connected to so much crap. He had been stabbed, arrested, accused of beating his wife, turned nasty to his friend Lou in a restaurant, and finally discovered new emotions with a prostitute. He felt like he was living inside the perfect soap opera.

With his memories coming back in bits and pieces, he could see that he'd been living inside a chaotic world longer than he had imagined. Feeling happy for himself had always been troubling. Who should he blame? Memories of his uncle's constant putdowns and emotional outbursts weighed heavy on him. Together with Nora's criticism and complaining, he couldn't rid his mind of the low self image he had.

The more Marc attempted to be strong, to stand up to Nora, she still tugged at his heart, not out of sympathy or compassion that a loving husband would have, but more from guilt that he was worthless and had no choices. Nora's most recent attempt to bring him back into her fold had him confused and befuddled. Having stage-4 cancer did not make any rational sense. The more he thought about her illness, the more he knew she was lying and trying to manipulate him. Nora was like a pesticide, killing whatever life that was trying to grow between them.

Either way Marc knew he was responsible for allowing Nora to treat him the way she did.   When he was with Lou or Lisa and away from Nora's clutches, he started to believe he was a nice guy. Those moments were fleeting. He just couldn't absorb the kindness they were trying to give him. His self doubt kept interfering with his desire to walk through new doors, slamming them shut.

Last night's melodramatic outburst by Nora once again had put him in a compromising light. She had always been skillful with her victim performance in the confines of their home. But this time she had exposed her ugly side to the world. This was not like her. Was her cancer real and affecting her emotionally, or just another manipulative attempt to control him?

Marc tried to think how Nora could have possibly known he was going to Meritage last night? He wondered if she had her own private detective following him. Right now, anything was possible. What were the odds of all three of them being at the same place at the same time? Something just didn't smell right to him.

All Marc could come up with was that he should have told her he was dating. He was trying to picture if that would have made a difference. The words of his divorce attorney exploded in his head: *"Nothing you do will ever make her like you or be nice to*

*you, so stop being such a pathetic fool. She hates your fucking
guts. Deal with it and get over it."*

His cell phone rang, snapping him back to the present. His heart
had started pounding reading the caller ID. It was Officer Perez.
Another woman in his life that wanted him strung up by his
testicles and whipped.
He answered in a cold tone. "Officer Perez, what can I do for you
this time?"

"You don't sound happy to hear from me," she said mockingly.
"I thought we were becoming such good friends?"

Her obnoxious tone gave him the chills. "My attorney doesn't
want me talking to you or your partner without him present. So
please call—" She rudely cut him off.

"We know that you and Lou Hart had a serious fight last night
at the Meritage Restaurant. Care to explain what happened?"

Marc bit his lip. He was puzzled how they even knew about
that. "Oh, my wife called you?" he said angrily. Officer Perez did
not respond.

"Can you account for your whereabouts between eleven last
evening, and say two this morning?" Her tone was now serious and
accusatory.

"Why do you want to know?"

"Mr. Richards, please answer my question."

He did not like where this was going. "I was with a friend until
five this morning."

Officer Perez sighed deeply. "If you can give us her name, so
we can verify your alibi—"

"Alibi? What's going on here?" he asked raising his voice. "Is
Lou okay?"

"Lou Hart was attacked. She was beat up to within an inch of
her life around 1:00 A.M. this morning. You were the last person
seen with her. So please stop stalling and tell us your friends name
so we can either arrest you or move forward with our
investigation."

Marc couldn't believe what he had just heard. He knew he
couldn't have done it. He was with Lisa. She'd verify it. So who
could have done this?

"Call my attorney. You've got his number. I'll give him her
name and address, but right now I've got to go," he said ending the
call abruptly.

Immediately, he dialed Lisa's cell. He needed to warn her that the police would be calling. Then he realized that he did not know her last name.

He was feeling guilty that her perfectly sheltered life was about to be turned upside down by him.

"Lisa, pick up the damn phone," he whispered. After ten rings, her voicemail clicked on. He thought of leaving a detailed message, but thought better of it.

"Lisa, it's Marc. Call me as soon as you get this message. It's important," he said in his most calming and relaxing voice, even though he was crawling out of his skin thinking about Lou.

FIFTY-THREE

Nora had cornered Lisa next to her car. Her daughter was sitting with her seatbelt fastened in the backseat. Nora put her finger to her lips, indicating to Lisa's daughter to remain quiet.

In a menacing tone, Nora spoke, her crazy rage showing. "I thought we had an agreement. You just wouldn't listen, would you?"

Lisa just smiled keeping her eyes focused on Nora. "Marc's divorcing you. Get over it and move on," she said calmly.

"It will never happen. Marc's a weak bastard and won't leave me. He tried once. Did he tell you that the first bitch just disappeared? Like the little coward he is, he ran back to me after his whore girlfriend vanished. When push comes to shove, he'll back out of the divorce," Nora said her voice quivering. "We have twenty-five years of a mixed history, mostly good, if I do say so myself. He'll never turn his back on a solid marriage like ours," Nora said swiping a lonely tear off her cheek.

"That's not what Marc's said. I really don't think you're listening to him. Maybe that's been the problem with your marriage?"

Lisa's cell started to ring. She glanced at the caller ID. It was Marc. "Here," she pointed, "Marc's calling. Perfect timing. You can speak to him if you'd like," she said, her tone challenging.

Nora's face turned beet red. Her face contorted with anger. "Don't answer it," she said quickly, lifting her blouse and revealing a gun in her waistband. "Here's the deal. You stop seeing my husband or I'll go to child services and report you as an unfit mother. Exposing your kid to a whorish life…well, child services frowns on such things. Don't challenge me, others have and lost. Do I make myself clear?"

Lisa felt the blood drain from her face. For the first time in a long time she had something to worry about. She had created a simple life for herself and daughter. Her work had been kept far away from home as possible. Now her house of cards was about to crumble at her feet all because she had met Marc.

Nora sensed a weakness and pounced upon it. "Picture your daughter living in one of those foster homes. They won't allow you to see her. What do you think it would do to her?"

Lisa was not one to cry or show her emotions to strangers. But, she couldn't control the tears that had started to roll down her cheeks.

Her daughter Melissa was watching intensely, her eyes wide with fright. She snapped off her seatbelt and opened the door, jumping to her mother's side. She shouted. "Leave her alone!" She was now screaming out of control.

Lisa put her arm around her daughter, allowing her to bury her face against her stomach. Melissa's screams had become muffled.

"Just go away and leave us alone," Lisa begged. "Don't do this in front of my daughter."

Nora just smiled and said. "Is Marc worth it? The police will be calling you wanting to know where he was last night. I know he was with you, but if you want me to be your friend, you'll have to forget that you ever saw him last night. I hope we have a deal?" she said, abruptly turning around and walking toward her car.

Nora turned to look back at Lisa and Melissa, and with a broad smile waved happily.

Lisa put Melissa back in the car. She sat silently behind the wheel gathering her thoughts. She glanced in the rearview mirror—her heart ached that her daughter might have heard what Nora had said.

"Who was that mean lady, mommy?"

"Just one of those adults I've told you about that have lots of problems. Don't you worry about anything. I'm going to call your uncle. She won't bother us anymore…I promise," she said crossing her fingers.

FIFTY-FOUR

After Lisa dropped Melissa off at school, she stopped at Pannikans', a converted train depot/boutique coffee shop off of Coast Highway in Leucadia—her cell phone was pressed tightly against her ear waiting for her brother-in-law, Detective Ray Allen of the Carlsbad police department to pick up.

Ray had remained a good friend to Lisa after his brother had died in Iraq. As Melissa's uncle, he spoiled her rotten. Lisa was sure he'd deal with Nora.

"Ray, it's Lisa," her voice was quivering. "I've got a serious problem."

"Lisa, calm down. What's up?"

Lisa took in a deep breath, but it wouldn't settle her nerves. "You know that I've been slowly closing down my business and turning over everything to Samantha, right? I've met a great guy. His soon-to-be ex-wife threatened me an hour ago…shit she had a gun."

"A gun? Did she show it to you? Did she get physical?" Ray's voice was getting louder.

"She never threatened me with the gun. Just made sure I saw it. It was mostly words. But, it was the way she said them. She even threatened Melissa." Lisa had lost whatever resolve she had. She was now sobbing. "I don't want Melissa going into foster care."

"How's that going to happen?" he asked.

"She's going to tell child services about what I do. That can't happen…or for Melissa to ever find out. That would kill me."

"Look, I've never liked what you had to do to make a life for you and Melissa since Duncan died, but you've done a great job keeping that part of your life separate from Melissa. You've done a great job as her mom and nothing's ever going to change that."

"But—" She interrupted him.

"No buts about it. All of your clientele would never confirm being with you. They would have more to lose than you. Let me have your boyfriend's name and phone number. I'll go talk to him now. Maybe I can find out what's up with his crazy wife?" Ray said, his tone soothing.

Lisa sighed deeply. "Thanks. She's a real nutcase. I'm scared that she'll come around again."

"I've got two detective buddies that owe me a favor. I'll have them hanging around when they get off their shift for the next week or so just in case she comes back. Don't worry about a thing. Just close down your business and live a long and happy life with my niece."

"Okay. My guy's name is Marc Richards. He's been under a lot of stress lately, so don't scare him, okay?"

Detective Allen laughed loudly. "I'll be my most charming self."

"That's what I'm worried about," she said.

* * * * *

Nora called Rita, totally upset. She was at the point of fainting, as she punched in her friend's phone number.

"Rita, you and Gail need to do something about that whore my husband's seeing. I tried to reason with her. I'm sure she's not going to listen," she sobbed.

"Stop the melodrama. It's me you're talking to. I know you better than anyone. You want us to do your dirty work, just ask," said Rita callously. "Have you decided what to do about Marc?"

"I'll be handling it. You just handle that Lisa bitch." Nora's tone had become seductive. "Be sure you remember every detail, you know how that turns me on."

"I've played your kinky game since high school. Whatever it takes to get you horny, sweetie," she said hanging up her phone. Rita immediately dialed Gail.

"Gail, we've got some loose ends to tie up. Be here in twenty-minutes," Rita barked into the phone, her tone left no room for argument.

Gail coughed nervously. "I can't. Not tonight. It's my kid's open house at school. I just won't miss it. Can't this wait?"

Rita moaned. "No it can't. Nora needs this done tonight or she's going to pass out."

"Well, I can't, not tonight. You'll just have to handle this on your own. It's not like you really need me anyway," said Gail sheepishly.

Rita let out a frustrated groan. "Go to your fucking kid's open house. It won't make you a better mother anyway," she said and then abruptly cut off the call.

FIFTY-FIVE

Marc couldn't wait any longer for Campbell. He wanted to go see how Lou was doing, but Officer Perez had told him that she was in ICU and not taking any visitors. He then decided to go to Chip's apartment. He knew that if something had happened to him, it would be another nail in his already oversized coffin.

He knocked at first a little too hesitantly against the weather-worn front door. Then he pressed the doorbell, but it didn't work. He gave the door three good bangs with his closed fist causing the door swing open. His heart started pounding, he was feeling dizzy. He knew this was not a good sign.

He called out. "Chip, Chip, Chip. He sounded like a nervous bird wondering if a large cat was going to attack. He was terrified and had every right to be. The apartment looked like a bomb had gone off inside it.

He tiptoed in, kicking the door closed with the back of his foot. *Don't touch anything,* he told himself. If something had happened to Campbell he did not want to leave any evidence that he had been there. He had just seen a Law and Order episode and felt comfortable that he had enough knowledge so he could enter and leave a crime scene properly.

After searching Campbell's entire apartment he remembered that he had left him a message earlier. He hoped the message was gone. It might mean that Campbell had been home…but then why didn't he show up at the restaurant? No message meant something was wrong.

He found a pen on Chip's desk and hit the message button on his answering machine. He heard his voice and immediately erased the message. If Chip was still alive he would tell him he was in his apartment.

He had taken a paper towel from the kitchen and opened the front door, wiping any area he might have touched. He stuffed it, as well as the pen in his pants pocket. He made a mental note to toss the pen and paper towel later. He wasn't sure if the police could pull his prints from a paper towel or if any of his perspiration had accumulated inside Campbell's apartment. He realized he was watching way too much Law and Order and CSI. Right now he wished his life would be a little bit more like Two and Half Men and not so much like the Sopranos.

He was walking back to his car, nervously looking around to see if any neighbors were watching him. He noticed a garage that had Chips apartment number on it. He didn't think that peeking inside was a crime?

At first, going from the bright sunlight into the dark garage made him blind. It took him almost a minute for his eyes to adjust. He massaged them a few times, until he had acclimated to the faint light. He jumped when he noticed a man's head behind the wheel of Campbell's car.

Marc faced the driver side window and immediately recognized that it was Chip, his chest covered in blood. He was becoming lightheaded on the verge of hyperventilation. He covered his nose and mouth with both hands.

Campbell's expression was frozen, his eyes wide opened and his mouth stuck in a silent scream. The pain on his face was real. Marc jerked back hitting a storage unit when his cell phone rang.

He bolted out of the garage unable to check the caller ID. His adrenaline was rushing through his veins, his pounding heart echoing in his ears had drowned out the ringing from his phone.

He was inside his car trying to take a few deep breaths to calm down. He was scared stiff.

He had just seen a dead body.

He had just broken into the dead body's apartment.

He was innocent, but felt extremely guilty. Calling 911 was the right and moral thing to do, however his survival instincts told him to flee and deal with it later.

As he sped away, his car fishtailing out of the parking lot, all the police dramas he watched were swimming inside his head once again. How was he going to explain why he didn't call the police when he first found the body? He knew he needed time to think.

He pressed hard on the accelerator skidding while making a right turn. He prayed that no one had been watching.

He went back to the Armenian Café and was seated in the same section with the server who had helped him an hour ago.

"You're back again," she said smiling.

"Went for a nice walk along the beach and got hungry again," he said awkwardly.

Marc's cell rang again and this time he picked it up immediately. "Hello," he said as calmly as he could under the circumstances.

"Is this Marc Richards?" the deep voice asked.

"Yes. And, who this?"

"I'm detective Ray Allen from the Carlsbad Police department. I'd like to talk to you if you have some time."

A cold chill blanketed his body. He could feel the moist sticky sweat dripping down his spine. He wondered if he was on the Carlsbad Police department's most popular list. Marc said, "I have an attorney. You'll need to call him to set something up," he said defensively.

"This is unofficial. A mutual friend asked that I talk to you. It seems that your wife Nora has made some threats that have scared my sister-in-law Lisa Cunningham."

He exhaled with relief. At least he now had her last name. "Why's my wife threatening her?"

"That's what I want to talk to you about. Right now Lisa's scared that your wife, Nora, will report her to child services…well I don't have to tell you what might happen. So, can we meet now?" Detective Allen asked.

"I'm at the Armenian Café, Coast Highway, Old Carlsbad, and eating lunch now. You can join me there."

"See you in fifteen minutes," said detective Allen.

FIFTY-SIX

Detective Ray Allen wore a serious expression, extending his hand in a congenial greeting. Flopping down at the outdoor umbrella table, he removed his San Diego Chargers ski hat and unzipped his windbreaker, revealing his shoulder holster that rested snuggly on his left side, maybe for intimidation, which made Marc squirm.

Marc couldn't stop nibbling his lower lip, a nervous habit he had perfected over the years living with Nora. Under the table he was nervously rotating the spot where his wedding ring had been affixed for twenty-five years, anxious about what the detective had to say.

Detective Allen was now staring, looking with malicious intent into Marc's eyes. His intensity was that of an attack dog. Marc's nerves had not unraveled since seeing Chip's bloodied body and things were beginning to come apart even further with detective Allen's deadpan attitude.

"For someone who's here unofficially, you're freaking me out with your staring and exposing your weapon. Like I told you on the phone I have an attorney that you can talk to—" The detective raised both hands feigning innocence.

"Just thirty years of experience," he pointed to his face, "etched on this tired face. Didn't mean to frighten you. Unless you have something to be frightened about," he said, the corners of his mouth curling ever so slightly in a grin.

Marc shrugged his shoulders, biting his lip so hard that he drew blood. "Since leaving my wife two weeks ago, I've been stabbed, arrested for assault. To top things off a friend of mine was attacked and is in critical condition. I've had two blackouts where almost ten hours of my life disappeared, and I've had two episodes with my heart that's landed me in the hospital. To make matters worse, if that could even happen, my wife has gone from a helpless victim, to going postal with Lisa, and now to make matters even more complicated getting a mysterious bout with cancer. I've become very paranoid. Can you blame me?"

Detective Allen rolled his eyes. "No, not really. Just try to relax so I can get to the bottom of what's going on with your wife."

Marc let out a slow nervous breath. "I'm just so tired. I just want a divorce and to get on with my life. When all of this started I didn't think that would be too much to ask for, but apparently it is?" he groaned.

"That's a lot shit," detective Allen said. "It's not uncommon for a jilted spouse to show her fangs. I've seen it a million times. Sometimes it subsides once she has a chance to see the reality of what's really going on and sometimes…well it can take an ugly turn. I'm here on behalf of my sister-in-law. I don't care too much about your divorce, just which way your wife is going with all of this."

Marc knew he needed to tell someone about what Chip Campbell had uncovered about Nora and her friends. Detective Allen seemed sincere. He decided that this was about as good a time as any to get it off his chest. "My divorce attorney, Lindsey Warren, had hired a PI. The other day he told me that he had discovered that my wife has a past that she's hiding. In fact, her other two friends are in the same boat with her. Chip—", Marc could see Allen was puzzled. "Chip Campbell, he's my private investigator…he believes that there's something that the three of them don't want anybody to know about. He called me earlier this morning and we were supposed to meet here. He said he has some important information to show me. But, he's not shown up. I'm a little uneasy about it, especially with all that's been happening lately."

Detective Allen smiled. "I know Campbell very well. He was my partner when we were with LAPD. He's one hell of a detective. Until the scandal that rocked the Parker building in Los Angeles, he was a god. I never wanted to believe what he was accused of doing, but when he resigned without benefits, well it destroyed our friendship. Anyway, if he found something, I'd be a little suspect about its credibility."

Marc saw an opening. "He had something to tell me. He also said that my life might be in danger. I've been waiting most of the day for him. He hasn't shown up. Do you think he's making all of it up?" Marc was now doing his own staring, trying to detect if Allen was buying his story. With Chip dead, it made Marc believe that what his PI had found was quite real.

"It's not like Chip to miss a meeting. He did start drinking a lot after leaving the force. Maybe he's sleeping one off right now. First, tell me everything about your wife, your marriage, and her two friends, and then we'll go over to Chip's place and rattle his cage."

They spent the next two hours sipping coffee and going over everything Marc could remember from the first day he met Nora. He even told him about his aunt and uncle's hit and run accident, to Ashley disappearance, and everything up to the present. Marc was impressed that detective Allen seemed genuinely interested.

"Got it," Ray said. "Let's go see Chip."

FIFTY-SEVEN

Marc couldn't stop his knees from trembling, as he stood in front of Campbell's apartment door again. He kept craning his neck toward the garage.   The visual of Campbell's body propped behind his steering wheel, his chest bloody, charged his nervous system.

Detective Allen banged on Chip's front door hard, his fist clenched tight. Slamming his fist in rapid bursts caused enough of a vibration that the door swung open like it had for Marc.

"I would take this as an invitation to enter the premises," he said slipping his hand inside his jacket gripping his gun. Marc watched intently, as Allen panned the room, caution stamped on his face. "Stay outside until I clear the room," he whispered. "I know that Campbell's a slob, but this isn't right. Someone's tossed his room looking for something…I don't like this."

Detective Allen had his gun by his side, pointed at the floor, as he stepped through the door slowly, turning his head from side to side, listening for sounds that were out of place. Marc's heart was racing, wondering if the person who murdered Campbell had returned, prepared to shoot an unwanted intruder. Detective Allen was now out of Marc's range of sight.

Marc was lost within his own worry, when Detective Allen tapped him on the shoulder, startling him.

"Uh, find anything?" Marc said his voice cracking.

"Campbell's not here. But, someone's been here looking for something. The apartment's too chaotic. There's no sign of a struggle, so I'll guess that Chip wasn't home when this happened.

Allen said, "Let's check the garage. You should call his cell again, just in case he's in a bar somewhere."

"I'll go get mine. I left it in the car," Marc said, with his most calm tone. He tried not to reveal what he already knew was inside the garage.

Marc nervously watched the detective peering through the four small garage windows using his police flashlight to get a better look. They heard the first ring of Chip's cell inside the garage and they both became stiff. Allen's gun was braced with both hands by his chest. On the second ring Allen hand signaled Marc to end the call.

Marc had started walking toward the garage, when Detective Allen once again gave him a signal like a traffic cop to stop.

Allen moved slowly, hugging the wall of the garage as he approached the side door of the garage. Without warning, the side door sprang open, knocking Allen backwards. He fell on the driveway his gun flying out of his hand. It skidded and stopped at Marc's feet.

The person standing over the surprised detective wore a black ski mask and a gray parka with tight leggings. The attacker appeared to be a woman of average size or a maybe a petite man with skinny legs. The masked woman pulled out a gun from under her jacket and pointed it at the Allen.

"Oh, shit," Marc muttered. "This can't be happening." He saw Allen's gun five feet from him and lunged toward it.

Marc was on his stomach fumbling, trying to steady his grip on the gun when he saw the attacker had placed the barrel of her gun against Allen's head. Marc had never shot a gun in his life, but had seen enough cop shows to know what to do.

"Don't think, don't rationalize, don't hesitate," Marc whispered as he lined up the masked attacker in his sights. The recoil vibrated through his body, as his trigger finger released three rounds.

The first bullet hit her in the right shoulder, causing her gun to discharge. He saw detective Allen fall over from the gun blast. Marc saw his next two rounds impact the attacker in the chest and neck. The impact of the bullets were powerful enough to drop the attacker hard against the cement driveway. Marc was breathing heavy.

At first Marc did not see Detective Allen moving. He was lying very still. He wasn't sure if the masked woman's gun had killed the detective? He saw some blood oozing from Ray's left shoulder.

"Are you okay?" he called out. Marc was relieved when detective Allen moved and propped himself up. He was noticeably hurt, but forcing himself to stand.

He was walking over to the lifeless attacker. "Where did you learn to shoot like that?" Allen asked, his left arm limp at his side.

"I watch way too many cop shows. It was a knee-jerk reaction." But, Marc knew at that moment it wasn't that. What he had done seemed familiar and natural, like he had done it many times before. With each round fired, Marc saw old memories flash across his eyes. Like a snake losing its skin, he was shedding the Marc he had grown comfortable with. He looked at Ray Allen and just shrugged his shoulders, trying to act shy about what he had just done.

"Good reaction. You saved my life," he said, his face white as a sheet.

"Does it hurt?" he asked, pointing at Ray's wound.

"Had worse gunshots than this one," he said matter-of-factly. Detective Allen bent over the attacker. He felt for a pulse and shook his head. He yanked off her ski mask, his anger showing. Marc was shocked when he saw who was lying in a large pool of blood.

Detective Allen fell back against the garage door, looking a little faint. He pressed his two-way and called for assistance.

Marc was now in a panic. If he would have told Ray the truth about Chip from the beginning this might not have happened.

FIFTY-EIGHT

Brad was dumb struck. He would have never imagined that Marc could have pulled the trigger on a gun, yet he did with a cold demeanor that made him proud.

Marc, even in his nervous, insecure, paranoid state, was evolving and it would be just a matter of time when he and Brad would be reunited. He just needed Marc emotionally stronger to be able to handle the truth about their relationship.

Brad knew it was now time for him to begin setting in motion the destruction of Nora so his protégé could come into his own.

He knew that Nora wanted him dead. He knew that the crazy bitch and her friends had to die so he and Marc could go back to being a fine-tuned machine of destruction. At least one of them was dead.

For his plan to work he had to walk on eggshells so Marc would adjust to his past and those horrible memories he's been blocking out. For Brad this would be easy. It was getting Marc to adjust to his past would be the difficult part.

What had Brad in a conundrum, was the fact that Marc had strong feelings for Lisa and Lou. For his plan to work, so he could step back out into the daylight, both those women had to be gone. He just needed to distract Marc long enough for Nora to do her part.

* * * * * *

Marc stared past detective Allen as the ER staff rushed him into their trauma room. His emotions were still spinning. He still

couldn't believe he had fired a gun…and one that had killed
Nora's best friend Gail. It didn't make sense at first, but things
were beginning to come into focus. He was starting to believe that
there might be something to what Chip Campbell had found out
about Nora and her friends.

Seeing Gail's horrid expression of death on her face had
triggered not a blackout, but a vivid flashback to the night his high
school friend was murdered. He realized that he had been there,
unsure if he had been an active participant, or a witness. He
remembered holding a baseball bat, standing over the bloodied
body of his friend. What Nora and her friends had done to his
friend that night was no longer being blocked out. He was
remembering how Nora (Rebecca) kept screaming at the
motionless body, spitting on him and yelling profanities. It was a
crazy mob hysteria that had triggered the brutal murder.

Brad had been there too. Then it all came flooding back. His
body started to shiver as his memory of his past exploded in front
of him.

Images of him and Brad made him lightheaded and forced him
to sit down on one of the ER's imitation leather armchairs in the
waiting room. Too many memories were cascading back. He was
beginning to feel sick.

The ER was packed: noisy children crying, a young man
passed out, and two handcuffed men who looked like they had
been fighting and in need immediate medical care. As Marc
flopped down, all the extraneous noises vanished, and he was
within his own world lost in a tornado of memories.

He cupped his head in his hands shocked and confused. It was
now becoming clear why for all those years Nora had brought her
high school sweetheart Brad into their marriage. And it had
become strikingly clear why she had faked Brad's murder.

Brad that night had done something horrible and needed to go
away. But, something about that night seemed more strange than
just the murder. Then more flashbacks were shooting around
inside his mind. He was seeing another murder: his mother and
father, as well as what really happened with Ashley's
disappearance. He then started seeing bits and pieces of his Aunt
and Uncle and their death, but nothing was really that clear.

However, the one connector that tied all of these deaths together
was Nora. At each specific moment those people had been the
catalyst that would have left her alone and abandoned. Something

she would not accept. It now made perfect sense to Marc why Nora stabbed him in a fit of rage once he told her he was leaving her.

Marc's eyes had become wide with fear. What had happened to Lou and Chip might be happening to Lisa right now and he had to warn her. He jumped up and ran out of the ER heading toward Lisa's house.

FIFTY-NINE

Rita parked her car a block away from Lisa's house. She was upset with Gail for not tagging along. It really didn't matter to her. She had killed before and did not need help.

Nora had not been specific on how she wanted Lisa killed. Rita thought it would be more humane to kill her daughter first, so the whore would go in peace knowing her daughter would not grow up in foster care.

However, compassion was not part of Rita's personality. When she planned her own parents' demise, she did not feel compassionate. The brutality of it was the result of years of physical abuse by her father and her mother's denial that it was even happening. It was supposed to be Nora and Gail's job to kill them back then. But, for personal reasons, Rita could not turn that over to them. She had too much rage inside her and needed to release it. She needed closure.

While her friends watched the brutal torture she had inflicted on her parents, she discovered that night a side of herself that gave her immense pleasure. That same sensation was now flowing through her veins approaching the back porch door of Lisa's house.

She heard talking and laughter in the kitchen. Lisa was preparing breakfast for her daughter. The smell of fresh pancakes and bacon was making Rita hungry. "A nice breakfast wouldn't hurt right now," she whispered. "I do get hungry after…" she hesitated before stepping up on the patio. She peeked through the window, verifying that it was just Lisa and her daughter inside the kitchen.

With the grace of a ballerina, she stepped lightly on each wooden step. While the wooden steps were warped from age and the damp beach weather, she was able to avoid making any creaking sounds. She gripped the doorknob finding it unlocked. Taking a deep quiet breath, she burst in. Her gun was immediately aimed at Lisa who was standing by the stove.

Melissa dropped her fork on the tile floor and filled the kitchen with a loud scream. Lisa turned abruptly, her eyes wide with disbelief, dropping the skillet with the sizzling bacon.

Rita's eyes were wide with anger. "Get over to your bastard child," she said in a menacing voice. "Now sit," she said, motioning with her gun.

"What do you want?" Lisa pleaded. "I have money. Take it, but don't hurt us, please."

Rita laughed mockingly. "Hurt you? I'm going to kill the two of you. First your daughter, so she won't have to watch her mother die. And, then you...but very, very, slowly so I can tell Nora how you begged for my mercy. You were warned to stay away from Marc and now you must pay," she said callously.

"Nora Richards sent you?" Lisa said with contempt.

"It doesn't really matter. The two of you will soon be dead and everyone in my life will be happy again. That's all that matters to me...making Nora happy."

Rita pointed her gun at Melissa. "Just close your eyes sweetie. You won't feel a thing," she said.

Lisa grabbed her daughter, holding her tight, her head burrowed against her mother's breasts. When she was born, her daughter suckled her first food from them. It was ironic that now she was about to die resting against her mother's breasts that had given her life.

Lisa couldn't stop pleading with Rita to spare her child's life. "Just kill me. I should be punished for not listening to Nora's warning. I'm the one, not my daughter," she sobbed. "She's innocent. Let her grow up." Her eyes were closed tight waiting for the explosion to happen.

"You're a whore and don't deserve to have a daughter. Sluts like you give women such a bad rap." Rita was not making any sense—her words irrational and incoherent. "Slide the fuck away from your daughter," Rita shouted.

Lisa did not listen, which made Rita even more furious. With the strength of a man, Lisa was pulled her by her long ponytail and dragged away from the kitchen table screaming. A loud explosion filled the kitchen, and Lisa felt a searing pain in her thigh. Rita had shot her in the leg.

Unable to move, she watched as Rita took aim at Melissa's head. Lisa closed her eyes unable to watch. "Sweetheart," she said softly with all the love she could muster trying to not show her fear, "We'll be together very soon. Don't be scared."

Lisa jumped hearing two loud bursts from the gun. Afraid to open her eyes, she buried her head in her hands. She heard her daughter crying and falling into her blood soaked lap.

Standing over the twisted body of Rita were two Carlsbad detectives, their shields dangling around their necks.

The first detective reached for Melissa who would not stop crying hysterically. She was holding her mother tight around her neck. Lisa's face was ashen. She was about to faint when the detective noticed the blood around her leg.

He brought his two-way to his lips. "I need a bus to 2217 Barcelona Ave. Civilian shot, another dead." His partner handed Melissa to him.

"It's going to be okay honey," he said, kissing her gently on the cheek. "I need to take a look at your mom. She's hurt and if you don't move I won't be able to help her."

He introduced himself to Lisa. "I'm detective O'Neil. Ray sent us to look out for you," he said calmly, as he pressed a dry kitchen towel on the wound. "An ambulance is on the way," he assured her. All he could see were her white globes. Lisa's eyes had rolled back. She had passed out.

His partner carried Melissa out of the kitchen and asked her to sit quietly on the couch in the living room. She was sobbing when she spoke. "Is my mom going to be all right?" she asked, her voice quivering.

"Detective O'Neil used to be a medic in the Army. He's seen worse. She'll be just fine. I'm detective Stanley. I'm a friend of your Uncle Ray," he said turning to go back into the kitchen.

"Is she going to be all right?" asked detective Stanley.

"The bullet hit her artery. She's losing a lot of blood. Where's the fucking bus?" Detective O'Neil shouted.

The two detectives heard the sirens in the distance. O'Neil had his fingers inside her wound, pinching the artery to slow her loss of blood. The kitchen floor was covered in blood, soaking the detective's pants.

"Get the medics in here and keep her daughter away. She shouldn't see this," O'Neil said. "Call Ray and tell him to meet us at Scripps Hospital."

Detective O'Neil searched for Lisa's pulse. It was faint. He knew she did not have much time. She had lost too much blood. "Stay with me Lisa," he pleaded.

The two paramedics were down next to O'Neil assessing her situation. "Where'd you learn to do that?" the first medic said.

"Desert Storm, 91," said O'Neil, as he continued to pinch Lisa's artery hard.

"Vitals are weak. We need to transport her now," the paramedic said nervously. She looked at O'Neil and asked. "Can you keep doing what you're doing until we get to the hospital?"

"Let's go," he said his voice unsure. "This is my best friend's sister-in-law and no way is she dying on me," he tried to sound confident.

SIXTY

Marc had not made it to his car when Ray's cell phone rang. He had forgotten that he was holding it for him. When he answered, the voice at the other end asked in an uneasy tone, "Who's this. Why are you answering Ray Allen's phone?"

Marc could hear in the background someone shouting: "Charge it to 250...clear."

"What's going on?" Marc asked fearfully.

Again the voice asked him who he was.

"Who the fuck are you?" he shouted into the phone. I want to know what's going on there."

"I'm detective Stanley. Now, who the hell are you and why do you have Ray's cell phone?"

"Marc Richards. Ray's in the ER. He was shot an hour ago."

There was a brief silence before detective Stanley spoke. "Is he going to be all right?"

"Just a shoulder wound, he's being patched up right now." Marc was afraid to ask, but he had to. "Are you the detective Ray had watching Lisa? Is Lisa okay?" he said tentatively.

"Not sure. The paramedics are doing everything they can to stop the bleeding. I can't talk. We just arrived at the ER." Then, Ray's phone went dead.

Marc couldn't believe what he had been told. He was numb with fear. He saw the ambulance screech to a halt by the Emergency Room bay doors. The back door sprung opened and two medics were yanking a gurney out, snapping the wheels to their upright position and running inside. Marc ran over to the ambulance. Someone was straddling Lisa, his hand inside her wound.

"What the fuck happened?" Marc barked.   When he didn't get an answer, he grabbed the detective's arm. "I'm Marc, you detective Stanley? What happened?" he asked extending his hand.

"Do you know a Rita Thomas?" his tone serious.

"She's my wife's friend and yoga instructor. Are you going to tell me what's going on?" Marc asked.

"Rita's dead. She shot Lisa in the leg right before she was going to blow away Melissa. We got inside in time and shot her."

Marc looked around and didn't see Lisa's daughter. "Where's Melissa?"

"She's with child services for now," he said detached.

Marc's heart sunk. He knew how Lisa felt about that and asked the detective to see if they could bring Melissa to the hospital. "She knows me and will feel safer being around me and her uncle."

"Let me see what I can do," detective Stanley said as he rushed into the ER.

* * * * *

Marc could hear Ray shouting at his friends. "How could you let her get by you?"

There was no response.

Marc noticed Ray slipping on his bloodied shirt, wincing in pain. He looked at the ER nurse and barked. "Where's my sister-in-law? I need to see her now," he said flashing his badge at her.

If anything could have made Marc's day worse than it had already been, it was seeing Lisa's unresponsive body on the gurney.

SIXTY-ONE

The garage was damp and dark. The Carlsbad PD and CSU officers eased their way toward Chip's car.   Blood had already caked on Campbell's shirt. The coroner checked the body's liver temperature and estimated he'd died around ten that morning.

A Carlsbad detective asked the CSU officer if he could look at the body before they did anything further. He knew that Campbell had been with LAPD and a friend of Ray's and wanted to make sure a fellow officer was not embarrassed. "No way for you to die," the detective said. He closed Campbell's frozen eye lids with his finger. He left the garage to allow the forensic team to secure the crime scene. He walked to his car and pulled out a roll of yellow tape every cop and detective carried and began cordoning off the area.

Something was bothering the detective about Campbell's murder. He had seen the initial blood spatter by the side garage door and the drag marks on the garage floor. In all his years of experience, the dead woman who tried to kill Ray did not appear large enough or even strong enough to have carried a two-hundred pound dead body that far, then lift him, and position him behind the wheel of his car. She wasn't working alone on this. He was sure of it.

* * * * * *

Marc did not see detective Stanley in the waiting room and pushed his way up to the nurse who was at her wits end answering questions from people who were complaining about their long wait. Marc had a fire in his eyes as he shoved a heavy-set woman and her boyfriend aside. "What the fuck?" the woman said angrily. She looked at her boyfriend, a White-Supremacist look-a-like, hoping to get some help from him. But, he just raised his hands and stepped aside. The woman tried to open her mouth to complain, until her eyes met Marc's. She too stepped aside and remained silent.

Marc rested both fists on the nurses counter and leaned forward. His voice was cold and menacing, as he asked her a question. "You just brought in a woman. I saw her go in. A gunshot victim? She's a friend. I have to see her," he demanded.

The nurse looked at Marc, emotionless and undaunted. "What's her name?" she asked with a cold monotone.

"Lisa Cunningham," he said.

"I don't see a Lisa Cunningham…" Marc cut her off before she could complete her statement.

"How many women just came in with a gunshot wound?" he said sarcastically, his voice noticeably loud. Before he could argue any further, a hand tapped his shoulder.

"I'm detective O'Neil. And, you are?" he said with suspicion.

Marc's eyes were wide with shock seeing the amount of blood on his shirt and pants. "Is that Lisa's blood?" he asked feeling his angina return. He fell back against the glass window that blocked the receptionist from the crazy people who wanted real answers to their questions.

"Answer my question, sir," he said more sternly.

"Marc Richards…I'm a friend. I was with detective Allen…when your partner called. Please tell me how she's doing?" he pleaded.

Detective O'Neil escorted him over to a chair in the waiting room. "Sit down. It's going to be while before we know anything. She's in surgery. The bullet punctured an artery in her leg. She lost a lot of blood. The doctors won't know until after surgery what her prognosis will be," he said. "Ray says you saved his life." He extended his hand. "You're a hero."

Sitting next to O'Neil was Melissa who had been brought to the ER by family services. She was sniffling, her head staring at the cold linoleum floor. She looked just like her mother.

Marc touched her arm gently. "Hi. Remember me? I'm Marc. Marc Richards, a friend of your mothers. We spoke the other day on the phone," he said.

She looked up, her blue eyes red from crying. "I remember. You sounded nice. My mommy was shot today. She's going to be all right. She's always told me that she'll be with me forever. I just know that she'll be okay," the young girl said holding back her true emotions. Marc saw her fear on her face.

Marc wasn't sure why he had put his arm around her, but it felt nice and it was the closest thing he had to Lisa at the moment. "You're mom's a fighter. I'm sure she's going to be all right also," he said kissing Melissa on the top of her head. She jumped off her chair and climbed on his lap, her thin little arms wrapped tight around his neck.

Feeling the softness of Lisa's daughter against his chest, sensing how scared she was for her mother, Marc's rage started to boil. He wanted to kill someone. Just then, as if a bolt of lightning had struck him in the head, he felt himself split apart. He closed his eyes and could see clearly, Brad staring at him and clapping, a big smile on his face.

SIXTY-TWO

Nora had not heard from either Rita or Gail, and was pacing across her living room, franticly worrying that they had failed. They were supposed to have checked in four hours ago. She checked herself in the mirror above her sectional couch, fluffing her hair, her most seductive look, mumbling to herself. "I just bet they blew it," she moaned.

Nora's mood was turning sour as each minute ticked. "Where the fuck, are you two?" she shouted at the telephone.

She dialed for the third time, Rita's cell, and got her voice mail once again. Then she dialed Gail's and got the same result. She tried text messaging them with no luck. She frantically called Gail's husband Peter, but he thought his wife was with her.

"She left early this morning. Said she was spending the entire day with you and Rita. She did say that she had a few errands to run before. Maybe she's tied up at some sale…you know how much she loves Chico's," he said sounding not too concerned.

"Oh, yes, I forgot. She was going to handle something for me before getting here. Sorry to have bothered you Peter," Nora said sweetly. "Jerk," she said, slamming the phone back into its cradle.

Finally, her phone rang and it was Rita's caller ID. "It's about time you called," she yelled. "Did you get it done? Is the bitch—" she was cut off before she could say another word.

"Mrs. Richards, this is detective Allen of the Carlsbad police department. What did you mean by *Did you get it done?*

Nora felt the blood drain from her face. "Detective Allen? Did something happen to Rita?" she asked nervously trying to deflect his question.

"She's dead. She was shot by the police while she was trying to murder my sister-in-law and niece. Now answer my question."

Nora hesitated before she responded. She was trying to come up with a logical answer. "She was going to Goodwill for me. You know the one on La Costa Avenue before the 5 freeway? What do you mean she's dead?" she said, a casual air in her voice.

He ignored her question. "I have a witness that puts you threatening Lisa Cunningham yesterday in front of her house. The next day a friend of yours tries to kill her. Now don't give me this bull-shit about the Goodwill. What the fuck did you mean by, "did you get it done?"

Nora tried to catch her breath. Her usually cool controlled demeanor was beginning to shatter. "Are you accusing me of something?" she barked back.

Detective Allen found it peculiar that the woman he was talking to did not show any emotion about her friend just dying. He figured he would give her some more bad news.

"Your other friend...Gail Sparks, or should I say...Carla Shortz, tried to kill me this afternoon. Now she's dead too. And, we believe that Rita and Gail killed Chip Campbell a private investigator," he said, his voice showing his anger. "Do you know anything about that, too?"

Nora was speechless. For the first time in a long time she was at a loss for words. "I have to go now. I can't talk. I'm too upset." She slammed the phone down hard on her coffee table. She ran to the bathroom and threw up her lunch.

She couldn't comprehend that her friends were really dead. They had always been there for her. She was steaming that they screwed everything up for her. She sat motionless, lost in thought. For the first time since high school, she was truly alone and it scared her. She was now wounded and very dangerous.

Rita and Gail had been everything to her. She wanted to recall their happy moments, however her mind drifted to the police and the reality of that they knew about Gail's past. She realized that they must know about hers and Rita's and that scared her even more.

"Story...I must have a logical answer to why I changed my name," she said thinking out loud. "Think girl." Nothing at first came to mind. Rita always helped her stay grounded. She needed to have Marc by her side. A supporting husband would look good to the police. "I've got to get him back," she whispered, a devious air to her voice.

Nora needed to return the two shoe boxes to her friend's garage. It was her fail-safe scenario if her cover had been blown. Now with both her friends dead, she couldn't be in possession of the boxes. She pulled down two shoe boxes from her closest shelf, slid into her parka, and headed toward the front door. She hoped that the police had not been to Rita's house yet.

She paused by the top the stairs on the landing outside her bedroom. She knew this idea was risky, but the victim role had always worked for her in the past, and she believed it would work again. "Get to Rita's first you moron. Then you throw yourself down your steps," she mumbled.

SIXTY-THREE

Marc couldn't sit still. His heart was still pounding since seeing Brad so vividly inside his head. He looked around. There was no nurse or doctor to talk to. He had to find out what was going on with Lisa. Melissa was now sleeping soundly on a small couch, her head on detective O'Neil's lap.

He remembered that Lou was also in ICU and decided to find her and see how she was doing. Once again, the two women in his life were in the same building. He wondered if Nora was going to show up unannounced.

The last few weeks seemed a life-time ago. His once quiet, unremarkable life had blasted into warp speed with no brakes. Most men would jump at the chance to have a beautiful wife, a great female friend, and a wholesome mother of the year type, who turned tricks on the side, all clamoring for his attention.

Not Marc. In fact, it was not just the women in his life that was changing him. His memories were returning rapidly. It was having a terrible affect on his equilibrium. He was beginning to shed the decades of Marc who allowed the world use him as a doormat and now he was letting another side of him to appear. The voice that spoke to him more frequently now, was pulling him away from his old life and into the new life the voice wanted him to start. Marc was now heading down a familiar path he had walked on before and knew he had to try to fight it before it was too late.

He had dreamt of bachelorhood, to savor the pleasures of being a playboy, to just be James Bond for a little while. He thought it would be a just reward after spending so many years in a dysfunctional marriage. But, that apparently was not in the cards.

His first and only female friend was lying in intensive care struggling for her life. His sexy and gorgeous new girlfriend was just shot by one of his wife's friends. Even the private investigator he had hired had been murdered investigating his wife and her friends. No one around him seemed safe, except Nora, the evil bitch who was right in the middle of everything.

The horrible thing for Marc was that it was happening all over again. Tragedy after tragedy was once again befalling him, and as before he did not know what to do. All he knew was that Nora was in the center of all his pain. The voice was now demanding that he deal with Nora with extreme prejudice, a phrase he had heard his attorney use, which seemed fitting.

Marc approached ICU and pressed the call button. He had remembered how "Nurse Ratchet" would not let Lou in to see him, so he was prepared to lie.

"Can I help you?" the nurse said.

Marc let out a long breath. "I'm here to see Lou Hart," he said nervously, his voice cracking.

"She's only allowed to see immediate family members."

"I'm her brother," Marc said not giving his name. He was holding his breath. He needed to see her and tell her how much he cared for her. Hearing the electrical buzz and the double doors popping open brought him some relief.

The nurse pointed to Lou's room. He was not prepared for what he saw. She was being incubated, with wires and IV's surrounding her hospital bed. Her eyes were swollen closed and her left arm was in a white cast.

She was being helped to breath, which what he remembered on the TV show ER was very serious. He couldn't control his tears. Seeing her like this and remembering their fight at Meritage made him feel like the lowest form of slime. He now knew that Nora had a hand in this too.

He pulled a chair over by her bed and held her hand. Her fingers were icy cold. It was a cold you experienced when you touched a dead body. He started shaking. His chest pains had returned.

Marc stood and leaned over to kiss her forehead. "Lou, it's Marc. I'm so sorry. Please don't die on me. You're my best friend…you can't…please fight. I miss my eggs and hash-browns and our great talks." He paused taking in a trembling breath. He continued whispering. "I promise, when you get better, I won't be the butt I've been," he couldn't stop rambling.

Marc pushed his chair back ready to leave when Lou squeezed his hand. Her eyes struggled to open. Her smiling eyes were masked with sadness or maybe fear—he wasn't really sure. She tried forcing a smile, as a solo tear rolled out of the corner of her eye.

Marc fell back in the chair, trying to put on a brave front. She lifted her hand that held his and brought it to the corner of her lips next to her breathing tube struggling to kiss his fingers. When he saw that she was awake and trying to comfort him, he lost it.

His voice couldn't stop quivering. He was shocked at the words that flew out of his mouth. "Lou, I love you. You need to get better. Then, we can go to some tropical island. You can recoup and suck down as many as you'd like of those funny drinks with umbrellas." The old Marc at that moment had returned. No strange voices talking to him. His mind seemed clear and focused.

Lou tried to respond, but the tube in her throat allowed only a grunt and a nod. After thirty minutes, the nurse told him that her patient needed her rest and that he could come back that evening, if he liked.

He told Lou he'd see her later. It had not been fifteen seconds when a cacophony of bells started ringing. Two nurses pushed him aside and a third was pressing an alarm button on the wall. Over the loud speakers came an alert: "Code Blue in ICU, Code Blue in ICU. It kept repeating itself until another nurse wheeling in a crash cart, followed by a doctor, hurried to Lou's side

Marc looked at the cardiac monitor and did not see the normal dancing lines of a happy heart. All he saw was a flat line. A nurse escorted him out of Lou's room and pushed him through the large double doors without an explanation. He slid down against the corridor wall, his knees pulled to his chest. "Don't do this to me," he chanted. "Lou…not now…please," he whispered into his cupped hands.

His cell phone rang. It was Detective Allen. "I can't talk now," he said harshly.

Detective Allen ignored him. "I'm in the ER. We need to talk about your wife. She's being brought in. She was pushed down the steps inside your house. Something doesn't seem right here and you're the only one who can make some sense of all of this," he said.

Marc took a calming breath. "I'll be right down."

SIXTY-FOUR

Marc was studying Detective Allen and Detective O'Neil, trying to listen to what they were talking about, as they huddled in the hospital corridor. Melissa was still sleeping soundly, something Marc was wishing he could be doing at the moment. He had never felt so exhausted. His brain was firing on all cylinders. He needed to be part of the investigation. He was feeling left out while the two detectives talked. He thought that saving detective Allen would have gotten him on the inside track to what was going on.

"Any word on Lisa?" Marc asked, trying to include himself.

Ray Allen craned his neck, a blank stare riveted Marc's body. His eyes were red from emotion. Marc understood that look. His legs felt rubbery, he looked for someplace to sit. "Not Lisa," he said despondently.

Ray remained silent, unable to speak. Marc kept his eyes focused on the floor, unable look at Lisa's brother-in-law's sorrowful face. He flopped down on a vacant couch, his head cupped in his hands. Someone had started to talk to him, but he couldn't hear the words. His mind was spinning out of control, blocking out all the other static that was invading his space.

Ray was struggling with his words, as he tapped on Marc's shoulder. "Marc, she's out of surgery. The doctor did the best he could. They have her in an induced coma to help her body heal on its own. She lost a lot of blood. The next twenty-four to forty-eight hours will be critical, if she's going to make a full recovery."

Marc looked up unable to comprehend what was happening. "Why is all of this happening?" were the only words he could muster.

Detective Allen sat down next to him and pulled out his notepad. "Right now what we do know is that Rita, or should I say Blanche Ruiz, and Gail, Carla Shortz, have a sealed juvenile record. I'm trying to get it unsealed, since they're both dead. Your wife, Nora, has a strong connection to the two of them, but like Teflon, Gail and Rita's problems are not sticking to her. Either she's that smart, or just a dumb blonde in never-never land."

"I would not describe Nora as a dumb blonde," Marc replied mockingly. "She's more a chameleon, able to change her appearance to suit her situation. I can't wait to see what she does next, now that her friends are dead." Marc's voice had become loud enough to wake Melissa.

When she saw her uncle she leaped into his arms crying. "Mommy's been shot. She's hurt real bad," she said sobbing.

"The doctor said she's going to be all right, princess. She's resting now, so she can be strong for you."

"I want to see her," she begged.

"You can't now. Soon, I promise."

Marc stood to get some air. He had to think. Nora had to pay and the voice inside his head had the perfect plan.

Outside in the emergency bay a speeding ambulance screeched to a halt. The paramedic that had been driving opened the back door to help his partner out with a screaming woman on the gurney.

Something familiar about that piercing sound brought a shiver over Marc's body. "Call my husband you idiot," she wailed. "He needs to know what happened to me. He'll be frantic," she kept hollering. "He's a worrier with a weak heart."

Bile coated Marc's throat, as his brain connected the banshee screams that were hurting his ears. It was Nora. He wanted to ignore what he was witnessing, but had to look her in the eyes first.

When Nora saw him, she escalated her cries. "Marc, you're here. How did you know? Someone tried to kill me at the house and in the struggle threw me down the stairs," she said grabbing his hand. She was now wildly kissing his palm trying to wrap his fingers around her face. He wanted to slip his hand around her neck, but thought better of it. It wasn't the right time. She had to suffer more.

Marc pulled his hand away abruptly. "I'll be in shortly," he said rudely. The worst of any nightmare, he could think of, was happening. All the women in his life were now staying at the same hospital. How crazy is this?

He was wound much too tight, ready to snap in half, trying to keep his scream at bay, while he tried to think.

He felt he was tip-toeing a fine line between controlling himself and letting his guard down. He had to step away from Nora before she captured him again. Marc could feel how he was changing, how cold his heart was becoming toward Nora. A satisfying smile formed on his face, realizing for the first time that the woman screaming in the ER had become a total stranger. He had to move quickly with the divorce and distance himself as far away as possible from her.

The transformation was swift. Old Marc was slowly disappearing and a stranger was being born inside his body and mind. He did not know if his rebirth would include Lou or Lisa, and it didn't matter. He knew right at that moment that he did not have the strength to be there for anyone, except himself.

Marc's reality was slapping him in the face, as Nora continued screaming in the emergency room, calling out his name. She was so alive, and so despicable, and still his wife after all. He turned, feeling the draw of twenty-five years, but kept walking away, toward the elevator, to find out how Lou was doing. He was going to let Nora figure things out without him.

SIXTY-FIVE

The boardwalk at north Carlsbad beach was empty of life at two in the morning. The marine layer was thick making the walkway wet and slippery. Splashes of moonlight broke through the scattered layers of fog, lighting up the pathway and whitewater that played its music against the shore. At least some temporary good news: Lou was not dead. She was still struggling to stay alive, after the doctors stabilized her.

Marc's instability had him talking to himself as he walked. The vivid image of shooting Gail was not as overwhelming as he had imagined. While he wanted to be at the hospital with Lou and Lisa, it was out of his hands right now and he had to lay out his plan. The first thing on his agenda was to find the answers to what Nora and her friends were hiding from him. Second, he would call Lindsey later in the day and begin to have his marriage annulled, if that was possible after 25 years. The faster Nora was severed from his life, maybe literally, Marc thought, the better.

Flashes of his aunt and uncle's death and Ashley's disappearance were beginning to make sense after the recent events with Campbell, Lisa and Lou, but those periods of time were not so clear just yet. The third thing he had to find out was if his blackouts where in some way being controlled by Nora?

SIXTY-SIX

Two days had passed and both Lou and Lisa had regained consciousness. They still had a long recovery ahead of them, but Marc had decided that for the time being, he would be committed to being there for both of them, if that was even possible.

More internal changes had started to materialize and for some unknown reason, the old Marc and new Marc were converging. It was a strange feeling for him, but he liked it.

Detective Allen had already turned up enough information on Nora and her girlfriends to start piecing together the morbid puzzle that haunted Marc's life.

Rebecca Morgan (Nora) had been linked to a series of brutal murders. However, the evidence was not pointing to Rebecca, it was pointing to her friends. Detective Allen filled him in with the next bit of news about his Aunt and Uncle and Ashley.

At Rita's house the Carlsbad crime scene investigation unit found videos and cassette tapes that tied Rita and Gail to Marc's Aunt and Uncles death and Ashley's disappearance, which now looked like a homicide. Rebecca (Nora) on the other hand, seemed to be out of the picture, and not connected to the crimes. He was assuming that she was the person taking the videos, but could not prove it at this time. It was still unclear why she had changed her name and disappeared with her friends.

Marc's settlement conference with Nora and her attorney proved very interesting, since Lindsey was going to lower the boom on them in front of the judge. The documents that Detective Allen had provided Lindsey Warren was all she needed to void Marc's marriage and turn the screws on Nora.

Marc had seen the preliminary division of assets and it looked great for him and horrible for Nora. There would be no alimony, no income from the corporation, and if he agreed, she could take some of the furniture with her when she moved out of the house, which Lindsey stipulated would have to be immediately.

Lindsey was drafting up the documents to file a civil lawsuit against Nora for fraud and embezzlement for all the money she stole from the corporation.

Marc couldn't stop thinking about Nora's vanity and how she pampered herself at his expense. One day, he thought justice will prevail and she'll discover that it is the beauty within that will sustain a person through life. For now, the only punishment he could inflict on her was to leave her penniless. For the first time he was truly enjoying the control and power he was feeling. "Brad you'd be so proud of me," he whispered to himself. To his surprise, Brad's voice whispered back. "I expected more out of you."

Sitting outside of courtroom 4, Lindsey sat by Marc's side reviewing her court brief. Nora arrived in full regalia. She was in a wheel chair being pushed by her attorney. On her lap was a banker's box and on top of that was an attaché case. She was dressed in a frumpy floral dress that partially covered the cast on her right leg. Covering her head was a large white bandage that wrapped under her chin and was tied in a big knot on top of her head. Marc could only imagine that she wanted to look like someone who was seriously hurt. Instead, she looked like a bunny rabbit with a toothache.

She tried to speak to Marc, but he turned his head unable to control his laughter. Rankin stopped pushing the wheelchair, anger in his eyes.

"I hope you'll be able to control your client today. I didn't want Nora here, but she insisted on coming so the judge could understand everything she's been through," said Rankin seriously.

Lindsey stood, a big grin on her face. "I hope you've brought a big shoehorn. You'll need it to pry your foot out of your mouth when I'm done with the two of you. I'd suggest you turn her around and just dissolve this marriage, as if it never existed."

Rankin looked confused. His face twisted as he spoke. "I just hope your client enjoys being penniless," he said confidently, pounding his fist on the banker box resting on Nora's lap, causing her to yelp from pain. He turned and continued pushing Nora into the courtroom.

"I guess your wife hasn't told him about her real name. This should be so much fun. Seeing Rankin get kicked in the balls will be a nice gift." Lindsey said chuckling.

The settlement conference took just under two hours because the paramedics had to tend to Nora who had passed out while throwing a temper tantrum on the cold courtroom floor. Rankin looked like he wanted to get down next to her and join in.

With all her theatrics, Nora had something up her sleeve, hoping to convince the heartless judge that she deserves something from Marc.

Fluttering her eyes and acting so much the victim, she spoke in her little girl voice. "Your honor can I please have a chance to speak on my behalf"— Nora was cut off quickly by the judge.

"That's what I tried to allow you to do, but you thought that throwing temper tantrums would control this court and my decision about you and your divorce. You'll have no more than five minutes to speak before I make my final decision. If I hear any theatrics from you, I'll put a muzzle on you," the judge said harshly. "Now speak, the clock is ticking."

Nora sucked in a quivering breath and started talking. "None of this was my fault," she said with conviction. "It was all Blanche and Carla. When they did their first murder, well the first one that I knew about I was shocked and wanted out of our friendship. But, they were stronger than me and threatened me and my family if I didn't cooperate and remain part of their group terrible things would happen to me and my mother and father."

The judge held up her hand. "This is a family law court, not a criminal court. You should use this when your criminal trial takes place."

Nora's face started turning blotchy red from the neck up and to both her cheeks. She knew that what she was telling the judge was not for her sake but for Marc's. "Just indulge me one more minute your honor, she begged. "As the years went on, and believe me I never helped either Blanche or Carla commit one murder, I did not know how to leave them for fear of my life. They already had killed my parents when I tried to get away once. I think I have what you would call 'Stockholm Syndrome'. I've been powerless all these years. Today is the first time I've felt free now that Blanche and Carla are dead. I just hope you can see in your heart that I deserve something from all the years I was married to Marc." She finished talking by dabbing the corners of her eyes with an already soaked tissue.

The judge's eyes grew wide with amazement. "That's some whopper of a story. Like I told you before your little speech, this is a family court and that line of bull-shit should be left to the criminal court. I've read your entire file and all the evidence the police have on you and your friends, and do not believe a word of what you just told this court. I am ready to make my decision after a ten minute recess," she said coldly.

Marc stood, ready to leave the courtroom, but had to lean over and whisper in Rankin's ear. "You know that song by the Dixie Chicks you play while your clients wait for you to pick up your phone, well here's my answer: *I'm not ready to play nice*, another poignant Dixie Chicks song."

Nora had heard Marc and did not know what to make of his new found confidence. *"Brad?"* she mumbled. The air in the courtroom seemed to grow heavy and the most garrulous talker had fallen silent. "Maybe there's still hope for me," she muttered to herself.

The ten minute recess went by quickly and everyone returned to their respective places. The judge had reviewed the police documents, Nora's birth certificate, as Rebecca Morgan, and her tie-in to her friends' criminal acts. Her decision was surprisingly too simple.

"Nora Richards, who this court now recognizes as Rebecca Morgan, you committed a fraud by signing your marriage certificate with an illegal fictitious name, which by California Law makes the marriage to Marc Richards invalid. I will ask the District Attorney to look into this and determine if criminal charges should be brought against Rebecca Morgan for identity theft. Ms Morgan, you should work on your statement a little more convincingly, you will need to when the district attorney arrests you. Further, Marc Richards has no financial obligations toward Miss Morgan, unless she can prove that she contributed any of her own personal money during their co-habitation. All assets, including savings and checking accounts in Nora Richards name will immediately be turned over to Mr. Richards' full control. The Corporation will also be Mr. Richards' sole property, since Nora Richards never existed legally. The judge continued on for the next thirty minutes, entering her ruling with prejudice.

Nora was white as a sheet, as she stormed out of the court room, knocking over her wheelchair as she jumped up. She hobbled on her cast, while tossing her head bandage on the floor.

Marc was surprised that he did not feel a bit sorry for her. He just hoped that her back was going to be the last thing he would ever see of her.

SIXTY-SEVEN

Two weeks had passed since Marc's marriage had been dissolved. Lisa and Lou were back at their homes recuperating. He was spreading himself thin between the two of them, wanting desperately to be in both their lives. Needless-to-say, the new Marc did not know what to do.

With Nora out of his life, Brad had returned and he and Marc were once again back as a team. He could not tell Lou or Lisa about Brad. It would just not be the right thing to do.

One important thing he did know was that the new Marc had emerged and he was finally able to enjoy himself without any guilt or insecurity. His emotions were finally blossoming in a fruitful direction. His paranoia had begun evaporating as Brad rekindled their old relationship, teaching Marc how to be strong in so many new ways he had never imagined. A lot of his new found growth had came from having both Lou and Lisa in his life and especially little Melissa.

He still had his moments of PTSD when old memories and his new personality clashed, enflaming his many painful scars that Nora had etched on his soul.

Marc went back to working with Dr. Kaplan. The doctor had his own ideas on how to help Marc cope with his past and the vivid images that continued to crop up when new happy moments filled his life. Marc felt comfortable with the doctor, and one day introduced the doctor to Brad, which was an unexpected bombshell that Kaplan had not expected.

During that session, Brad had become pissed and angry with Marc for telling his doctor about him. "You're a fool to think this fucking doctor will keep your secret to himself. If he finds out what we've done, what I've done, he'd have to report us to the police and we'd both go to prison."

Marc shook his head. "That would never happen. I only know from Nora that you have done horrible things. There's no proof, only the faking of your death, which I still can't believe worked. Did everyone at school actually believe that we were twins? Did anyone ever see us together? Until I see some evidence that YOU, ME, have hurt anyone or were part of the evil three's crimes, I will just believe that you and I were duped by Nora. So keep your anger to yourself. I won't support your violent temper anymore," he said, his voice rising.

"You've let the cat out of the bag and can't stop me," Brad screamed.

Dr. Kaplan had been listening to the conversation Marc was having with his alter-ego Brad. The doctor instantly knew that different convergence of personalities was about to happen and his life could be in danger. Marc seemed distant and lost within his own mind, arguing loudly with himself. The doctor reached for his phone hoping he'd be able to call 911 in time. He saw Marc had returned and put his phone down.

"Dr. Kaplan, I am in control now, not Brad. You'll be safe," Marc said.

But, then something unusual happened and Marc started to blackout again. For the first time, someone other than Nora was witnessing how Marc and Brad co-existed. There was no way for Kaplan to stop it. It was too late. Brad was now in charge and turned toward Kaplan, a murderous grin on his face. "You were thinking of calling the police, right?," Brad said in an eerie monotone.

Kaplan's hand was shaking. "You need to bring Marc back," he said with authority. "Marc's not going to like what you're thinking of doing," he said, trying to defuse the rage building on Brad's face. "You two are finally working together in a positive way. Don't rush it."

The doctor knew that sometimes mentioning the other personality could bring the calmer one back, but by the look on Brad's face it was not working. Marc was not in control at the moment.

"Brad stop it!" Marc screamed, the words flowing out of Brad's lips.

"Bull-shit. It's time you witness what I'm capable of. I've had to sit back and watch you acting like a weak idiot all these years. So just relax and watch. We need to blend together for this to work so we can survive. " Brad said in a cold menacing tone.

Marc tried to get control, but Brad was stronger.

He was now remembering how strong Brad's personality had always been. He tried to struggle to find the strength to overcome Brad's strength. Then a new voice entered his head. It was totally different than the voice he had been hearing lately.

"You can do this. You've always been able to do this. Brad no longer needs to be in your life. Together we can rid Brad from us, for good," the new voice said with a strength Marc had not heard before.

"Brad's always been the dominant one. I've been the one who comes out when Brad needs to run away from trouble," Marc said. Dr. Kaplan's eyes were wide with disbelief at what was unfolding before him. The doctor did not say a word, and just listened.

Brad surfaced again, but this time his voice sounded scared. "Marc, we've been a team all of our life. You cannot get rid of me that easy," his voice cracking. "I won't let it. I do not want to go away again. I need you Marc, and you need me," he said as his voice started to fade.

Marc puffed out his chest, a feeling of confidence showing on his face. "You've only existed because I felt weak and helpless. I am not that person anymore. Brad is dead and Marc has been reborn." And with that Brad had left the room.

Kaplan jumped up from his chair running toward his office door unsure who was in the room with him.

Marc shouted to the doctor to sit down and listen to him. Kaplan was frightened. He saw a completely different look on Marc's face and knew he had no other choice.

"Is that really you, Marc?"

"Yes," Marc said calmly. I can feel that Brad is totally gone. However, there is a new voice talking to me. It feels good. I think I am going to be all right now."

Doctor Kaplan had never seen anything like what just happened before. He had read about multiple personalities, but nothing like this. He wasn't convinced that Brad was totally gone, but very happy Marc was now in control…at least for the time being.

"That was very scary for awhile," Kaplan said. "We have a lot of work ahead of us."

Marc seemed shaken to the core, and Brad was nowhere to be found. Marc stood and thanked the doctor for all of his help. "I don't think I will need your services anymore," he said and walked out the door. He looked back with a big smile on his face.

Marc's Blackberry buzzed reminding him of an appointment. Looking at who it was with, he wasn't sure he'd be in any condition to handle it. The appointment was with Detective Allen. He had called earlier in the day and said he had uncovered some exciting evidence about Nora and her friends. Marc couldn't imagine what could be more exciting than what had just happened.

* * * * *

The Armenian Café in Carlsbad, where they first met, was crowded. It had become their place to talk about the case against Nora. It was a bright sunny day and the beach was crowded.

Marc would have rather found another location. It had too many bad memories and he did not need to keep rehashing them over and over again. He was Marc Richards at the moment, the guy who thought of other people's feelings before his, but now he wasn't sure when or if Brad would pop up again.   He needed some alone time to figure things out and see how he could talk some more to the new voice.

Ray Allen looked more serious than on previous meetings. He had a thick manila folder in front of him, which when Marc sat down, he slid over toward him.

"Open it up," he said in a calm whisper.

The top sheet had a photo clipped to it. It was of a dense wooded area with an exposed hole and a skeleton. When Marc saw the decomposed body and the Abalone Shell purse he had bought for Ashley, he recognized immediately that Detective Allen had found his girlfriend.

Detective Allen bit his lower lip, his face etched with frustration. "Rita had a map at her apartment with the exact location of the body. We're running some DNA tests to see what might turn up. It's a long-shot, but we have nothing else we can do to tie Nora to this in anyway."

Marc was relieved that there was now some resolution to Ashley's disappearance. He felt sad that she was not alive and happily living life somewhere. "Was there anything in Rita's stuff regarding my aunt and uncle's murder?"

Ray Allen lowered his eyes. Marc could tell he was uncomfortable looking at him. "You can tell me anything at this point. Nothing would shock me about Nora, I mean Rebecca."

"I'm concerned that what I've found won't be that easy for you to take. It's pretty shocking," he said, exposing a sorrow Marc had not seen before. "I know you have a thousand questions about your aunt and uncle's death, as well as Ashley's disappearance and now apparent murder. I have nothing for you on your aunt and uncles death. I think—"

Marc had to stop him. Seeing Ashley's remains and her purse flooded him with anger. He did want answers, but most of all he wanted to know what Nora had to do with it. Did Nora…shit…Rebecca, whatever her name is have anything to do with what you're going to tell me?"

Ray seemed exhausted. "You need to understand some of the history Gail and Rita had with Nora so you can understand their motives and what they did for their friend." Ray took a deep breath. "Rita and Gail, by all appearances, were blindly loyal to Nora. They acted out her every wish. I had Nora's juvenile record pulled. As it turns out she got angry for some illogical reason and Brad was the object of that anger. To punish him, she had accused him of raping her right after they started dating in High School. The charges were later dismissed when the police found out that she had admitted she was a lesbian.

"Nora's a lesbian?" Marc said shocked. For the first time he realized that Nora married him as punishment for what she believed Brad had done to her. Now he finally understood why she stayed with him. She was waiting for Brad to return so she could punish him. Everything she had said in court the other day was yet again a manipulative lie.

It was also making sense why she always made him feel like he was a sexual deviate for wanting to have sex with her. Another scar had started to hurt. "Go on," he said shaking his head.

"When the judge dismissed the rape charges and it spread all over her high school and everyone started calling her "Lesbo", her pristine image was shattered. A week later, before the prom, Brad was found brutally beaten to death with a baseball bat. Back then, DNA was in its infant stages and the West Covina Police did not have the facilities to process the entire crime scene. All they had to make an ID on the body was his wallet and two teeth that were knocked out."

Marc moved his tongue, rubbing against the bridge that formed his two front teeth. Nora had convinced him that they had been knocked out playing basketball in high school. Things were beginning to come together now. He had always been Brad.

Ray shook Marc's shoulder. "Are you with me?

"Yeah. Just got a little lost with my thoughts," Marc said sadly.

"Well, Blanche, Carla, and Rebecca were people of interest, but they covered for each other and the case went cold."

Marc understood Nora's need for revenge, but twenty-five years of punishing him? That didn't make any sense. "Do they still keep the evidence kits this long?" Marc asked, hoping for something positive to link Nora to murder.

Ray smiled for the first time. "West Covina's CSU has done us some good," he chuckled. "I have all the evidence being shipped to me. I should have it any day. If there's anything with Rebecca's DNA on any of the evidence the police saved, then we can nail her for Brad's murder."

"Now you're talking," said Marc, realizing that Brad wasn't really dead.

"There's more," Ray said, his emotions boiling. He had taken on this case not just for his sister-in-law, but for Marc. They had become close friends since Marc had saved his life. He wanted to help his friend put to bed the torment he's had for so many years.

Marc tapped Ray's hand. "I know what you're doing for me and I appreciate it. Just understand my anxiousness. I'm trying hard to understand all the verbal abuse and putdowns by Nora and that they were all lies. The bitch was just punishing me for what that Brad character had done to her."

"You should have realized on your own that they were not true," said Ray, a puzzled expression on his face.

"I know it's hard to imagine that I could be affectionately fond of a woman like Nora, but she had a certain power over me, something like she had over her girlfriends. I must admit I was a submissive husband, which continues to eat at me more than ever. I'm working on forgiving myself. She drove a wedge between me and my aunt and uncle, which I'll go to my grave regretting. So whatever you still have to tell me about Nora, don't humanize her. She's an animal."

Ray nodded and continued. "I could never make any of them out to be anything other than the sociopaths they were and in

Rebecca's case still is. We have sent the tapes to the FBI so they can determine if they have been altered. If Rebecca's on those tapes, they will find it. Right now my focus is on locking up your ex and closing this case for both of us. I've also sent to Quantico some hairs and a broken nail we found at Lou Hart's house after her attack. They also found blood on a window sill and a footprint from a flip-flop. It could be Lou's, but we'll know soon enough. If Nora was there, they'll find it. It's just a matter of time before we have something on her. These women were like a pack of coyotes, organized and vicious," Ray said, his frustration showing, "But they were not very smart."

Marc couldn't hide his anger. "I want Nora locked up so bad I can taste it."

Ray pursed his lips. "I'm hoping Nora was so enraged when she was outed that she actually participated in Brad Stevens' murder. We might never know, but believe me I'm doing everything in my power to find out. She is either a naïve dumb blonde or a very smart sociopath, my vote is for the latter, who might still have something left to prove before she skips town again."

"I agree. I can testify what a bitch she was to me. I can see how she controlled her friends to do her bidding. There just has to be something you'll find that will link her to all of this," he said despondently.

"We did pull something from Chip Campbell's fax machine. He had received a ten-page fax the morning he was killed. It came from the FBI. I've sent a request to find out who sent the fax and if we could get a copy of the file. If this is why he was killed, then we might have the evidence we're looking for."

"Any idea when you might hear from them?"

"The agent's out of town and will return tomorrow. I left a message for him to call me ASAP."

"You'll let me know if anything pans out?"

"You're number one on my list," Ray said without hesitation. Oh, one other thing. We found in Campbell's papers a strange letter addressed to you. Do you know anything about it?"

Marc nodded. He had almost forgotten about the letter and how it had triggered his flashbacks. "It was sent to me right when all of my flashbacks had started. I gave it to Chip to look into what the sender had written. That's all I got. Did Campbell find out anything about it?"

"I have a theory. I had a language expert look at it and she felt that it was written in the first person by someone who writes lefty. It was written as if YOU were trying to tell yourself something from your suppressed memories. Strange huh?."

Marc seemed surprised. "I'm righty. So that blows that theory."

Ray shrugged his shoulders and packed up his file. "Talk to you soon buddy. We're getting closer."

The marine layer had returned with a vengeance socking in the coastline with wet drizzly clouds. Marc needed to walk for awhile, alone, to process everything Ray had said and what Brad had done a few hours earlier. His last twenty-five years were a lie, something he was still unable to shake off. Nora was like a tattoo that was put on by mistake, only the mistake was permanently under his skin tormenting his soul. As he walked briskly he wished that the knife had not missed its intended target weeks ago.

He stopped and pulled out his copy of the mysterious letter. He turned it over and wrote the same first two sentences with his left hand. To his surprise, writing lefty was easy and even though he wasn't a hand writing expert, it matched. "Shit, Brad wrote that letter to jolt me back to who I really am." Marc did not want to believe that he was a murderer.

SIXTY-EIGHT

Nora had loaded her car with what little clothing she wanted to take with her. She did not know how she was going to access the money she had over the years siphoned from what was ruled Marc's savings by the judge. Rita and Gail had contributed to their emergency fund. She had to find a way to get into the joint safety deposit box, stuffed with $2,500,000, without sending off any alarms.

She prayed it would last her long until she found another man, another sucker that would lavish her with all that she wanted. This time she knew she'd have to be different. She would have to portray a sexy Southern Belle type so she could nab an older rich guy who did not need a lot of sex and would allow her the freedom to hang out with her new girl friends she would make.

However, looking for a new man would first have to take a backseat to her immediate plan. What she really wanted, what was owed to her from Marc, was Brad's hide, and she was going to get it before she skipped town. She just didn't enjoy being screwed over. Her anger was at a boiling point and she knew she had to do it fast or lose her opportunity to punish Marc and Brad once and for all.

She just had to gather her senses and figure out what would hurt them the most. She was thinking about her performance in court and wondered if it pressed any of Marc's buttons?

She was muttering to herself, something that was not a good sign, as she got ready to leave the house she shared with Marc for the last eight years. "You never should have messed with me, Marc," she said loudly. "Things were going just fine, before my two friends were brutally murdered…Brad's can't be out of the picture?" she rambled incoherently. She looked around the living room and threw a crystal candy dish at Marc's beloved Picasso that hung over the fireplace. She smiled, satisfied. The shattered glass was imbedded in his precious piece of art.

Ashley died way too quickly. You'll not have that luxury," she grumbled, tossing a framed photo of their wedding day on the tile foyer floor.

"First you'll watch the people you love suffer even more and then it will be your turn," she said with an eerie calm. She kept ranting, while using a big carving knife to slash the furniture she once thought was hers and where she made love with Rita.

Later in the day, Nora had checked into the La Costa Resort and Spa in Carlsbad. The sun was breaking through the thick cloud cover. It was still too cool to lay outside, so she decided a few hours at the spa for some pampering and mental processing.

She had to rid herself of her Nora persona, as well as the old Rebecca that was coming back to haunt her. It was time to create a new identity and start over. She thought that Europe sounded inviting. It would be easy to become some wealthy man's trophy wife, with her "Southern Belle" wiles, while being able to pursue her sexual preferences. In Europe it was more acceptable.

Her ego needed to see Marc and his friends suffer severely so she could begin formulating her new life. Lying with two cucumbers on her eyes, a mudpack drying on her face, she visualized the worst pain she could inflict upon Marc and it wasn't going to be his death. *He seems attached to the whore's little girl,* she thought. *What better way to get what I want and have him suffering for the rest of his life?* "Yes, that's it!" she yelled, startling the reflexologist working on her feet.

"Are you okay, madam?"

Rebecca cracked her masque with her big smile. "I'm just fine," she said in a menacing voice.

SIXTY-NINE

The phone call from Detective Allen could not have come at a better time. Marc had just left Lisa's house helping her with the little odds and ends she could not do for herself. He had dropped Melissa off at her school. He then had to pick up some groceries and her prescriptions. He loved being needed by Lisa and Lou, but was being torn by his strong feelings for Lou.

Marc wanted his cake, all of it, but knew he would soon have to make a decision. It had to wait until the two women were back to normal and finished with their physical therapy. It didn't make things easier that Lisa and Lou had become friends when they met at the physical therapist office.

Ray seemed abnormally happy, which for him was rare. "We've got the blood match and the 'flip-flop' sandal that made the imprint at Lou's. It's Nora's, I mean Rebecca's. We now can tie her to the attack on Lou. The DA has issued an arrest warrant and I've been given permission to pick her up. Care to tag along? She's staying at The La Costa Resort and Spa."

"Only if I can slap the cuffs on her," Marc said happily.

"You can watch. I usually don't get this wrapped up with a case, but I'm looking forward to squeezing the cuffs nice and tight on that bitch," he said angrily. "I almost forgot to mention. Your two best friends, Officer's Monroe and Perez are meeting us there. It seems that they want to be part of this arrest also.

"I'm on my way back to Lisa's. Pick me up in forty minutes."

Marc was so excited he had not noticed that he was going sixty on Coast Highway. Finally, the closure he so desperately needed, was going to happen.

With his adrenaline pumping, he felt Brad returning. He had thought that part of him was gone, but looking at his eyes in the rearview mirror told another story. "I'm stronger than you now," Marc said in a low stern whisper. "I won't let you come out to play. Not this time or any time again."

He heard Brad's voice change. It had become gravely and deeper. "Nothing changed. I've just been letting you taste a life you'll never have as long as I am part of it…I can't be gotten rid of that easy," Brad growled.

"I like the person I'm becoming. Can't you just enjoy it yourself?"

The car had become silent before Brad spoke. "Soon we're going to merge even further. We'll surface as a stronger and better us. I can see HIM now," Brad laughed and then disappeared.

SEVENTY

The door to the steam room opened. A cold gush of air blanketed Rebecca's naked body. "Shut the fucking door. I'm freezing, you moron."

"Still with that same vulgar vocabulary, Nora, Rebecca, or whatever your name is today. This is the police and you'll need to get dressed and come with me now," Officer Perez ordered.

Rebecca did not flinch. "I'm not ready. I need to let the oil from my massage sink in."

"Don't make me drag your ugly ass out of there. Put your towel around that skinny, anorexic body of yours and get moving," Perez said impatiently.

"What's this all about?" Rebecca said peevishly.

Perez sighed and walked inside the steam room. She grabbed Rebecca's sweaty wrist trying to snap the cuffs on her. "You're being arrested for the assault on Lou Hart and the murder of Chip Campbell. You have the right to remain silent—" Officer Perez was surprised by the timing of the hot steam shooting out of the wall, which blinded her vision. Rebecca pulled her hand away and vanished within the thick hot fog.

Before she could react, Officer Perez was struck hard across her head. Her knees buckled and she slipped on the wet tile floor hitting her head hard.

Rebecca stepped over the fallen officer, wrapping her towel around the gun she now carried with her at all times. It did not take her more that a minute to put on her jogging suit and slip out the back door that opened to the pool area. There were no police officers guarding the exit. She jogged up the stairs to the front lobby and was at the valet. Her luck did not run out, as the valet recognized her, he started running to get her car.

"Always did like the way they treated me here," she giggled.

She sped away realizing she had no direction in mind. Her joy turned to fear realizing she was now a fugitive. "How the fuck did they find out?" she yelled speeding down La Costa Blvd to Interstate 5.

* * * * *

Officer Monroe and Detective Allen could hear the screams coming from inside the spa locker room.

They had already drawn their weapons.

Detective Allen, without hesitation, pushed open the doors to what would be normally a forbidden area for men, especially a man with a gun in his hand.

Marc followed both officers with curiosity. *What did Nora do this time?* He thought.

The door to the steam room was partially opened by two very attractive very nude women. They were staring down at Officer Perez and the moist blood that was oozing out on the locker room tile. The women did not notice the three men trying to get to the downed officer, as they continued to scream.

Once Officer Monroe barked out, "ladies please step aside." The two naked women finally realized the voice was attached to a man and fumbled for their towels, shocked looks on their faces and ran back to their lockers screaming.

Officer Perez was regaining consciousness, rubbing her head with her hand. "That bitch had a gun in the steam room. Who the fuck does that?" she complained.

Detective Allen shrugged his shoulders. "I guess a sociopath who's always prepared."

Detective Monroe was calling for a bus to attend to his partner. "Officer injured at The La Costa Resort and Spa women's locker room. BOLO, Nora Richards, armed and dangerous." Monroe also gave a full description of Nora's car.

Marc was not surprised at what Nora had done. His memory drifted back to the days she and Brad were together and her violence did not surprise him. "Aren't you guys going after her?"

Officer Monroe gave me a curious look. "We have a BOLO issued. She won't get far. The entire Carlsbad Police force will be out looking for her, as we speak. Within hours every city in North San Diego County will be looking for her."

"I don't want to pop your bubble, but she's disappeared before and right now she's like a wounded tiger looking for someone to hurt."

SEVENTY-ONE

It had been one month since Nora had vanished off the face of the earth. Not even the FBI had any viable leads to her whereabouts. Her face had been pasted on every news channel. The two most popular reality crime shows did a piece on her life with her two co-conspirators. Marc posted a fifty-thousand dollar reward for anyone who could lead the authorities to her.

Once again, Marc's life had become a waiting game. He felt like a grieving husband whose wife had been abducted, hopeful she'd turn up alive and back in his arms, except he wanted her back in the arms of the FBI and locked up for the rest of her life.

Nora's fugitive status was not traumatizing Marc, as much as it was keeping Lou and Lisa on pins and needles. Brad's prediction was slowly coming to fruition with small noticeable changes that Marc seemed to like. He was becoming stronger, more assertive and most importantly, able to keep Brad's anger at bay. The new Marc was not paranoid anymore.

Lisa had officially retired from her less than perfect profession and Lou had sold her coffee shop to a retired New York couple. Nora had not only changed Marc's life forever, but that of the two women he had grown to care about.

Marc tried not to blame Nora for every problem in his life. There were times he wanted to thank her for finally allowing him to see what a sad pathetic life he had with her. He constantly played his mind games wondering what would have happened if Nora had not been so egotistical and had given him just an ounce of passion. Would he have been happy with crumbs? He knew the answer and it scared him.

Now that he was experiencing being totally on his own, that is, totally without Nora or Brad in the picture, he had to deal with the old emotional misfit he was and the new transformation he was now experiencing.

Marc was slowly regaining his early memories, coming to grips with what his Brad personality was responsible for and trying to make a fresh start for himself. It was still unclear to him or to detective Allen if Brad had committed any of the murders or if he was just a bystander.

Lou had adjusted to her new life, doing all the things she always wanted to do. Lisa on the other hand had become over involved with her daughter's life and activities, trying to erase the stigma her career etched on her soul.

With all of his time, Marc had not felt energized to pursue any hobbies, even golf. Finding Nora and helping Detective Allen had become his full-time obsession. He sold his financial consulting firm and with his other investments and the sale of Nora's Lake Tahoe house, he had enough money to live on for the rest of his life.

Marc understood that his obsession to find Nora was stifling him and it was putting a large wedge between him and the two women he cared about the most.

Lou kept up her pestering, hoping that one day Marc would realize he needed to get over Nora and move on, but the umbilical cord she still had on him remained connected. He knew that it would only get cut when he saw her locked up or dead.

There were times while walking at the beach, Marc could sense Nora lurking, watching every move he made. Today, it wasn't his paranoia that was confronting him. He could sense she was close by.

When he's with Lisa and Melissa at one of their soccer games, or at one of the Karate tournaments the young girl competes in, he could feel Nora's piercing eyes on the back of his neck, knowing she was calculating how she will hurt all of them.

Lisa had become very keen to Marc's moods and emotional swings. She tried being polite and caring, but when it affected Melissa, that's where she drew the line.

Marc's capricious behavior had gotten him into the doghouse with Lisa way too frequently, affecting their intimacy.

Lisa would talk to Marc about her concerns constantly, to the point that he started feeling unwelcomed around the two of them.

"Marc, we both love having you spend time with us. Melissa especially loves the attention you give her. She's never had a real father in her life. Uncle Ray's great with her, but he's just her uncle who works his butt off, especially now with you. I sometimes feel that the two of you are chasing windmills. Nora's not coming back. She's long gone. We all need to get on with our lives, especially you."

Marc understood the reality of his obsession, but he just couldn't let it go that easy. He now fantasizes that Nora's death would be the only solution to his problem.

"I don't want to mess things up with us. You and Melissa have become the family I've never had. But, I keep seeing Nora everywhere. There are times that I can smell her perfume clinging to the fog as I walk on the beach. I feel her eyes burning on my neck when I'm with you and Melissa…I just don't know what to do."

Lisa looked away, as a stream of tears cascaded down her cheeks. "Until you can get over this thing you have with your ex, I can't have you hanging around. It's only going to hurt Melissa and me. It was hard enough explaining to her what I did for a living, another by-product of your ex, and I just don't want that woman in my life anymore.

"I'm sorry," Marc said.

"I am not so sure you are. You bring her with you every time we see you and it's just not right. We need a break. Please don't come back until you and Ray are over this thing. It's destroying you and us," she said unable to control her tears.

SEVENTY-TWO

Nora sat inside Lou's old coffee shop, her dark glasses and brunette wig seemed the perfect disguise, as Marc and Ray discussed one of their new leads. She had been finalizing her plan to get the money from Marc that she believed she still deserved. Today, what she had planned was going to set it all in motion.

She tried to contain her laughter, but hearing Marc complain to Detective Allen warmed her heart.

Marc seemed frustrated. "Lisa has given me the boot. I don't know what to do. She's right about how I've been, but I just can't get Nora out of my mind. So much needs to be said to her. Doctor Kaplan has had me write letters to her, but that's not helping. I need to do it face-to-face and get everything off my chest."

Ray nodded. "Women just don't understand about things like this. Trust me, Lisa will get over it. She really likes you, especially how you and Melissa have bonded. You do know that you can count on me with this investigation. You deserve to be happy. Cops have the worst track record when it comes to staying married and you don't need this life-style."

"Yeah, but the scars I have from Nora won't be healed until I see her dead or locked up. If I'm not helping you, I'd just be hanging around my house, becoming a vegetable. I need this. If Lisa or Lou can't understand, then there's nothing I can do about it right now."

"Bitch, am I? Wait until you see what I've got in store for your precious Lisa and her bastard child. You'll beg me to kill you," Nora thought, sipping her coffee.

Nora stood and walked toward the booth where Marc sat. She dropped her cell phone on purpose.

"Let me get that for you," Marc said. He looked up and handed her the phone.

"Thank you. You're such a gentleman," Nora said in a low seductive Southern drawl as she sauntered away.

Detective Allen looked up from his notes and stared at the tight beige Capri's that hugged Nora's firm butt. "Nice ass," he said, just out of earshot of Nora.

"Yeah, her breasts didn't look too shabby either," Marc said, returning to what they were doing.

"You dumb bastard. You can't even recognize your own wife," she muttered. "You're going to pay for that one."

* * * * *

Melissa was waiting for her mother, nervously pacing outside by the school buses. She glanced at her Barbie watch, realizing that she was going to be late for her big soccer game.

* * * * *

Lisa had a flat tire in the Forum Shops parking lot in Carlsbad. She had called Melissa's school, but couldn't get through to the administration office. Fear gripped her when she noticed that her tire had been slashed. Marc's obsession about Nora now had her really upset and scared.

She tried Ray's cell. He didn't pick up. Then she tried Marc's to no avail. "Please, please, where are you guys?" She cried.

* * * * *

Melissa was sitting on the curb in the parking lot when a woman with dark glasses walked up in front of her. "Are you Melissa?" she asked in a soft non-threatening voice.

Melissa looked up and nodded. "Yes. Who are you?" she asked politely.

"I'm Officer Rebecca Morgan. I work with your Uncle Ray," she said flashing a fake badge. "You're mother can't make it. She got a flat tire and Uncle Ray's busy working. He asked me to pick you up and bring you to the police station. I just cleared it with your school and its okay for you to go with me."

Melissa was staring at the woman officer. Something about her seemed familiar. "You work with my uncle Ray?"

The woman patted Melissa's cheek, a broad smile on her face. "I met you the last time Ray brought you to the station, don't you remember?"

Melissa was now lost in thought. Her lips twisted as she tried to remember the familiar face. "Oh, yes. I do remember you," she said nodding confidently. "But, I can't go to the police station. I have a soccer match. Can we use your siren, so we can get there on time?" she said excitedly.

"That's a great idea. I'll call your uncle and tell him there's been a change in plans."

Melissa stood and turned to see her teacher near the school steps. She waved at Mrs. Smith, who then waved back. "I guess it would be all right," Melissa said.

SEVENTY-THREE

Lisa arrived by taxi to Melissa's school thirty minutes late. Panic raced through her body. Her daughter was nowhere in sight. Only a few children were still waiting to be picked up.

She threw a twenty at the taxi driver and ran toward the front steps, her head panning the playground in case Melissa was playing with a friend. She was breathing hard, her mouth dry as sand. Her nerves had overtaken her sense of reasoning and she was now screaming for her daughter.

Inside the administration office she saw the principal talking to a parent. She barged in and screamed, "Where's my daughter?…have you seen Melissa Cunningham?…she's not outside…I was late…but she should have been outside waiting for me." Lisa was out of breath and acting like an uncontrollable distraught mother.

The principal excused herself from the parent she was talking to and walked over to Lisa. In a calm patronizing tone said. "Now take a deep breath and let it out slowly, then tell me what's going on."

"Melissa Cunningham? Where the fuck is she?" Lisa barked.

Principal Edwards blushed at Lisa's cursing. "Let's not use that foul language here. I expect you to conduct yourself in an adult manner if you want me to listen to you," said Mrs. Edwards, a little too insensitive and condescending for Lisa's liking.

Lisa grabbed the principal's lapels on her suit jacket and shook her hard. "Don't talk to me like I'm one of your students. My daughter's missing and I need answers." She noticed the fear on the principal's face and released her grip.

Lisa knew that she had to get a hold of her emotions and took a deep breath. "Sorry. My daughter's not out front. I was late. I had a flat tire, but she knows to wait for me no matter what," she said her voice cracking with panic.

Principal Edwards straightened out her jacket and picked up her two-way. She was punching the keyboard on a computer. "Here we go. Mrs. Smith is your daughter's teacher. I'm sure that when you did not arrive, our school policy is to take all students back to the classroom to wait for their parents. I'm sure that Melissa is doing her homework as we speak. Let me give Mrs. Smith a call and we can resolve this matter right now."

Lisa did not wait to hear if Melissa was in her classroom. She was out the door at full stride anticipating seeing her daughter right where the Principal said she would be.

Lisa skidded to a halt in front of the classroom. Inside was Mrs. Smith working at her desk grading papers. Melissa was nowhere in sight. "Where's my daughter, Melissa Cunningham?" she said her voice very loud.

Mrs. Smith stood, alarm on her face. "A woman with a police badge said that you had a flat tire and that your brother-in-law sent her to pick up Melissa. I saw them go off together. Melissa looked like she knew the woman. If I thought something was wrong I would have never let her go with that person. For god's sake, she was a police officer…I thought."

Lisa fell to the floor, her body banging against one of the small desks. "How could you let this happen? The only other person besides myself is Detective Ray Allen, her uncle, who has permission to pick up Melissa. Didn't you think of calling me or my brother-in-law to verify this change in procedure?"

Principal Edwards was now inside the classroom trying to act like a referee. "Let's stay calm. There must be a perfectly good explanation for this. Let's call the police station and speak to…" she looked at Mrs. Smith, "Did you get the officer's name?"

Melissa's teacher looked at her sign-out sheet. "Officer Rebecca Morgan," she said nervously.

Lisa screamed. Her eyes were wide with fear. "She's no police officer. Call 911, my daughter's been abducted." She flipped open her cell and dialed Ray. This time he picked up.

"Hey Lisa, what's up?"

"Where the hell have you been all day? I tried to call you, but you wouldn't pick up," Lisa was now hysterical.

"What going on?" he said, panic in his voice.

"Melissa's been taken by that crazy bitch you and Marc are looking for. I got a flat tire…it was slashed. I tried calling you and Marc to pick up Melissa, but you didn't pick up. How could this happen?"

 Ray looked at Mar, terrified. "Lisa where are you?"

"I'm at Melissa's school," she said sobbing. "Please find her. She's my entire life."

"I'll be there in ten minutes," he said.

SEVENTY-FOUR

Marc had wanted to go with Ray and comfort Lisa, but Ray thought that under the circumstances it would be best that he wait until he assessed the situation. Marc felt responsible. He walked Ray out to his car, feeling lightheaded.

He thought he'd go back to his apartment and wait to hear from Ray, but he needed someone to talk to and Lou was the first person to pop into his head. He did not want to talk on the phone and with her house close by he decided to pop over.

Her car was in her driveway, her morning newspaper had not been brought in and her mailbox was full of the normal junk mail. It was unlike her to neglect even those simple mundane chores, but since her attack, she was not her normal self.

Marc scooped up her newspaper and carried her mail to the front door. It was partially ajar, which started his heart racing. "Hey, Lou, you in the mood for a visitor?" he called out tentatively. The hair on the back of his neck stood at attention. He was sensing something was wrong.

In the background, coming from the direction of her kitchen he could hear her radio playing. "I'm coming in, I hope you're decent?" he warned.

Lou's place, while old, was usually kept in immaculate condition, but, not today. It looked like an earthquake had wreaked havoc with her stuff. Her books from her bookcase were scattered on the floor. Her photos that rested neatly on her fireplace mantle were lying broken on the marble tile in front of the hearth. Marc was beginning to get nervous. He was transported back to

Chip Campbell's apartment remembering how he found the body. Panic had consumed him.

"Lou, it's Marc. Are you all right?" he shouted, as loud as he could.

Inside the kitchen on a small table was what looked like her un-eaten breakfast of two eggs over easy, with bacon and a toasted English Muffin. He felt her coffee cup and it was cold. Now he was thinking the worst after what just happened with Lisa.

Marc rushed toward her bedroom, and when he did not find her there, he slowly opened the bathroom door, expecting to see her lying there. He couldn't get control of his breathing. His thoughts were racing, faster than his pounding heart.

He couldn't stop imagining what Nora had done to all the women in his life and now with Melissa being abducted, he was afraid of what he would see behind the bathroom door. He slowly pushed the door open, relieved that Lou was not lying there dead. *But, where the hell was she?* He knew the answer was not going to be good.

Marc called Ray and told him what he had found. Ray at first did not think it was relevant, but after re-thinking about it, he dispatched a patrol car to Lou's house.

"I'm worried about Lisa. She might also be in danger," Marc told him.

"I'm sending her home with two detectives. We're going to be monitoring her phones, waiting for word from Nora. I need you to go home and wait for me to call. It's possible if this is really your ex, she might be contacting you instead of Lisa."

His words did not make sense to him at first, but with Lou possibly missing, he realized that Nora would want to let him know that she was back in control of his life.

Marc was now shouting at Ray through the phone. "This is Nora's work, and you know it! Is there a Rebecca Morgan at the Carlsbad PD? Do you really think she'll want to negotiate with us after what I've done to her?"

"Until we hear from her, we just don't know what's inside her sick mind. Just get home and wait," Ray said, sounding hopeless.

* * * * *

Marc had returned to his apartment feeling isolated and distraught. He wasn't sure if his imagination was getting the best of him, but Nora's perfume hung in the air like a stale cigar.

His computer screen was on and his inbox had a new email message.

He was not ready for what it said:

> *You thought you could screw with me. Well...see who's the one doing the screwing now. I've got the whore's daughter and the other slut you've been seeing. Here's the deal. I want five million dollars for both of them. Don't bring in the police or FBI or they will die and you'll never find their bodies. I'm watching you, like I've always been able to watch you, so don't think you can fool me. You'll have twenty-four hours to get me the money or Lou will be the first to die and you'll get a few of her body parts delivered by one of those cute men in brown uniforms.*
> *Forever, your loving wife*

Marc tried to reply, but the email instantly came back as a mailer-demon. He wanted to call Ray, but he wasn't sure what Nora meant by she's watching him. He immediately called his securities broker and told him to liquidate his entire portfolio. His broker was surprised, and tried to reason with Marc, and when he was told the money was needed, in cash, by tomorrow, he said it couldn't be done.

"You have no choice. I need my money. If you ever want business from me again, you'll pull some strings." Marc slammed the phone down and sunk deep into his couch trying to not think about all the horrible things Nora was capable of doing, but the flashbacks were returning.

"Brad, I need you," Marc whispered.

SEVENTY-FIVE

It had been an hour since Marc read Nora's email, but it seemed like an eternity. He wasn't optimistic he'd have the money she demanded in time. The thought of Nora hurting Lou and Melissa was making his body shiver. He felt totally responsible for this mess.

Marc couldn't stop thinking how Nora still occupied his time and every thought. It didn't help that Ray had told him how Lisa blames the two of them for all of this. Ray didn't put much stock into her venting, but it cut at Marc's heart in the worst way.

He couldn't stop reliving how Melissa had been abducted and the stupid choice he had made to turn off his cell phone while he and Ray worked on finding Nora.

Marc was not convinced that Nora just wanted the money. He knew she was out to hurt him in a bad way. He just needed to figure out how to give her what she wanted and bring Lou and Melissa home safely. He needed help to formulate a plan. Someone who knew Nora better than he did. It was a poor choice, but Brad was his only option.

Marc's swirling mind got interrupted by a loud banging on his door. He heard Ray's voice. He sounded agitated.

"Marc, open up. We need to talk."

Ray looked like his life force had been drained from his body. He looked like he had been crying, as he barged into the apartment. Marc signaled him not to speak and walked him over to his computer screen. Once Ray read the message, he knew immediately what was going on.

On a piece of paper Marc scribbled a location where they could meet privately. Ray left first, then Marc followed fifteen minutes later. Nora had both of them paranoid. It still baffled him how she had known what he was doing before he even knew.

* * * * *

The seawall at Carlsbad beach was Marc's fortress of solitude, but unlike Superman, he had no super powers to get Melissa and Lou back. When he finally got there, Ray was tossing large stones into the breaking waves, lost in the moment. Marc could only imagine what was going on inside his head by the force he exerted with each toss.

Marc tapped his shoulder gently. Ray craned his neck, acknowledging his arrival, and kept throwing the remaining two rocks he had in his hands. Marc could see in his eyes the contempt he had for him for even coming into his life and Melissa's.

"Is she serious about the five-million dollars?" Ray said in a low whisper. "How the fuck does that idiot you were married to know how to bug your apartment?

Marc knew it was a loaded question. "I don't know. She keeps surprising me every moment she's in my life," he shrugged helplessly. "There is so much I still don't know about her or my past."

Ray turned and grabbed Marc by his lapels. Marc had never seen such anger in any ones eyes before. "Why did you have to choose my sister-in-law? Couldn't you have called Samantha?" his voice cracked with every word.

Marc pursed his lips. "I called Samantha first. She didn't answer..." he stopped mid-sentence. "Does it really matter? I can pay the five-million dollars. It's only money. I just don't know what Nora's endgame is. If she's bugging my apartment, I'd think she has some help. Just that the only other two people, other than me, in her life are now dead," he said.

Ray was massaging his hair with his sandy fingers. "What little I've learned about her when she was younger and what she was accused of doing to her high school sweetheart, I'm with you. I'm really not convinced this has anything to do with the money. I think we need to look into any other friends she might have that you didn't know about."

"I barely knew Rita and Gail. If she had other friends like them, then I'm more scared than I've ever been." Then it hit him. Brad knew all of Nora's (Rebecca's) friends. Marc knew he couldn't trust Ray with that fact.

He had to talk to Brad. *He should know if Rebecca-Nora had any other friends when they were younger. Maybe she has been in contact with him before I sent him away.* Marc kept looking beyond Ray as he pondered his next move.

Ray did not notice that Marc was in his own world before he spoke. "I'd like your permission to pull all of your phone records and go back as far as I can. We can start there. I just want Melissa back safe. I don't want to spook Nora. We'll let her play her little game for awhile and hope she makes a mistake."

"How much time do you think we have…you know, before she might hurt Lou and Melissa?"

"She said twenty-four hours…but, I don't know. If it's not the money and she wants to hurt you, then maybe we can stall her just a bit if she believes she winning. We're just going to have to wait until she calls. Right now she's in the driver's seat."

SEVENTY-SIX

Nora was pacing erratically inside the storage locker. She was acting like a caged tiger, sensing danger. She was waving her gun in the air, mumbling to herself. In a dark corner, Lou and Melissa sat on the bare cement floor tied up in a prone position against the wall. Duck tape bound their hands and legs. A small strip was pasted over their lips.

Melissa had stopped crying and leaned her head on Lou's shoulder. That scene set off Nora's rage.

"Get your fucking head off her shoulder. She's not your mother. She's a slut who took away my husband," she screamed. "You do know what a slut is, don't you?"

Melissa's small frame got rigid, her eyes grew wide, exposing her terror as she watched the crazy woman yelling at her. She didn't know what the word slut meant, but it was just another word that didn't sound nice coming from Nora's lips.

"Answer me you, illegitimate bitch."

Melissa shook her head. The duct tape muffled her voice.

"Then I'll tell you. It's like what your mother is, just this woman doesn't charge for it," Nora said laughing. "She probably wouldn't make as much money as your mother," she grinned.

Melissa closed her eyes tight, hoping the bad woman's words would go silent. Her head fell again upon Lou's soft shoulder, only to incite another tirade from Nora.

"I'm not going to tell you again. Get your fucking head off her shoulder," Nora's eyes were burning pits of fire as the venom spewed out from her mouth.

Melissa was whimpering again, her little frail body heaving with each sob. Nora walked over and pulled Lou by her hair away from the wall. With her gun, Nora pistol whipped Lou until she blacked out. Her head was surrounded by a pool of blood.

"Next time you don't listen, I'll shoot her. Now be a good little girl and sit up straight. It's time I call your mother."

SEVENTY-SEVEN

Ray had decided to go back to the Police Station to look at the video tapes they had gotten from Rita's garage and all the evidence one more time. He needed something fast and looking into Marc's phone records was just a desperate response to his frustration.

He was frantic.

He believed he had missed something on his initial investigation.

He knew that Marc had to return to his old house and wait for Nora to call. That was her rule. Even though it had too many bad memories for Marc, he was glad that he had agreed. What Ray did not know was that Marc was going to utilize Brad to help him find Nora and try to end it all by himself.

* * * * *

The house had a stale smell. Not from being vacant for the last several weeks, but from the toxicity of a horrible marriage that hung in the air.

Marc had a strange feeling, some unconscious knowledge that somewhere inside the master bedroom, Nora's sanctuary, the answers to his past, the past that included a sociopath, Brad, would allow him to finally put the pieces together in his strange puzzle. He knew Brad was locked deep inside him, but still didn't have a clue as to who came first. Was he the real person or was Brad?

He stepped inside Nora's large walk-in closest, knocking down hundreds of her shoe boxes. Spewed on the shag carpet was a history in each shoe. It was a history of a woman who walked in strange circles. One who traveled a path that had finally led to the kidnapping of two people he cared about. Looking at each shoe felt strange. The person who walked in them, a woman he had known a quarter of century, had been a sociopathic killer during their entire marriage.

At first he did not notice the spiral notebook. Upon closer inspection his heart started racing. It had his handwriting on the outside. It was volume one, book one. It was the notebook that had been missing from his collection.

Marc had started to tremble. He felt cold, a cold that seemed familiar. A cold that he knew was going to expose a past he most likely did not want to remember.

He clutched the book tightly, pressing it to his chest, feeling its life-force radiate throughout his body. He flopped down on the floor, his back propped up against the closet wall. He knew that once he opened it up, there would be no turning back.

His eyes grew wide, as he read the first sentence. He couldn't believe what he was reading. It was written in Brad's voice not his. He had finally discovered the most important answer about himself and Nora. He now knew he had a little window of hope to save Lou and Melissa.

* * * * *

Ray had been inside one of the interrogation rooms for an hour watching the videos found at Rita's house. It revealed nothing new. He re-read Rita's diaries. He couldn't believe he had missed it. The notation on the day Brad was murdered seemed obvious now.

He opened another evidence box searching for the yearbook that had the memorial page for Brad. When he saw the photo, it was the eyes that he knew, the eyes he had seen recently. He was now more scared than ever. He knew that Lisa was next.

He tried to dial her cell and got no answer. He dialed her home and got the same result. She had agreed to be available in case something had come up about Melissa. He knew that the worse had happened.

"How could I be so stupid?" he yelled, as he tossed the yearbook across the room. "There was a fourth person."

SEVENTY-EIGHT

Nora had gotten to Lou's coffee shop and saw that Lisa was already there, her face ashen, her eyes red from crying. She was sitting in the same booth that Marc had called his own. Nora had been in this situation before. She had killed many times, but now she seemed more desperate and irrational. Not having Rita and Gail by her side prevented her from thinking clearly.

She knew that today, people would die, and the beginning of a new identity would be born. She still clung to the hope that Brad would overtake Marc and be back in her arms living the life she had dreamt about for a quarter of a century. She knew that her plan to shock Marc back to being Brad, his true reality, had to be swift and brutal. Then, she would punish Brad when she was tired of him.

Killing, the thing she knew he loved about her, was the only alternative at the moment she had to bring Brad back to her. It had worked before when she killed his aunt and uncle and Ashley. The only problem was that Brad did not permanently take over Marc's personality. For Nora, at the moment, it was worth the risk.

Nora had to do her job quickly and with such cruelty, as to erase all of the memories, all of the life Marc had with his other side, his good and wholesome side that always got in the way of her happiness. That was the only way Brad could come back permanently or so she believed. Oh, how she wished she had her friends by her side.

Nora slipped behind the table facing Lisa. "Thanks for coming. You're daughter's still safe and unharmed. You understand my terms?" Lisa nodded. "They need to be followed to the letter or you'll never see your daughter again," she said with an eerie calm that got the right response from Lisa. "I'm so glad you believe me."

"I just want her back. I'll do whatever you want, just don't hurt her," she begged nervously. Lisa's hands could not stop shaking no matter how hard she rubbed them.

Nora gave off a sadistic smile. "Very good. Once I know that Marc's on his way, I'll release your daughter."

"You haven't told me where to tell Marc to go," Lisa said puzzled.

"He'll know if you give him the message I gave you. You never should have thought he could be yours. In fact, he's never really been Marc, at least the Marc you thought you knew. He's been mine almost all of his life and that will never change," she said, cracking her knuckles.

"What about Lou? Are you going to release her?"

"That slut is none of your concern. She's the one who started getting inside Marc's head and caused him to leave me. Just keep to your end of our deal and you'll have your daughter back. I'm being overly generous, so don't push your luck. Remember, *only tell* Marc. If I find out that you've told your brother-in-law, the deals off and Melissa will die a horrible painful death."

Lisa nodded. Her eyes had a sadness that excited Nora. "You know you've left me no alternative," she replied. "All you had to do was break it off with Marc and you and your daughter would be home right now."

Nora stood and briskly walked out of the restaurant. She disappeared into a white van with no license plates.

Lisa immediately dialed Marc's cell. She was relieved he picked up on the first ring. "Lisa, I'm so glad you've called—" she cut him off in mid-sentence.

"I don't know what you have to do with all of this, but I just met with Nora and she has this message for you: You need to meet her at your mausoleum by four this afternoon". What does all this mean," she said sobbing.

Marc tried to act like he didn't know what the message meant, but he was a bad actor. Brad had already told him where the location was. "I'm so sorry for all of this. I'm discovering thing about myself that I never knew," he said in his defense.

"What are you talking about?"

"I'm not who you think I am…", there was a long silence before he spoke again. "I'll do my best to get Melissa back to you, before I change back into someone who scares me," Marc said nervously.

"Marc, you're scaring me. Please just get Melissa and Lou back safely and then you can explain everything to me if you like. Right now I just don't care about anything except my daughter's safety." She hung up her phone.

Marc had heard Lisa's bone chilling anxiety in her voice. It had him breathing way too rapidly. He was hyperventilating, getting lightheaded, the same way he's gotten right before one of his blackouts. He tried to calm down, taking in slow deep breaths, while trying to exhale through his pressed lips. He sounded like a hissing tea-kettle. He heard a faint voice calling his name: "Marc, I've got to come back," Brad said.

Marc stood in front of a mirror that hung over his couch. It was Brad staring him right in the eyes. The face he was now looking at had become contorted. His eyes grew wide, spewing rage he had never seen in himself before. Marc sucked in a deep breath unable to move.

"It's time for me to take over," Brad said. "Nora wants us to be at the mausoleum where she's keeps our past locked away. We have to be there at four this afternoon. You need me again to resolve the mess you've created."

Marc was confused at how Brad knew so much.

Was Brad's memories hidden so far away inside Marc's brain that he had no clue or memory of what was going on? He could see himself in the mirror, but it was not the Marc he knew.

"I'm not going anywhere with you," Marc said. "I can handle Nora on my own. She pretended you were dead and I want you to stay that way. I am not the person you are. From this day forward I am going to live a normal life," he said, his voice showing confidence.

"You've always been in denial," Brad replied. "I've just been hibernating. It's time for us to move on again and start over."

A cold sticky sweat clung to Marc's body like Saran Wrap. He felt himself drifting back into to a place that he had tried to forget. Flashes of his past.

Marc tried to close his eyes to block out the horrible memories, but they were erupting inside his head like a fourth of July firework display.

"This can't be true," he shouted at Brad. "I'm Marc Richards and I'm a nice guy." The one thing his memories could not show him was that he had performed any of the murders. It was as if he was seeing his memories from the outside looking in.

In the mirror, Brad winked at him and said, "Let's just go see Nora. She'll straighten you out once and for all. It's time you found out who you really are."

Marc closed his eyes tight and when he opened them again, Brad had vanished as fast as he had appeared. Marc adjusted his eyes, looking unblinkingly at the mirror. This time he was left staring at himself. The only thing Brad had left him was the location of the "mausoleum" Nora was talking about.

SEVENTY-NINE

Detective Allen didn't fully comprehend what he was reading in the files he had on Nora's gang and the evidence boxes he had gotten from crimes that went back over twenty-five years.

The Brad Stevens who Nora (Rebecca) allegedly murdered with her two friends Carla Shortz and Blanche Ruiz were also persons of interest when his mother and father died in a hit and run accident. Witnesses recalled seeing a black Ford cargo van, the kind that Brad always drove, fleeing the accident that night. The police had just two numbers on the license plate, and with Rebecca as Brad's alibi, the police had no other leads.

This all happened a week before Brad was purportedly found murdered. The article in the newspaper mentioned how the Steven's family had suffered tragedy after tragedy. First, losing their older son, Marc Stevens, age ten, in a mysterious drowning accident. The article reported the accident happened when Brad and his brother Marc were out on a row boat during a family camping trip up in the Sierras.

Detective Allen picked up a hair brush inside Brad's evidence box. It was unclear if this was Brad's brush or Marc's, but there were enough hair fibers to perform a DNA match. Ray always went with his gut and this time it was telling him very loudly what to do. If he was right, then everything was beginning to make sense to him. He immediately dialed Lisa's cell. To his dismay, he got her voicemail. He thought of leaving a message, but if she was with Marc, he did not want to alert him to his suspicions.

He decided to call Marc and see if he'd meet with him and answer a few questions. Once again, he was relegated to leaving a message, which again, he decided against.

One thing he knew he could resolve about Brad Stevens was going to happen at the forensic lab. He prayed he was wrong, but the evidence was pointing toward Marc.

EIGHTY

Marc was not surprised that he understood what Nora meant by their "mausoleum". A lot of his memories were returning, especially the bad memories that had been kept hidden for so long. He could feel it happening, he had no more control over Marc. Brad had taken over his motor skills and was driving him to the location. He didn't know what he was going to see there, but he prayed Lou and Melissa were still very much alive.

He glanced up, Brad's face was in the rearview mirror. "We're almost there," Brad said calmly. "You're going to have to let me do the talking. What I'm going to do won't take too long and you might not have the stomach for it."

Brad was scaring Marc. The energy flowing through his veins was overwhelming to the point that a blackout was coming on way too fast. His eyes were now focusing on the street ahead. The traffic light was yellow and he tried to apply the brakes. When he lifted his right foot off of the accelerator, it was instantly slammed down, pushing the car to a speed that made it through the intersection as the light turned red. Brad was yelling now to step on it.

It had happened so fast. The dark curtain came down as Marc ran the red light. He could hear Brad screaming profanities at him, just as the blackout had taken effect. The strange thing was that Marc was still conscious this time, in a dreamlike state, inside Brad's body, watching him maneuver the car, avoiding the other cars in his way.

Brad was now in full control, yelling at all the motorists to get out of his way, honking his horn wildly and flipping everyone the bird, as he sped to where Nora was waiting for him.

Brad was adjusted the rearview mirror, tilting it enough for Marc to see his face. Marc tried to scream, but he had no more control over his body. He had been consumed by Brad. He felt nauseous, as he felt Brad's rage and hate flow through his veins. He was in a nightmare that was giving him real pain. Was this the coming together that Brad had been telling him about?

Marc's innocent face, the one of a mild mannered man had been replaced by a twisted snarl, which exposed his teeth. Marc watched through Brad's eyes with startled emotions, as he became Brad. He was turning into a monster that wanted to satisfy his hunger. He was wishing for a blackout. He did not want to witness what Brad was thinking of doing.

The car came to a screeching halt in front of a storage unit. Nora was waiting, a big smile on her face. Marc tried to step out, ready to yell at her, but some other words floated out through his lips.

"Honey, I'm back!" Brad said with an eerie chuckle.

Nora could tell instantly that her plan had worked. She opened her arms wide, waving Brad over to her. "Oh have I missed you. Is Marc gone this time forever?" she said sweetly.

Brad was now in control, even though Marc tried to jump out and choke Nora. "Maybe this time he'll stay away permanently, but I really doubt it." Brad said stepping into Nora's arms, kissing her passionately. "I missed you too."

Nora was massaging Brad between his legs, lost in some perverted embrace. "I want you so bad right now, but first we have some unfinished business to attend to." She led him inside the storage unit.

Sitting huddled together was Lou and Melissa. They at first seemed happy to see Marc, but that quickly changed when Brad starting speaking and they instantly knew something was terribly wrong.

"Am I going to do it here?" Brad said puzzled. He handed Nora the duffle bag that contained the ransom money. He looked around the storage unit and saw that Nora had made it a shrine of all their personal memories, all their memorabilia that defined who they were as a couple. All he could do was laugh at how silly she had become. Bradley, her teddy bear was resting next to a picture of them from their first date. He knew he had to keep his comments to himself for a while. Then, Nora brought her lips to his ear.

She said in a whisper. "We have to. The police have a BOLO for me and I would guess for you now too, if Detective Allen's as smart as I think he is." Nora said that to complete Brad's transformation, he had to finally murder someone who was close to Marc. This way it would send Marc away permanently. Nora was certain it would make Brad's change final. She knew that Marc would never return knowing what Brad had done.

Marc, through Brad's eyes, watched Nora hand Brad a gun.

Marc tried to take control of his body, but he was powerless to rein Brad in. Nora kissed his cheek and said. "Make it quick. I'm real horny and can't wait. I'll be waiting in the car."

Marc heard the metal door slam and felt Brad walking over to Lou and Melissa. The young girl was huddled in Lou's lap, whimpering.   Lou was emotionless, disappointment in her eyes.

Brad was now pacing nervously, waving the gun erratically, pointing it at them. "This won't hurt," he said in a soft calm voice. "Just a loud bang and it's over."

Marc felt powerless, wanting to shut his eyes, but that was what he had done all of his life, at least the life that he knew. He had to reclaim himself, but didn't know how.

Brad was now pressing the cold barrel of the gun against Lou's temple, then he switched to Melissa's, apparently confused. He was acting like a drug addict in need of a fix.

"Who should go first?" he giggled. "Maybe the whore's kid? No, maybe Miss Lou who wants to befriend everyone? Maybe you? No maybe you?" Brad teased alternating the gun back and forth, his face in a twisted rage. "No, the little girl. No reason for her to see someone die."

Marc felt Brad's finger pressing on the trigger. He heard the gun cock. He tried to block it all out, but he was a helpless voyeur trapped inside the mind of a crazed killer.

EIGHTY-ONE

Nora sat impatiently inside her BMW. She was playing their favorite song by Ronnie Millsap—*I wouldn't have missed this for the world.* She wanted their official reunion to be perfect.

She leaned her head against the headrest, her eyes closed, daydreaming about the life she and Brad could have had if only he'd not vanished and become Marc. The old memories of their beginnings flowed back in a rush. She was once again back as Rebecca.

She could recall how her life at age twelve was boring and uneventful. She hated hanging around with the girls her age, mostly from embarrassment of what her mother did for a living. As cruel as young girls could be, the girls at her school were even crueler when they discovered what her mother did.

Even that was not as bad as what her mother exposed her to. She hated even more being around the adult men who would come to their house to visit on a regular basis. Some would spend the night; others would just be there for a few hours. At first she thought they were real boyfriends, but as the girls at school teased her about her life, she soon realized those men had been paying her mother for her company.

On school nights, she had to remain in her room and on weekends she was asked to hang out with friends, while her mother conducted her business. "A young beautiful girl like you should not be alone with older men," her mother would say in her encrypted way, always seeming somewhere else when she spoke to Rebecca. "These are mommy's friends. They might get confused and want to be with you instead of me…you wouldn't want to hurt mommy…would you?" she'd pretend to pout. As if it was yesterday, Rebecca could remember how selfish and self-centered her mother was and how possessive she was about her men.

It soon became apparent to Rebecca why her mother did not want her around. She was blossoming into an attractive, desirable young woman, who looked older and sexier than her age. Her mother, at thirty-four, was slowly aging and becoming afraid that her daughter would steal away her clients.

Rebecca did not like those kind of men anyway and did not see the problem her mother was having with her. But that was going to rapidly change for her. It happened one evening when she was in her room watching TV. One of her mother's friends had come early and was complaining about having to wait. Her mother in a desperate tone and high on Cocaine, told him he could wait with her daughter until she was finished.

Rebecca was listening to the argument, when it suddenly turned into a calming discussion that involved something like a freebie for his trouble. She jumped back away from the door pulling *Bradley,* her stuffed teddy bear, to her chest.

The man walked in and sat down on her bed. It was the first time anyone other than her mother had come into her bedroom. He smelled of stale cigar smoke and alcohol. He had a peculiar look on her face, one she had never seen before on any of her mother's clients.

"You shouldn't be in here," Rebecca said, her voice trembling, as she tightly clutched her teddy bear.

"Your mother's busy and said I could be with you for a while," he replied, stumbling toward her. "You're more beautiful than your mother, you know," he said, slurring his words.

Rebecca was confused. Her mother had always told her to lock her bedroom door when she was "entertaining", as she would say. "Never let anyone in unless I tell you its okay," her mother would tell her over and over again. Unfortunately, this time she had forgotten to lock her door.

Why would she tell her friend to come into my room this time? Especially, without first telling me it was okay, she thought. "You need to leave right now," she said nervously squeezing Bradley.

"Not until I get my freebie," said the man callously.

Then, it had happened way too fast for her to scream or react. The man put his large hand over her mouth and ripped off her flowered underwear. He had slipped off his pants, his throbbing penis coming toward her mouth.

"This won't hurt," he said breathing heavily. "Don't even think of hurting me," he said pressing his hard manly part on her lips.

Rebecca tried to move her head to the side, but his hand was too strong and held her mouth in place. "I don't want that ugly thing near me," she shouted.

He was now laughing. "You're old enough to learn about this part of life," he chuckled. "When you're done, it will be my turn to enjoy a virgin. Now suck on me gently. Remember, you hurt me and I'll kill you and then your mother."

Rebecca closed her eyes and opened her mouth. She felt his throbbing cock moving in and out, while he moaned. This went on for almost five minutes until something exploded inside her mouth making her gag.

"That's disgusting you pervert," she screamed spitting out what had been injected into her mouth.

Before she could raise her arm, he slapped her hard. She felt blood on her lip and started crying. "I'm no pervert you little bitch of a whore. Now, I'm going to show you what a real man expects from a woman so you can learn how to be a good little girl for the next time I'm here."

During the next hour, the man did to Rebecca what most women don't experience in their life-time. When he was finished with her, he left her a hundred dollar bill.

"Not bad for your first time," he said with a bellowing laugh. "See you in a week and if you improve, your tip will be larger."

Over the next six months Rebecca had sex with thirty-six different men who had become her regular companions when her mother was busy or passed out from her drugs. However, none of them paid her any money. They all gave their payments to her mother, who never said a word to her about what she was being put through.

It was on March twenty-fifth, five years after she was raped by one of her mother's clients, that Rebecca's life was about to changed. That was when Brad Stevens transferred into her high school. Rumor had it that he was trouble. He had been kicked out of three other high schools for fighting, one where he put a boy in the hospital. For Rebecca, it was love at first sight, a way for her to be protected. Brad, being two grades behind her, did not matter. She liked younger boys. Plus, he had the same name as her teddy bear, which she thought was a positive sign that they were supposed to be together.

He too seemed to connect instantly with her and a week later they were going steady and talking about their dreams and hopes for the future. They both promised that nothing would ever keep them apart. Brad had never asked her to do anything sexual—he knew they were too young for stuff like that. They just kissed and hugged until he had to take her home.

They both believed they were soul mates and would be together forever. Then, Rebecca confided in him about what her mother was forcing her to do with all the men that came to her house. That was when Brad promised her that he would take care of it. It was the first time she saw Brad's rage explode in his eyes and she fell more deeply in love with him.

"You will never have to do those horrible things again. When you decide you're ready, it will be with your free will," Brad said.

Two days later her mother was found shot in the head and the man that first raped Rebecca was found with his penis cut off and stuff inside his mouth. The police had no clue which one of her mother's clients could have committed the gruesome murders. It was to be the beginnings of a great love affair for Rebecca and Brad.

Social services found a kind and caring foster home for Rebecca, which was close to her high school. It worked out perfectly, so she and Brad could remain together.

The night her mother was murdered, Brad told her about his blackouts and his alter ego, Marc. He told her that during those blackouts he would not remember anything. He then told her that the Marc personality was that of his dead brother, who he believed had died at his hands, on a lake, during a summer family outing.

Brad's only memory was from the blame his parents had dished out to him. As it turned out, his brother had died from an unfortunate drowning accident.

That night Rebecca, who thought Brad was joking about his other personality, witnessed a frightening convulsive episode that transformed him right before her eyes.

When Marc came to and saw her, he screamed as if he had come out of a nightmare, not recognizing Rebecca. He fell back into another blackout, this time returning as Brad.

"You're one great actor," Rebecca said laughing.

"That wasn't an act. You scared the shit out of Marc. He's a real pussy," he said nervously.

"I don't like Marc Stevens. I want Brad with me forever," she begged.

For the first time, Brad seemed scared. "The police are starting to ask too many questions about your mom's murder. I just know that it's only a matter of time before they figure out I did it."

Rebecca shook her head wildly. She knew the truth, but kept it to herself. "I'd never tell them. Maybe we should run away?" She knew he had not murdered her mother, but needed that leverage over him to keep him in tow.

"If we do that, the police will for sure know I did it. I don't want you mixed up with my problem."

Rebecca kissed his cheek, brushing his long forelock back away from his eyes. "Your problem has become my problem. We could tell the police what my mother was forcing me to do—" Brad raised his finger to her lips.

"It's too late for that. You never complained before. You don't have any proof. It's hopeless. I have to disappear from the police's radar. This way we can have a happy life," he said his tone desperate.

Rebecca was now sobbing. "I can't live without you. You saved my life. There has to be another way. I'll run away with you."

"No. I need to let Marc emerge as a new person. Brad Stevens has to be out of the picture until things cool down."

Rebecca thought for while and then smiled. I have a wonderful plan, but it will take some time to work. Let's not worry about anything for a while and see where the police go with their case." That night they devised what they believed was a foolproof plan. Plus, Rebecca learned how to control Brad and Marc, or so she thought.

Brad did not know that Rebecca had a few other people on her list that needed to be out of the way before he could truly go away.

Two loud gunshot explosions startled her abruptly back to the present. Walking out of the storage unit with a silly grin on his face was Brad. She knew the sadistic look he always wore after watching someone die.

"Is it over?" She asked anxiously.

"It's so over. Let's go somewhere. I need to rest," Brad said.

EIGHTY-TWO

Nora sat on the king size bed in their hotel room. She was naked and had her knees pulled up to her chest. There was nothing left to the imagination, as Brad stared at her.

"Tell me how it felt when you pulled the trigger," she begged.

Brad hesitated, unsure of what to say. "I've never killed a child before. It didn't feel real good. Lou was easy, but the look on Melissa's face was just horrible."

Nora seemed puzzled. "Since when do you have a conscience? I wish I could have seen their looks," her tone more disappointed than curious.

"You're one sick bitch," Brad said angrily. He kept staring at her beautiful body thinking about how she loved sex with women and men. He did not understand it, but she was great at it and that's all that mattered at the moment.

"But, you've always loved this sick bitch. We're a great pair," she said lying back on the bed and spreading her legs. "Now come and satisfy me. I've missed you so much."

For the next hour they made love until they both passed out in each other's arms. Nora was sleeping soundly when Brad awoke. He propped himself up against the headboard, staring at Nora—his pillow on his lap. He seemed lost in thought, his hands squeezing his pillow tightly.

He loved staring at her. That was about the only thing he like that Marc did each day. As he gazed down he noticed how quiet and peaceful she slept. The voices in his head were quiet, as he raised his pillow and placed it over her face. "It's your time to die. Justice must be served."

Nora was jerking wildly scratching at Brad's arms, but he was stronger and kept pressing harder.   The harder he pressed the pillow, the more she thrashed about on the bed.   She arched her back, attempting to twist to her side so she could breathe, but Brad was not letting up on the pressure. With each second, her struggle got weaker, until she was almost not moving.   It was about over and Brad was feeling relieved.

Then from out of nowhere, Marc took over from Brad.   He immediately eased off and lifted the pillow off of Nora's face. Her skin was bright red, the blood vessels in her eyes were broken, but she able to cough and struggled to catch her breath.

Marc took her left wrist and snitched it with some rope to the headboard and proceeded to do the same with her right arm.   Then he did the same with her ankles and fastened them to the baseboard of the bed. An evil grin had formed on Marc's face.

Nora first looked at Marc and then lifted her head to see that she was tied up. "I did not know you were into such kinky stuff, Brad, I like it," she said smiling.

"I'm not Brad, you silly bitch. Killing you would have been too good for you. I want you to rot in prison, alone and without Brad to comfort you. That would be the best punishment for a sociopath like you," he said calmly. He then put some duck tape over Nora's mouth so he wouldn't have to hear her voice anymore.

Marc got dressed, wiped down the room and placed the "Privacy Please" sign on the door and left.

He had some unfinished business to attend to before he disappeared once again, but this time forever.   He had finally discovered who he really was and wanted to learn to love that person. He was no longer a stranger to himself. There was a new voice talking to him.

He had to drive to Lisa's house and finish what he had started. It was the only way for him to have closure on Brad Stevens and Marc Richards.   He felt sorry for all the pain he had caused her, but soon it would be over for her too.

In his car he texted detective Allen the location of Nora and asked him to lock her up and throw away the key.

EIGHTY-THREE

Detective Ray Allen had thought he had put the pieces to the Marc Richards/Brad Stevens puzzle together. Doctor Todd McHugh, a leading psychiatric specialist on multiple personality disorders, felt confident that Marc fit the definition perfectly.

What scared Ray was that McHugh believed that the two personalities were in a conflict stage and that there was going to be a spontaneous and involuntary implosion within one of the already tormented alter personalities.

Doctor McHugh was confident that time was running out and that one of the personalities was going to take over permanently and it usually turned out to be the stronger one that prevailed.

Detective Allen sucked in a nervous breath. "If Brad takes over he might not ever leave until all his unfinished business was completed."

Panic was now his worst enemy. His sister-in-law's safety was his only concern. He drove like a wild man, sirens blasting, to Lisa's house. He prayed he wasn't too late.

A manila folder lay on the passenger seat like a witness ready to provide testimony in front of a jury. Inside was the proof of the next convergence of a disturbed mind. While he had all the proof he needed to convict Nora (Rebecca) of all the murders, he did not have enough proof that showed Brad or Marc had a hand in any of them. The only problem Ray had with all of this was that he was acting alone. It was his gut that was his partner for the moment.

This pattern of murder and disappearance and once again murder and disappearance, when analyzed through the eyes of an FBI data analysis program made what was going to happen next

obvious. He just couldn't share what he found, especially with the
FBI. They would immediately upstage him and take over the
entire case. Lisa and Melissa did not have the luxury of waiting
for the FBI to formulate a plan. He knew it was up to him to save
them before Brad and Nora murdered them and moved on and
disappeared.

He knew if he captured or killed both of them, it would be his
crowning glory. He was going to solve twelve murders that took
place over the last forty years, all cold cases, all now so very hot,
and all so ready to be closed. Finally, after so many years of not
getting the recognition he deserved, Detective Ray Allen was
going to get the promotion to detective first grade with this
remarkable police work. He knew that he had a small window of
opportunity before Nora and Brad disappeared again with perfect
new identities that would make them virtually untraceable until the
next murders surfaced.

How he never noticed Marc's fingertips with the acid burns that
erased the unique pattern that gave every individual a forensic
identity surprised him. That was his job to notice the unusual and
he missed it. Each murder scene had identical sets of the scarred
prints.

At Marc's studio apartment his forensic team had turned up
Brad Stevens DNA, at first he thought Brad Stevens had returned
from the grave, but when he compared it to Marc's DNA from his
last hospital stay, he understood what Doctor McHugh was talking
about. The forensic team pulled the only finger prints found at
Marc's apartment and when Detective Allen compared them to the
one's found at Ashley's apartment the night she went missing, he
knew Marc and Brad were one and the same killer. Marc was just a
nice guy suffering from a personality disorder. But, Brad was the
dominant one and it was Brad he had to find now.

It all started the night he saw the striking resemblance with
Brad's senior high school photo. There was no doubt that Marc
was Brad. It was not enough to arrest him, but when his forensic
team pulled the same prints inside Lou's apartment the night she
was brutally beaten—he knew Brad and Marc acted with Nora and
her friends.

Ray was shocked when he pulled up in front of Lisa's house
and saw Marc's Mercedes. His drew his gun running toward the
front door.

EIGHTY-FOUR

Brad had been pacing wildly, the barrel of his gun pressed against his temple. "Marc's trying to control me," he said. "He's always tried, but it never lasts too long."

Lisa's hands were cupped in front of her mouth. She was trying to control her temper. She did not recognize the face that looked like Marc. His bulging veins on his forehead, his clenched jaw, had transformed him into a stranger. Even his voice did not sound like Marc. Did he have a twin he had not told her about? she thought. Feeling her tears cascade down her cheeks she reminded herself of the danger her daughter was in.

She struggled for the right words to ask him. "Is Melissa all right?" Her voice cracked with fear.

Brad was nervously banging his pistol against his head, trying hard to think of a response. "For now. Marc was able to stop me, but he's gone now and I'll be going back to finish what I started."

"Please don't hurt my little girl. She's all I have," Lisa pleaded.

"Your boyfriend is getting my Rebecca locked away. Now I have nothing and so will you soon," he shouted.

Lisa heard a car come screeching to a halt in front of her house. She craned her neck and saw Ray running with his gun drawn. Brad must have heard it too and went into a frenzy, spinning and darting back and forth in her living room.

"Time for you to die, whore!" he screamed.

Lisa closed her eyes, a whispered prayer flowed from her lips. "Melissa, mommy will be with you soon. We will be in a better place. Don't be scared my love."

Lisa heard the front door burst open and two gun shots exploded muting Brad's vulgar cursing. She couldn't open her eyes. She was afraid to see what was happening. Two more rounds were discharged and then there was an eerie silence.

She heard Brad's painful yelp and watched him limp out of her house. Ray was on his back not moving.

"Ray," she screamed. "Ray, are you all right? Don't die! Not you too." She was by his side feeling for a pulse. She couldn't find one and was immediately dialing 911. "Officer down," she yelled and gave her address.

* * * * *

Brad was speeding down the freeway back toward the storage container to finish off Lou and Melissa. His wound in his thigh was painful, but missed his artery. He had tied his belt above where the blood was flowing, trying to stop the bleeding. He could not stop the severe pain that was throbbing through his leg.

"Brad, it's over," Marc said. "We're both going away forever. This has to end right here and right now."

Brad looked in the rearview mirror and saw Marc's angry eyes. "You don't have the guts to do it," he barked. "You've tried before and failed. You'll fail again. So let me finish this and we can move on together and start over again. I promise that this time I'll be better," Brad begged.

Marc was tired of arguing with himself, but Brad was so alive he had no choice. "That's what you said last time and look what you've done. I was finally moving on tasting some happiness. But, no, you can't stand seeing me happy, not for even an instant," Marc barked into the rearview mirror. "You will always allow a woman like Nora to control you and I won't stand for it anymore."

"Happy?…you can't be happy," Brad argued. "I'm the happiest when I'm hurting people and you stop me from my pleasures. Is that fair?"

Marc slammed his foot on the brake pedal causing the car to fishtail on the shoulder of the freeway. "My happiness doesn't hurt anyone you moron. I'm going to take what I can from our pathetic life and you're not going to interfere with me this time. Marc will prevail and you can't stop me."

"I did once before."

"Just like the time you watched me drown?" Marc mocked. "My body might have died, but my spirit will always be here alive inside your fucking head, seeking my revenge."

Marc couldn't stop laughing. He actually heard the insanity in the voice that was echoing inside the car. He pictured his hands around Brad's throat squeezing tighter and tighter.

He imagined he was back on that small rowboat on the lake, where he drowned, watching the life drain from him as his brother laughed. But, this time, in his car, it was Brad's thrashing that was inside his head. He pressed harder and harder until the image of his sick brother had vanished. It was over. He was free.

He knew it was not going to be over until he finished what needed to be done with Lou and Melissa. He slipped Brad's gun in his jacket pocket. He drove to the storage locker and fumbled with his keys looking for the right one to open the lock.

EIGHTY-FIVE

Lisa was sitting on her couch watching the paramedics attend to Ray's wounds. One of the bullets had lodged in his vest, the other in the same shoulder that he was recovering from. He was sitting up on the gurney when Lisa's cell rang.

She started crying hysterically. "Marc, where's Melissa? Please don't hurt her. She loves you," Lisa sobbed.

"Lisa, understand that Brad's finally gone. He and Nora won't be able to hurt you or Melissa anymore. Nora's location is on Ray's cell phone so he can lock her up. And, I'm dead for all intensive purposes. Melissa and Lou are fine. I called 911 and they're on the way to pick them up. It's the least I could do. I'm so sorry for everything that's happened. Please tell Ray that too."

Lisa's eyes grew wide as she spoke. "They're alive?" she said, crying hysterically. "Thank you so much. But, I'm so confused. What happened to you? You seemed like such a gentle man. I saw it in your eyes. I know I wasn't wrong," she said, her voice calmer.

"I can't explain it. I don't fully understand it. I have to go, the police are on their way and I can't get caught at least not now. I've discovered the real me, a stranger of sorts, and I need to get to know him. In a way…I owe it to you and Lou. I had to come out of my shell so I could meet the real me. I'm so sorry for hurting you and Melissa, but it's best this way if I go away forever."

Lisa took a deep breath. After all she's been through, she still liked Marc. "You need help. We can do this together," she said.

"It's too late for us, but not for you. Melissa needs her mother and you need to enjoy your new life. A package will be coming to you and Lou shortly. Use it to have a wonderful life." With that, he hung up the phone. Lisa just stared blankly at Ray.

"Was that Marc or Brad?" he asked.

"It was Marc. He called 911 and the police are on their way to get Melissa and Lou. He said that you have a text message from him giving you Nora's location. He's leaving," she said.

Ray pulled his cell from his pocket. He gave the Highway Patrol a full description of Marc and his car and told them to find the location of the call that just came into Lisa's phone. He was confident that with all the new Amber Alert billboards on all the freeways, that the capture of Marc Richard would be completed before the end of the day.

* * * * *

One hour had passed and Lisa paced anxiously in front of her living room window. When she saw the patrol car pull up she was out the door running towards her daughter.

Melissa jumped out of the car, her eyes still red from crying. Like a happy puppy, she leaped into her mother's arms her thin legs wrapped around her mother's waist. They were both kissing each other laughing and crying with each breath.

Lisa looked inside the black and white for Lou. "Where's Lou?" she asked Melissa.

"The mean lady hit her too hard with her gun. She's at the hospital. I don't know how she's doing. She saved my life, you know," Melissa said swallowing hard.

"Maybe we should go to the hospital and see how she's doing," Lisa said.

Melissa took in a quivering breath. "I'd like that. Maybe we can all be friends?"

Lisa smiled sweetly, kissing her daughter's cheek. "I'd like that too."

EPOLOGUE

It had been four months since Marc vanished. Melissa and her mother had moved to Palm Desert. Marc had quick claimed his home there to her. Lou moved to Tahoe with the money she had gotten from Marc and opened another coffee shop. Lou, Lisa, Melissa and Ray were given a million dollars each to start their lives over.

Ray had been promoted to detective first grade, but soon quit his job after receiving Marc's million dollar gift. It came with a note that challenged him to manage the money smartly, doing some real detective work. Marc knew Ray had always wanted to be a private eye. As it turned out, his first case was to find Marc Richards. It was something he had to do so he could sleep at night. Twice he had been close to death and twice it involved Marc.

* * * * *

Rusty's Tavern overlooked Puget Sound, its big picture windows faced Mount Rainer. It was a sunny clear day in Seattle, a day that made putting up with the usual rain worthwhile.

Harrison sipped his Bombay Sapphire and Tonic, daydreaming, wondering what his day would be like. He savored his drink, it made him feel worthy and special. He disliked whiskey, it had too many bad memories. He could no longer drink beer, especially the flavored beer, he was not that person anymore.

He had become friendly with the bartender, Troy, learning about Vashon Island and all the important gossip that every small community had. The horn of the incoming ferry echoed loudly, like a flirtatious whistle, as two attractive women pranced in and hopped on two barstools.

They were beautiful and in many ways this scene seemed very familiar. As he sipped his Gin and Tonic, he watched with a curious eye the two men sitting a few stools down from them, their eyes riveted on the two chatty ladies. One of the men stood up and walked in between the two women, interrupting their lively conversation.

A smile grew on Harrison's face. It was as if he knew what was coming next. His thoughts were interrupted by Troy. "Another Gin and Tonic my friend?" he said loudly.

Harrison looked at him and nodded. "Sure, why not? I just have something that needs handling first."

Troy took the empty glass from him and was staring at his customer's fingers. "Some nasty scars? What happened man?"

"I used to work with some corrosive chemicals. Had a bad accident a few years back. Now I have no fingerprints. I guess it's a good thing if I were a criminal," he laughed.

"I'm a good judge of character and you're not even close to what I'd call a criminal." He handed him his drink. "This one's on me."

Harrison took one quick sip and stood. He walked over to the two ladies that seemed to be having a problem convincing the man to leave them alone.

"Don't you know what NO means?" Harrison said sternly.

The man turned and took a swing at him. It was happening again. Brad and Marc just watched, unable to help. They were locked away, as Harrison began his new life.

www.ingramcontent.com/pod-product-compliance
Lightning Source LLC
Chambersburg PA
CBHW051941090426
42741CB00008B/1229